BEYOND GRAUSTARK

William Cotton

George Barr McCutcheon

BEYOND GRAUSTARK

George Barr McCutcheon Playwright Discovered

A. L. LAZARUS and VICTOR H. JONES

National University Publications
KENNIKAT PRESS // 1981
Port Washington, N.Y. // London

Manufactured in the United States of America

Published by
Kennikat Press Corp.
Port Washington, N.Y. / London

Library of Congress Cataloging in Publication Data

Lazarus, Arnold Leslie.
    Beyond Graustark.

    (National University publications) (Literary criticism series)
    Bibliography: p.
    Includes index.
    1. McCutcheon, George Barr, 1866–1928. 2. Authors, American–20th century–Biography. I. Jones, Victor H., joint author. II. Title.
PS3525.A187Z75   812'.52[B]   80-27566
ISBN 0-8046-9280-7

To three of our teachers

Hazard Adams
Howard Mumford Jones
Louis B. Wright

CONTENTS

Kennikat Press
National University Publications
Literary Criticism Series

ACKNOWLEDGMENTS

Throughout the search for what has gone into this biography the authors have enjoyed the enthusiastic support of the McCutcheon family— George Barr McCutcheon II, a son of GBMc's brother John; John T. McCutcheon Jr., Editorial Director of the *Chicago Tribune;* John McCutcheon Raleigh, a son of GBMc's sister Jessie; and Theodora McCutcheon, daughter-in-law of GBMc's brother Ben. We are everlastingly grateful for the letters and anecdotes that these McCutcheons have shared with us.

Our other benefactors include the following; Laszlo Kovacs, Helen Schroyer, Barbara McCorkle, Jenny Knauth, Cheryl Knodle, and Janet Huettner of the Purdue Library; Ellen Dunlap, Erika Wilson, Lois Garcia, John Kirkpatrick, Trudy Prescott, Charlotte Mitchell, and Betsy Cornwell of the Texas Humanities Research Center; Lois Szladits and David Pankow of the New York Public Library; Mardel Pacheco of Princeton University Library; Rodney Dennis, the Houghton Library; Ted Grieder, the New York University Library; Louis Hieb, University of Arizona Library; Heddy Richter, University of Southern California Library; William Roberts, the Bancroft Library, Berkeley, California; Joan Echtencamp, the University of Virginia Library; Gwenna Wishinskey, the University of Illinois Library; Maureen Duffany, Library of St. John's Seminary, Camarillo, California; D. C. Weber, Stanford University Library; William Cagle, Saundra Taylor, and Susan Godlewski, Lilly Library, Bloomington, Indiana; Peggy Sinko and Diana Haskell, the Newberry Library; Leslie Needham, Cook County, Illinois, Bureau of Vital Statistics; Robert O'Neill, Karen Chittick, Carol Chapman, Mary Ann Phillips, and Taokan Huang, the Indiana State University Library; the Indiana State University Committee on Research; Gayle Thornbrough, the Indiana Historical Society; Paula Woods, Carol Waddell, Lyda Hilt, Mildred Paarlberg, and Mary Lou Bilsborough, the Tippecanoe County, Indiana, Historical Association; Virginia Miller, Wells Library, Lafayette, Indiana; Lucille Washburne and Lois Andrew, West Lafayette, Indiana, Public Library;

Donald Thompson, Librarian, Wabash College; Jared Carter of Indianapolis; Robert L. Lowe, Richard Cordell, H. B. Knoll, Paul Fatout, Darrell Abel, Russell Cosper, Jacob Adler, and William Stuckey, Purdue University Department of English; Audry Arellanes and Barbara McCrimmon of the Manuscript Society; Ted Berkman, Bernell Warren Smith, and June Evans Smith of Santa Barbara, California; Cornell Jaray and John Parke of the Kennikat Press.

Special thanks go to our forbearing spouses, Keo Felker Lazarus and Shirley L. Jones.

For permission to publish excerpts from certain manuscripts* and to reprint from published works, thanks are due the following:

The Beinecke Rare Book Room and Manuscript Library, Yale University, for excerpts from GBMc's "The Wedding Journey" and his short story "The Gloaming Ghosts" (unpublished ms.) in the Collection of American Literature.

The Bobbs-Merrill Company, Inc. for excerpts from John T. McCutcheon, *Drawn from Memory* (1950).

Butler Library, Columbia University, for brief excerpts from GBMc's letters to Brander Matthews, the Brander Matthews Collection.

Fales Library, New York University, for GBMc's typescript "Blind Man's Buff."

Farrar, Straus, & Giroux, Inc., for an excerpt from Edmund Wilson, *The Twenties* (1975).

Harcourt Brace Jovanovich, Inc. for an excerpt from Mark Van Doren's Introduction to Carl Sandburg, *Harvest Poems* (Harcourt, Brace, 1960).

The Houghton Library, Harvard University, for GBMc's "Tribute to Howells."

The Lilly Library, Indiana University, for excerpts from GBMc's Letters to James Whitcomb Riley, the Riley Manuscripts Collection.

Macmillan Publishing Company and Marguerite Fetcher for excerpts from Harriet Monroe, *A Poet's Life* (Macmillan, 1938); rights reverted to Mrs. Fetcher.

Newberry Library, Chicago, for GBMc's and Ben McCutcheon's letters to John T. McCutcheon, the John T. McCutcheon Collection.

Northwestern University Library for a brief excerpt from John T. McCutcheon's letter to Charles G. Dawes.

Oxford University Press for the excerpt from Walter Blair and Hamlin Hill, *America's Humor* (1978).

Purdue University Library, Indiana Collection, for excerpts from GBMc's letters to George Ade and George Ade's letters to GBMc. NOTE: Although A. L. Lazarus owns publication and production rights to all GBMc's plays, the Purdue Library has mss. of the following GBMc plays

---

*By special arrangement with the executors of the literary estate of George Barr McCutcheon, all rights to the publication and production of his plays have been assigned to A. L. Lazarus. Inquiries should be addressed to Mr. Lazarus, 945 Ward Drive No. 69, Santa Barbara, California 93111.

(among others): *The Double Doctor, The Flyers, George Washington's Last Duel, Judith Verne, Midthorne, A Mythological Malady, Old Dominion, The Reef Bell,* and *Vashti.*

Putnam Publishing Group for an excerpt from James Montgomery Flagg, *Roses and Buckshot* (G. P. Putnam's Sons, 1946).

Stanford University Library Rare Book Room for excerpts from the American Art Association catalogue of GBMc's *The Renowned Collection of First Editions of the Works of Charles Dickens and William Makepeace Thackeray* (ca. 1926).

Tippecanoe County, Indiana, Historical Association for GBMc's verses in *Several Short Ones* and for numerous selections in their archives, cited specifically in the NOTES.

University of Arizona Library, Special Collections, for excerpts from GBMc's typescript "Courage."

University of Chicago Press for a brief excerpt from Walter Jackson Bate, *The Achievement of Samuel Johnson,* originally published in 1961 by Oxford University Press; rights reverted to the author and to the University of Chicago Press.

University of Southern California Library, Hamlin Garland Collection, for GBMc's letters to Hamlin Garland.

University of Texas Humanities Research Center, McCutcheon Collection, for numerous selected materials cited specifically in the NOTES.

Yale University Press for excerpts from Peter Brooks, *The Melodramatic Imagination* (1976).

A. L. Lazarus is Emeritus Professor of English, Purdue University.

Victor H. Jones is Associate Professor of English, Indiana State University.

PROLOGUE

A Purdue professor was commissioned by an Indiana academic society to compile an anthology of Hoosier writers. While exploring for selections, he happened upon an unexpected treasure. Covered with dust in the attic of the Purdue Library lay a carton of play manuscripts by George Barr McCutcheon (1866–1928). McCutcheon was the author of *Graustark, Brewster's Millions,* and many another romance which Hollywood adapted as movies in the early 1920s and which enjoyed immense popularity.

The manuscripts, written in neat longhand on foolscap, edges fraying, consisted of some juvenilia, some fragments, and some completed plays, including *The Double Doctor* and *The Flyers.* Other play manuscripts of McCutcheon's, along with his two privately printed plays, later turned up in the Beinecke Library at Yale and in the Berg Collection of the New York Public Library. Most of his other papers, along with his personal library, have been acquired for the McCutcheon Collection at the University of Texas Humanities Research Center in Austin.

On reading these plays—even the juvenilia—the professor (a former play director in college and little theaters) was struck by their charm and wit, by their universal and controversial themes, and by McCutcheon-the-playwright coming through as a different, more intellectual, person than McCutcheon-the-novelist, whose Dodd, Mead romances had made him a millionaire before the advent of the Sixteenth Amendment.

Why did GBMc's good plays remain unproduced when his novels were selling in the millions? Some answers to that question—after three years of research (and thousands of miles of legwork by the professor and his colleague Victor H. Jones)—comprise much of this literary biography. But it is not just literary detective work; McCutcheon's life and times generated their own dramas, enigmas, paradoxes and ironies. Undistinguished plays by McCutcheon's Purdue friends Ade and Tarkington achieved successful production on Broadway whereas GBMc's plays met with rejection by the New York theaters, especially by the all-powerful Frohman syndicate. McCutcheon's heart and best work were in the theater, but the theater was not ready for him or his satires of Victorian mores. Even some of his short stories and essays remain more creditable than is generally realized. His contemporaries saw him only as a romanticist, and he was stuck with that label.

Except perhaps for Samuel Johnson's *Lives of the Poets,* few biographies have reckoned with writers of minor but creditable achievement. What was it like, in the early 1900s in this country, to have published forty novels, some justifiably dismissed as kitsch and most eluding the notice of reputable critics? What was it like to have done one's best with melodramas and comedies which rarely if ever (except for adaptations) breached the Broadway theaters? What was it like—breaking one's back and heart, trying to escape one's persona as a provincial? Trains and washed-out bridges and other images of escape and frustration permeate GBMC's writings. Could a writer win the applause of the multitudes yet despise himself as a Hoosier yokel because the Eastern establishment ignored his more serious work?

Students of popular culture know that *Graustark* (1901) was the first of a series of edelweiss romances set in a mythical Alpine principality. Its Princess Yetive falls in love with and marries a young American, Grenfall Lorry. The author created such an illusion of reality that for several months after the publication of that novel prospective tourists inundated travel agents with orders to book passage to Graustark. The novel was adapted as a movie and its name was transferred—long before the era of decals and T-shirts—to a two-step dance and a Kentucky Derby racehorse. *Graustark* was no doubt one of the "current spate of romances" disparaged by William Dean Howells in his lectures at the Plymouth Church in Indianapolis.

McCutcheon's progress beyond *Graustark* toward realism was not, however, an act of contrition—not a late atonement for having written things romantic. Rather, his journey was perennial and had started quite early in his career; one of the purposes of this biography is to show his precocity. Whether or not "he preferred realism to romance," as Sarah Bowerman writes in the *Dictionary of American Biography,* he was a split personality. In most of his novels, he indulged in romantic idealism; in most of his plays and short stories, he reveled in satirical realism. His plays are also energized with ironic humor, especially *Brood House* and *One Score & Ten;* they often reach literary distinction.

In short, McCutcheon was a frustrated playwright. The Frohman syndicate, which owned or controlled most of the playhouses in the United States, rejected him along with Ibsen and Shaw. The syndicate stockholders disliked McCutcheon's controversial themes and his lampooning of stuffy nineteenth century melodrama. Since Charles and Daniel Frohman, the syndicate managers, were successfully staging more melodrama at the turn of the century than any other genre, they were not about to kill that lucrative goose, even though Daniel himself conceded that such plays "had not a spark of humor." The Frohmans antagonized many of their artists, among them the celebrated Minnie Maddern, who wearied of stereotyped roles. She was also embarrassed by the syndicate's monopolistic practices, and she eventually resigned. With Miss Maddern, McCutcheon carried on a love affair from afar.

McCutcheon poked fun at his contemporaries' mores and conventions. Half a century before Jessica Mitford's *The American Way of Death,* he lampooned unctuous cadaver snatchers in his comic melodrama *One Score & Ten* and in his comedy *The Flyers.* In the latter, he also satirized lovers' formal engagements. He had some reservations about the practical consequences of activist feminism, as reflected in his story "When Girl Meets Girl," but in his melodrama *Brood House* he takes Mr. Brood to task for his chauvinistic treatment of Mrs. Brood. In the same play, the sets of which are strewn with lion skins and elephant tusks, GBMc satirizes the senseless hunting and killing of wildlife. Here he was slapping the wrist of his brother John, the *Chicago Tribune* cartoonist and war correspondent, who had joined Theodore Roosevelt on a safari and later published *In Africa: Hunting Adventures in the Big-Game Country* (1910).

Aside from social criticism in the comedies (e.g., in *The Double Doctor, One Score & Ten,* and *The Man Who Loved Children*) GBMc's triumph remains his contribution to popular culture through the melodrama in his fiction and the parody of melodrama in some of his plays. In fact, he need not have taken as seriously as he did the browbeating that Eastern reviewers (those who noticed him at all) gave his melodramatic mode. Even when parodied for its excesses, that mode is not necessarily beneath critical notice, as Eric Bentley, Peter Brooks, and other contemporary critics have argued.

McCutcheon wrote several of his better novels—*The Flyers, Mr. Bingle, Black Is White, From the Housetops, Oliver October,* and *Yollop*—in play form first. In his forties and early fifties, as a pattern, two to three years elapsed between one or another of his unproduced plays and its rein-carnation as a published novel. (Similar patterns obtain for certain works by Dickens and by Henry James.) No doubt, McCutcheon's marketable image as a novelist was too well established by the time he moved to New York to make him a credible syndicate playwright either of comedy or of melodrama. Theater people of his time had an idée fixe that novelists could not write plays.

Although we deal briefly with his novels, our emphasis is on his more serious works—namely, his short stories and, especially, his plays. We do make connections between certain episodes in his life and certain passages in his writings regardless of genre: his struggle to transcend what he re-garded as a backward milieu; his discovery that there was a theatrical establishment controlled by people like the Frohmans and that he was not a part of it; his discovery that he was also not a part of the Eastern literary establishment—that the best magazines were controlled by people like William Dean Howells; his vicarious participation in Minnie and Harry Fiske's battle with the Frohmans; his abortive and fatal skirmish with those who pigeonholed him as an incorrigible romanticist.

Of course, he did write too many ephemeral romances, too many pot-boilers, to be taken seriously by the critics. He himself knew when he was compromising his art, his better self. Knowing better, doing worse; that was his tragic flaw. Still, his novel *The Sherrods,* which traces with psychological realism the experiences of a bigamist and his wives, remains a distinguished sleeper, along with his best plays, *Brood House* and *One Score & Ten.*

Finally, certain episodes in McCutcheon's life and times, including his relations with George Ade and Booth Tarkington, evoke poignancy and hilarity.

BEYOND GRAUSTARK

It is not the illustrious only who illustrate history; all grades have a hand in it.

Mark Twain

As a biographer you would never feel a success unless you had shown the darker side. . . . How a man's life fell into disorder can serve as a kind of parable from which we might learn the lessons the man himself was never able to learn.

Walter Jackson Bate

The literary work is not a mere artifact. . . . It can never possess the virginity our "new critics" would like it to have. It persists in remaining a part of something larger.

Leon Edel

1

BEHIND THE SCENES

The McCutcheons of Lafayette, Indiana, were descended from the McCutchens (no "o") of Wigtomshire, Scotland. Their first foothold in the new country, in the 1700s, was in Fairfax County, Virginia. From there they emigrated during the early 1800s to Fairfax Township, Ross County, Ohio, where John Barr McCutcheon, George's father, was born in 1828. About five years later the family moved to Tippecanoe County, Indiana.

George's mother's family, the Glicks—originally Glück from Germany—had settled in Lancaster, Pennsylvania in 1749. Like the McCutcheons the Benjamin Glicks later emigrated westward. In the 1830s, with a group of Pennsylvania Lutherans, they helped found Lancaster, Ohio, where George's mother, Clarissa Glick, was born in 1841. Shortly afterward the Glicks moved to Tippecanoe County, Indiana.

Both families were attracted to Tippecanoe County because of its reputation for abundant rich soil at bargain prices. The Glick farms, of which there were several, were established earlier and prospered more rapidly than the lone McCutcheon farm. In fact, the Glick farms fronted nearly a mile on the planked toll road between Lafayette and Crawfordsville.

Here the grassy plains were relieved only occasionally by gently rolling hills. Each spring more and more fields were planted to corn, some stalks growing as tall as eight feet. Tall oaks and silver maples clustered around the Glicks' water wells and two-storied clapboard houses. The Glicks and the McCutcheons later planted walnut trees, at the tops of which flamboyant cardinals proclaimed their possessive "paree, paree, paree" calls.

The air was also filled, in the humid summers, with sweet smells from the alfalfa fields. During the bitterly cold winter nights one depended for warmth on billowy German featherbeds. But the winter days were brightened by the snow and by crackling oak logs in the fireplaces. According to *Drawn from Memory,* John T. McCutcheon's autobiography, the Glick homestead served almost from the beginning as "headquarters for the meetings of young people for miles about, at no time less than twenty at the table."

During the 1850s those young people included the drover John Barr McCutcheon, who from 1847 had been in charge of shipping cattle and hogs as far east as Pennsylvania. For over ten years John enjoyed the gemütlichkeit of the Glick family—their very name, German for happiness. And on his return from the war between the states he was to be welcome there for the rest of his life. His affection for Clarissa may have begun in 1854, when she was only thirteen. Even then she was accomplished in household skills and the finer arts and crafts; she sang an enchanting alto; she read good literature; she rode horses (she often read while riding); and according to her son John T. "she was universally loved." Clara, as she came to be called, may have set her demure white *Fräuleinhut* for the handsome drover when she was a teenager, but they were not to be married until she was twenty-five because of—among other reasons—John's service in the war.

In 1861 John Barr McCutcheon organized a company of his Tippecanoe County neighbors and friends and, commissioned as Captain of Company K, 15th Indiana Volunteers, joined the Union cause. He was the second youngest of all the Indiana captains. He fought in the Battles of Shiloh and Stone River, among others; but after receiving a severe wound in 1864, he was sent home from Murfreesboro. To regain his health he began working again as a drover, and on weekends he resumed his visits to the Glick homestead.

In October, 1865, he and Clara were married, their ages thirty-eight and twenty-five, respectively. Their first child, George Barr McCutcheon, was born on July 26, 1866. He was to enjoy the attentions of unusually mature parents, his father a proven leader of men, his mother gentle and intelligent. Clara's father had given her as a wedding gift one of the Glick farms on the Romney Road in South Raub, a short distance from the Glick homestead. It was not long before this McCutcheon household, like the Glicks' before it, became a rendezvous—but now, for Captain Barr's friends who had served with him in the war. By 1870, when a second son was born, the McCutcheons had moved to the farmhouse across from the Yellow Barn. For many decades a familiar landmark, this huge, two-storied structure served not only as a storage house but also as an overnight accommodation for transient drovers.

Clara was more formally educated than Barr, who was nonetheless (according to the *Dictionary of American Biography*) "a drover with literary tastes; he had won local fame by writing a five-act play." On surrey rides, also before the bright hearth, he retold tales from Walter Scott's romances. He recited excerpts from *The Lady of the Lake,* characteristically the gallant fight between Roderick Dhu and James Fitz-James. Both parents were well-read and they furnished their homestead, and indeed all the homes they were destined to move into and out of during the 1870s, with reputable literature. Their library included the Bible, Plutarch, Homer's *Iliad* and *Odyssey,* Shakespeare's plays, and Bunyan's *Pilgrim's Progress,* the edition containing an introduction by Edward Eggleston, author of *The Hoosier Schoolmaster.* In good times they also bought the works of such contemporaries as Emerson, Mark Twain, and Lew Wallace. Clara's older brother Elias, a physician and surgeon, whose tastes were literary and musical, invariably gave them books for Christmas and for birthdays. "I was obliged to read good books," George later said. "There was never anything about the house but good books." "House" excluded the Yellow Barn, where George did his surreptitious reading. During a few months before he was eight, in the hayloft of the Yellow Barn, he read many of Beadle's dime novels, including Castlemon's *Frank on a Gunboat.* George would read the classics at Ford School and, later, at Purdue, most of Dickens and all of Thackeray. But his fondness for Oliver Optic, Horatio Alger, and Dead-Eye Dick would die hard.

George's loving but strict parents frowned upon "such trash." From time to time he was bodily chastised by his father, a disciplinarian dedicated to woodshed and switch, as reflected in George's earliest doggerel:

> The boy was bad,
> His pa was mad,
> And the switch was a holy twister.
> When his pa got through,
> Poor boy—he knew
> How it felt to bear a blister.

John Tinney ("Johnny") was born on May 6, 1870, and George adored him from the beginning. Their mutual affection was rarely diminished by sibling rivalry, although many years later John T., as Pulitzer prize-winning cartoonist and celebrated war correspondent, overshadowed George—at least in George's self-effacing estimation, which was to develop almost to masochism. When George was not doing chores or attending school, he and Johnny sledded in the winters, and in the summers swam in the cold waters of Wea Creek, not far from Fort Ouiatenon and the former camp grounds of the Wea Indians. (The Wea swimming sessions were to inspire John T.'s cartoon series "Boy in Springtime" and "Injun Summer.") Both the boys were popular with their peers, and the entire family basked in reflected glory when, in the fall of 1874, Uncle Elias ("Doc") Glick was elected Mayor of Lafayette.

One of the earliest extant pictures of George, in *Drawn from Memory*, reveals a handsome boy about eight years old with animated expression, broad forehead, curly dark hair, and large piercing eyes. From another source one learns that he had a ruddy complexion which was accentuated when he blushed: "My symphony in scarlet gave away my bashfulness," he would say in his maturity.

During the early 1870s George walked with shining morning face to one of the County's one-room schoolhouses, which concentrated on mastery of the three Rs. Although his parents often muttered about the "superior educational opportunities in the City" and ultimately transferred him to Ford School in Lafayette, George did enjoy solid foundations at Old Red-Eye. He received high marks for reading and penmanship, and his biographers must be grateful for the legibility of his manuscripts. A report card issued for him by the Wea Township School Number 8, Tippecanoe County, May 1876, gave him high marks, indeed, in every category. "None" appears after the entries for "Times absent" and "Times tardy." He received a general average of 92, a 95 in reading, and 100 in orthography. That that grade of 100 was not inflated is borne out in a perusal of his manuscripts, in which the spelling is indeed impeccable.

Still, George, along with Johnny, sought intellectual stimulus and the exercise of the imagination outside Old Red-Eye. Early on, George scribbled stories and plays, as did Johnny. At the age of eight George wrote a draft of "Panther Jim: A Tale of Adventure," which he later rewrote as the play *A Scout's Revenge*. The McCutcheon brothers produced their plays (including *Bashful Dude*) in the Yellow Barn, in school yards, in churches, and later behind the County Jailhouse. George, no mean artist, taught John how to draw, especially scenic backdrops on butcher paper.

On May 31, 1875, George acquired a second brother, Ben Frederick, who was destined to give him the basic idea for the best-selling novel of 1903, *Brewster's Millions,* and with whom he would share the royalties. Both George and John idolized Ben and—far from excluding him—involved him as soon as he could walk and talk in many of their thespian activities. They made him first an usher and ticket taker; later, at age four, one of the actors in their home-produced plays. Though lovable, Ben was reticent and at times enigmatic—much like the sealed-off Ben in Thomas Wolfe's *Look Homeward, Angel.*

As for Barr, one of the reasons the family admired him was that he seldom complained about his war wound, which they knew caused him intermittent pain. At Shiloh he had caught a shell fragment behind his right ear, and although the fragment had been removed, he had to wear a clean dressing every day for the rest of his life. (The infection that set in in 1888 proved fatal.)

Another reason Barr's children idolized him was that he was given to playing more or less harmless practical jokes, some of which George would be incorporating, many years later, in his short story "Anthony the Joker." Barr's repertoire of humor included giving Confederate nicknames to all the members of the family. He called George, "Tyler"; Johnny, "Simeon P. Jack"; Ben, "Medders"; and Clara, "Mrs. Warner" ("another cup of your delicious coffee, Mrs. Warner, *if* you please!") No doubt the soubriquet of Tyler reflected George's special, almost aristocratic, status. The Tylers, one of Lafayette's first families, were descended from the early Virginia Tylers.

The Panic of 1873, which pitted financiers against farmers, especially those with over-extended credit, hardly affected the Glicks. With consistent conservatism they had managed to stay solvent. By 1876, however, the slump had sagged down to the livestock trade. Drovers' incomes dwindled to such an alarming low that Barr was forced to seek a livelihood outside the world of cattle and hogs. John Barr McCutcheon—"rarely called Captain, never Mister, more frequently and affectionately Barr"—accepted a position as Manager of the Commissary at Purdue, the new university that had opened in 1874.

For the next year, his family lived in the west end of Ladies' Hall and took their meals at The Boarding House. Here the men and the (outnumbered) women dined together. George, age ten, and Johnny, age six, were enrolled in the Chauncey school. (The Town of Chauncey was later incorporated as the City of West Lafayette.)

Barr's job at Purdue proved to be short-lived—little more than a year, although he could have stayed as long as he pleased. One of his friends, James Baird, who had just been elected Sheriff of Tippecanoe County, offered the post of Deputy Sheriff to Barr provided he and his family would live in the Sheriff's residence adjoining the County Jail, downtown, and look after the prisoners. The salary and fringe benefits were too good to resist, even if the appointment could not last beyond the two-year term of 1877-1879.

Thus in August, 1877, the McCutcheons moved downtown, where Barr assumed practically all the responsibilities of Sheriff. The Sheriff's residence on Fourth Street was an imposing brick house with four huge rooms on each of two floors. Wide hallways separated the rooms. In the basement were the kitchen, laundry, and service quarters; and backed up against this residence was the jail, surrounded by a high brick wall.

As for Lafayette itself in the late 1800s, the City remained laid out east of the Wabash River as it was from its beginnings (early 1800s; incorporated 1853), the numbered streets running north and south, and parallel to the River. Most of the downtown streets were paved with red brick. The other streets remained dusty or muddy according to the weather. Main Street intersected the numbered streets at right angles and was flanked by Columbia and Ferry. The western extension of Main Street, via a bridge across the River, became State Street and led up the hill to the Purdue campus.

In downtown Lafayette the Square—bounded by Main Street, Columbia, Third, and Fourth—was dominated by the Courthouse, a Victorian structure of redoubtable granite. Opposite this matron, like siblings at a mother's skirts, stood the bright-faced law offices, the *Morning Call* Building, the dry-goods store, the Wells Yeager Pharmacy, and—as a kind of father-of-the-family—the four-storied Loeb's Department Store. (Solomon Loeb of Karlstadt, Germany, had arrived in Lafayette in 1869 and in competition with the Gimbels of Vincennes had peddled goods for a year before opening his store.)

By 1877 few of the barges formerly drawn on the Wabash and Erie Canal (1832-1875) tied up at the First Street and Ferry Wharf. The First Street packing houses, which had earlier bustled with Canal commerce, were now converted to less noisy warehouses for hides and wool. Livestock shipments were handled by several railroads, which had put the Canal out of business. Freight yards sprawled among the inland streets. The Monon Line occupied huge yards to the northeast, and its main tracks ran along Fifth Street right through town. Except for these trains vehicles were for the most part horse-drawn, so that pedestrians had to take care where they stepped; they had to exercise vigilance to sniff—not just to stop, look, and listen.

Even with the pungencies of horses the air smelled clean and sweet. Commerce lumbered along during the days, but the evenings furnished such excitements as town socials (some of them in the basements of the churches on Sixth and Seventh Streets), country dances, amateur plays in the Grand Army Hall, and professional theatrical performances at the new Opera House on Sixth Street—from the McCutcheon residence a short walk under the glow of gas lamps.

2

AT CURTAIN RISE

While living in the Sheriff's residence on Fourth Street, Barr and Clara attended the Opera House at least one evening a week, leaving George, age twelve, in charge. One evening a bold burglar, who had secreted himself under the bed in which George and Johnny were sound asleep, made off with over one hundred dollars' worth of family belongings. Since Barr was fond of playing practical jokes on the family, George may at first have suspected that the burglary, which was real enough (the culprit was later apprehended) was just another of Barr's pranks. It is not clear whether the teasing George later received was because of his groundless skepticism or because he had let the burglar get away. Teased he was nonetheless.

Characteristically thin-skinned, George spent many an exasperated moment living the episode down. To put it out of mind, he returned to his story "Panther Jim," rewriting it as a play "for production among the neighborhood kids." Later he collaborated with Johnny, who was even more precocious, in writing "a few other thrillers," including *The Red Avenger,* which they produced in the basement and, weather permitting, in the yard behind the jail. Given John's testimony in *Drawn from Memory,* there is good reason to believe that they tried out some of their plays on the prisoners, with whom they often fraternized. Johnny became better acquainted with the prisoners than did George, who, more often than not, had his head in a book when he was not writing melodramas or delivering newspapers. In fact, at a remarkably callow age Johnny made a daring capture of an escapee.

"Somewhat abruptly about this time," George wrote in "My Maiden Effort," "I concluded that my forte was playwriting. At the advanced age of twelve I *produced* my maiden effort *Panther Jim.* I also wrote a few engaging dramas for Miss Annie Pixley." No such dramas that can be specifically identified as written for Miss Pixley are extant, although they may be embryonic versions that turned up among his juvenilia. Moreover, these "engaging dramas" were probably meant in an imaginary way. He may well have been smitten at this time with a fantasy-fixation on Annie, which was soon to be replaced by his longer-lived adoration for Minnie Maddern. In Miss Pixley's triumphant appearances at the Opera House she played the heroine in *M'Liss,* based on Bret Harte's short story of the same name. This melodrama was to return to the Opera House for several engagements between 1877 and 1887.

Many a dime that George earned for delivering newspapers he spent on Saturday matinees. Gallery seats went for ten cents. Indeed, "twenty seconds after the box office opened," he writes, he was seated in the front row:

> I lived in a beautiful Indiana town, remote from Broadway, yet not one of the places on the map that the stars . . . could afford to ignore when planning their tours of one-night stands. It was, in the proper parlance, a good show-town. Booth and Barrett, Jefferson, Skinner, Robson . . . Modjeska, Julia Marlowe, Minnie Maddern . . . and all the top-notchers made annual visits to the Opera House and played to capacity audiences. If any of those luminaries had ventured a direct stare in a certain spot in the front row of the gallery, they would have beheld a youngish sort of person with curly hair (and a rather superior collection of front teeth) stationed there with his elbows on the rail; and if they had gone to the trouble of making a personal inquiry, they would have discovered that they had taken the last cent out of his pocket within twenty seconds after the box office opened.

The Lafayette Opera House, which had opened in February, 1873, at Sixth Street and Columbia, afforded George a variety of entertainments, including what he himself later called lowbrow when he was teasing his fellow journalist George Ade on the latter's tastes. In 1878, for example, the young McCutcheon might have seen and probably did see Buffalo Bill in *Lost and Won* on February 13; Frank May in *Davy Crockett* on April 12; the New Orleans Minstrels on April 19; the vaudeville of Tony Pastor's troupe "direct from New York City" on September 2; and *Mazeppa and the Wild Horse of Tartary* on November 29.

Through the influence of his parents George was no doubt also exposed to more intellectual fare—on April 4, for example, to Henry Ward Beecher on "The Wastes and Burdens of Society" and, a few weeks later, to the uplifting lectures of Lew Wallace, author of *Ben-Hur*, which in 1880 was added to the McCutcheons' library. There was also plenty of humor—Josh Billings, for example, on January 15 and on several return engagements; even Mark Twain (somewhat later) in a double bill with George Washington Cable.

The Opera House did present operas, to Clara's delight, among them *Aida, Carmen, La Traviata, Mignon, The Bohemian Girl,* and *Lucia di Lammermoor* (McCutcheon alludes to the last in his melodrama *Judith Verne*). But the most reputable offerings during the years George grew up in Lafayette consisted of tragedies and comedies; also adaptations of fiction by George's favorites, Dickens and Thackeray, especially *The Old Curiosity Shop* and *Becky Sharp*. There were as well adaptations of Brontë's *Jane Eyre* and Stowe's *Uncle Tom's Cabin,* with Minnie Maddern as Little Eva. All these were repeated during 1878 and, indeed, annually for several years after, not only in the evenings but also during family matinees at 2:30.

Among the tragedies presented in 1878 were Shakespeare's *Hamlet, King Lear,* and *Romeo and Juliet;* among the comedies, *As You Like It* and *A Comedy of Errors* (the last probably influencing McCutcheon's *The Double Doctor*); Goldsmith's *She Stoops to Conquer* and Sheridan's *The Rivals* and *The School for Scandal* ("minors admitted only if accompanied by adults").

From the beginning the Opera House featured companies on tour; by the end of the 1880s, the Frohman roadshows from New York and an occasional Belasco group from San Francisco in the days before Belasco joined the Frohman syndicate. Even to a boy as young as George it soon became apparent—from the "presented by" on playbills and advertisements—that the best performers belonged to an organization that owned or controlled the theaters and that certainly controlled the bookings. Such contracted performers who appeared in the Lafayette Opera House as early as 1878 included—besides Annie Pixley and Minnie Maddern— Thomas Keane, David Warfield, Richard Mansfield, Maurice Barrymore, Julia Marlowe and E. H. Sothern. Sothern was a young American idol, whom Charles Frohman would later bill as "from England."

One of the most memorable performances of the decade was that of Helena Modjeska in Corneille's *Camille*. Madame Modjeska had emigrated from Poland in 1876 and within a few months became a sensation.

She had stopped in Lafayette (for one performance only) on her way from Chicago to Indianapolis, where she was booked by the Frohman syndicate for a week's run at English's new Opera House. She would portray Nora in *A Doll's House* at Louisville, a few years later, in the first Ibsen production in the United States. It is not known whether the McCutcheons went down to Kentucky to see Modjeska. They did occasionally take the train into Indianapolis, an hour's ride from Lafayette, to see plays at English's. They saw Sarah Bernhardt there, for example, in Rostand's melodrama *L'Aiglon,* a performance described in Booth Tarkington's story "Great Men's Sons."

Occasionally Clara persuaded Barr to visit backstage and extend the stimulating conversation of accomplished thespians by inviting them home for an after-performance supper. On October 4, 1878, at the Lafayette Opera House, the McCutcheons attended a production of the romance *The Rose of Killarney,* starring E. H. Sothern and Jennie Hight. Later that evening, after the performance, Mr. Sothern and Miss Hight were supper guests at the McCutcheon residence. As they walked the two blocks from the Opera House to the Sheriff's quarters, the October air like wine, the two actors jokingly wished to be assured that they were not being arrested.

It is not known how many times after this, if at all, E. H. Sothern was their guest. He did make at least twenty more appearances on the stage of the Opera House (from 1880 on, the Grand Opera House). If he was invited again, he would have been accompanied not by Jennie Hight but by Julia Marlowe, with whom he starred in many plays and who later (1911) became his wife. It is also not known whether George's favorite actress, Minnie Maddern, was ever among the after-theater guests of the McCutcheons. But there is reason to believe that she was. At this time, little did George realize, as the line might read in one of his melodramas, that his path would cross one day in New York, however briefly, with the paths of Minnie Maddern Fiske, David Belasco, and the Frohman syndicate.

In inviting actors, no matter how reputable, to their home, the McCutcheons were risking ostracism by Lafayette's first families, although that was not the circle in which George's parents moved most of the time. First families relegated theater people to a social status only slightly above that of gypsies. In giving performers the recognition generally accorded to lecturing preachers, moreover, the McCutcheons also risked the disapprobation of their church elders. The Presbyterian congregation to which they belonged appears to have held to more Calvinist tenets than George could comfortably live with. In his story "The Marriage Models" he has the unlikable narrator condemn "the microbe of passion" and "Sabbath desecrating." George also rejected the kind of hell fire he satirized in his poem "Lucky It Was a Dream, Being the Chronicle of a Dream After a Sermon Against Dancing." Thus his attending the less fundamentalist Methodist Church in Elston was motivated by considerations other than joy of singing in their choir. Nor was there much promise in his singing. As brother John teased, "The Methodist choir only liked to have him around."

The social status of the McCutcheons, somewhat below that of Lafayette's first families—the Tylers, the Fowlers, the Perrins, the Van Nattas—and somewhat above that of rank-and-file policemen, was to haunt George for much of his life, perhaps because he was something of a snob even if unconsciously. (Still, a daughter of the Van Nattas would one day become quite fond of the author of *Graustark*.) Only George's mother's side of the family truly belonged. They had been clergymen, physicians, and landed gentry. Captain Barr, on the other hand, had acquired no land except what his wife had brought him as dowry. He did enjoy popularity as a drover, a war veteran, and a sheriff—even as a Democrat in a politically conservative stronghold, in which most people, the Glicks among them, registered as Republicans. Aside from their political and denominational ties, indeed, few families in Lafayette would have invited theater people to their homes. Yet it was in such after-theater suppers that young George, when he was permitted to stay up, absorbed the table talk that contributed to his love of the theater and his passion for playwriting.

If a connection can be made between the melodramas he would write and the types of plays that made the deepest and most persistent impressions on him, with or without his parents he must have witnessed more melodramas at the Opera House than any other kinds of plays. The hundreds of playbills preserved in the Tippecanoe County Historical Association's archives indicate that melodrama led far and away all the other offerings from 1878 to the turn of the century—the years in which George grew up in Lafayette and worked as a reporter, later as an editor.

The word melodrama derives from two Greek words: *dramein,* to run or move or do; and *melos,* a melody or song. The lyrical elements in melodrama, when present at all, can be heard in the rhythms of the heroine's impassioned pleas, vestiges of the ancient Greek chorus's pleas and comments, as if from the playwright's own mouth, on certain actions and moral themes. In melodrama the conflicts between good and evil are exaggerated; and the characters, stereotyped and larger than life. Invariably the dramatis personae includes a coal-black villain (in the earliest plays not necessarily hissed and booed by the audience) and a sinned-against heroine of snow-white virtue. In the most stereotyped plots the villain, much older and richer than the heroine, demands the daughter in marriage in return for bailing out the father, who is on the brink of financial ruin. The heroine, goodness incarnate, agrees to sacrifice herself but is at the last moment saved by the handsome young man she loves, a hero whose ambition invariably exceeds his financial assets. In the early melodramas, especially the French versions, the villain perpetrates the most dastardly deeds, while the heroine's behavior is angelic. In *La Fille de l'exile* by Pixérécourt, for example, the victimized heroine pays a kindness to, even saves the life of, her depraved persecutor. The typical melodrama focuses on an oversimplified, almost allegorical conflict between good and evil. How audiences in McCutcheon's era could have been captivated by the melodramatic mode is explained in psychological terms in a 1976 study of melodrama by Peter Brooks. Brooks finds it quite natural for audiences in any era to empathize with, experience a catharsis in, the unfolding drama of good versus evil:

Melodrama regularly simulates the experiences of nightmare, where virtue, representative of the ego, lies supine while menace plays out its occult designs. The end is an awakening brought about by confrontation with the expulsion of the villain, the person in whom all evil seems to be concentrated, and in a reaffirmation of "decent people." . . . We, the audience, feel the need for a melodramatized reality both within and without ourselves. . . . Melodrama offers us heroic confrontation, purgation, purification, recognition.

Brooks, along with Eric Bentley, also finds in melodrama an aesthetic integrity, although different in intent of course from that of tragedy and poetry. Whereas tragedy and poetry signal meanings via symbols and "internalizations," melodrama signals meanings through overt signs or "externalizations." At heart, melodrama represents "the theatrical impulse itself," writes Bentley, "the impulse toward dramatization, heightening, expression, acting out." And in the observation that melodrama "is of the utmost importance to an understanding of Dickens" Brooks contributes a clue to understanding how McCutcheon's lifelong love of Dickens and Thackeray could have been kindled early by adaptations of melodramatic episodes in their works, which he saw in Lafayette.

The Opera House from the beginning imported British and French melodramas, the French in translation. There were as well melodramas by such Americans as Augustin Daly (1838-1899), Augustus Thomas (1857-1934), and David Belasco (1853-1931). Belasco was one of the most prolific adapters of melodramatic episodes in Continental, British, and American novels. A perusal of the playbills of the era in which McCutcheon grew up in Lafayette affords a virtual history-in-outline of melodrama.

For example, Guilbert de Pixérécourt (1773-1844), generally acknowledged founder of melodrama, was represented not only by *The Banished Maiden* but also by *Celine; or the Mysterious Infant,* both of which enjoyed several return engagements. Similarly, *The Octoroon* and *The Jilt* brought perennial attention to the name of Dion Boucicault (1820-1890) even if not always on the playbills themselves. For as Frank Rahill observes in *The World of Melodrama,* playwrights' names during this era were often relegated to minor billing or none at all. The star performers were the thing, scripts remaining secondary in importance, or so it would seem. The playwright and actor Dion Boucicault (to be distinguished from his son of the same name, whom the Frohman syndicate later hired as a manager of one of its London theaters) was an Irishman of French descent. In middle life he moved to the United States and became one of the most influential figures in melodrama. For the Frohmans he worked as chief adapter of foreign plays until he was replaced by Augustus Thomas.

Other favorites included Sarah Bernhardt's friend Victorien Sardou (1831-1908), for his melodramas *Andrea,** *Fedora,* and *Thermidor;* Adolphe Dennery (1811-1899) for his *Two Orphans,* starring Minnie Maddern as Louise. Such melodramas as *The Unequal Match, The Governess,* and *The Ticket-of-Leave Man* by the British playwright Tom Taylor (1817-1880) apparently captured McCutcheon's imagination. He would be adapting Taylor's play *The Fool's Revenge* during an ill-fated road show with his cousin Charles Homrig during the summer of 1884 (the Clifford interlude below). One of the most sensational of the melodramas McCutcheon witnessed was Augustin Daly's *Under the Gaslight,* in which the heroine was tied to a log about to be sawed in two. David Belasco's productions of *The Millionaire's Daughter, The Mighty Dollar,* and Bulwer Lytton's *Money* may well have planted in McCutcheon

---

*In 1885 Steele MacKaye adapted Sardou's *Andrea* as the musical *In Spite of All,* starring Minnie Maddern.

one of the seeds that later germinated in his and his brother Ben's novel *Brewster's Millions*. McCutcheon was impressed above all, as reflected in one of his reviews, with Augustus Thomas's Americana series of plays, especially *Arizona*, and by Thomas's melodrama *The Burglar*, which enjoyed a ten-year run.

Among other American melodramas perennially brought back to Lafayette "by popular demand" between 1878 and 1887 were *M'Liss; East Lynne; or, The Elopement* (GBMc later satirized elopements in *The Flyers*); and *Ten Nights in a Bar Room*, with Minnie Maddern as Mary, singing the hit song "Father, Dear Father, Come Home with Me Now." Runners-up included *Heroine in Rags, Out of Bondage, Two Little Vagrants, A Mother's Prayer, The White Slave, The Factory Girl; or All That Glitters Is Not Gold*, and *The Double Marriage*, which may have given GBMc the idea for his best novel, *The Sherrods*.

Except for Augustus Thomas's, perhaps, these melodramas could boast little literary distinction, and not one of them was informed by any intended humor. With his precocity, therefore, McCutcheon, viewing them from the gallery, developed not only a logistical but also an aesthetic distance, a detachment that no doubt prompted some of the parody in his own melodramas. The characters and dialogue of Opera House melodramas struck GBMc as patently unbelievable, and he poked fun at them in *Vashti* (1882) and *Judith Verne* (1885). In protest against unintended naiveté he made Vashti and Judith perversely complicated and blew up their hifalutin lines to the point of farce. Several years later he and his friend George Ade, both reporters for local newspapers, hooted at some of the foolish solemnities on the local stage and elicited cutting stares from some of the more innocent devotees in the audience.

Still, as a child of his milieu, McCutcheon must have identified with the sense of justice vs. injustice dramatized in these Opera House plays, as he did in the novels of Dickens and Thackeray, which he was now reading avidly—a few on school assignment, many more on his own.

3

OLD DOMINION, MINNIE MADDERN, AND PURDUE

At the end of Barr's two-year term, when a new sheriff was elected, the ex-drover returned to managing shipments for livestock owners. Instead of moving back to South Raub, however, the McCutcheons moved to Elston, only two miles south of town. There the Wabash Railroad station was more convenient to shipping, and the boys would be closer to Old Red-Eye.

At least once a week the McCutcheons drove their surrey into Lafayette for provisions, taking all three boys. (Little sister, Jessie, had not yet arrived.) On such occasions Barr entertained the family with songs and stories. "George's skill in colorful narration," wrote John T., "was inherited from our father, a rare raconteur, who thrilled us. Once the family surrey, loaded with the five McCutcheons, headed south to Romney to see a traveling troupe enact the melodrama *Ten Nights in a Bar Room*. All the children from miles around attended this as their first experience of a theatrical performance." It was old stuff, of course, for George.

As a drover, Barr made a comfortable living, but he was not the "man of means" young George boasted about. Hence Barr allowed the boys to earn spending-money as long as their odd jobs did not interfere with school work. George deferred to Johnny when it came to canvassing neighbors for work. George only "helped John-the-entrepreneur" in his Sunday newspaper route (forty subscribers). To get the papers and divide the load, both boys jogged the four-mile round trip between Elston and Lafayette. In below-zero weather they used the buckboard and were back for breakfast by eight.

Nor was George the only playwright in the family. When John wrote the comedy *Blunders of a Bashful Dude,* which was produced in the yard behind Old Red-Eye and later in the basement of the Lehman Church, George was type-cast in the leading role. Female parts were played by even younger boys in the neighborhood, and a walk-on female role was played by little brother Ben. The producers were probably unaware that they were thus observing a convention of the Elizabethan stage. At the Opera House George was to see a reversal of that convention: young male roles played by females—Rackstraw, for example, played by Minnie Maddern.

Other pastimes in Elston included spelling-bees (George spelled everyone down) and exchanging tall tales around the cracker barrel or the pot-bellied stove in Johnston's General Store. In the countryside surrounding Elston there were occasional barn raisings and perennial corn huskings in the summers. Summer also ushered in float trips down the Wabash, swimming, picnics, baseball games, and horse racing. Purdue's football games brightened each chilly grey fall. Basketball had yet to turn the winters into Hoosier hysteria. But the winters did provide God's plenty of sledding, pond-skating, and sleighriding. Spring came suddenly, turning the snow to slush, seducing the elms into displaying their nubile buds through gauzy green mists, and triggering students' excursions out of town. In every season interesting visitors brought word of Chicago, the great urban magnet to the north, which attracted young people from Lafayette and Purdue.

Barr and Clara, sensitive to how far their children were "advanced beyond the curriculum of Elston School," sent George—and later Johnny—to Lafayette's Ford School, which since 1869 had stood at the corner of Fourteenth and South Streets. At this time (the late 1870s) Ford School was accommodating all grades from elementary through high school. (Lafayette High School was not built until 1890). In 1879 four of Ford's teachers were assigned to ninety-two high school students, a ratio of one teacher to twenty-three students. The curriculum was impressively educative, as outlined in the Annual Reports of the Trustees. In grades 9 through 12, for example, the students were exposed to solid doses of Latin (including Caesar's *Commentaries on the Gallic War,* Cicero's *Orations,* and Virgil's *Aeneid*); English and American literature, grammar, and composition; arithmetic, algebra, geometry, and trigonometry; astronomy (there was an observatory on the roof); botany, zoology, and chemistry "or" physics; history, geography, and music. George majored in English and history.

George worked hard at Ford School and at home on assignments, but he also managed to keep up with his own writing projects, including plays and stories. One of his stories, "The Countess Thalma," in eighteen neatly penned pages, is a Poe-esque tale set in Italy. Thalma was "the daughter of Ravenelli, cousin to the King." This story is unique in its daring eroticism: "He [Antonio] moistened those fatal lips and then they met the soft white skin, clinging to it as with the fierceness of starvation. . . . Almost as his lips left her flesh, a cry of pain escaped them." McCutcheon at fourteen! Not for twenty-eight years—not before *Brood House*, his best play—would he write anything as erotically passionate. For in spite of fancying himself an enemy of prudishness, he was more deeply committed to his Calvinist heritage than he himself realized.

Almost surely, George's father did not see "The Countess Thalma," but he did see other pieces of George's early fiction and did not approve. Barr preferred that George spend less time on creative writing, more on practical exposition. At the end of George's first year at Ford School, and just as he was planning to devote his summer to intensive playwriting, he was sent to work at an uncle's farm:

My father did not believe I could write even a fairly intelligible school composition . . . and undertook to convince me of the error of my ways by sending me to my uncle's farm, where I was expected to work off a portion of my ambition and at the same time cultivate corn instead of literature. . . . [At this time in George's productions, one could hardly tell the difference.] My employment as a farm hand covered a period of three weeks, and I did not do enough hard work to acquire a calloused hand.

In 1881, when he was fifteen, George composed the melodrama *Old Dominion; or the Banshee of Bathurst Hall,* subtitled *A Comedy in Five Acts.* Later in the year, he sent a copy of that opus to an actress he admired ever since he had been patronizing the local Opera House—Miss Minnie Maddern.

Miss Maddern was to become a favorite in New York and in road tours throughout the country, including Lafayette. In 1890, two years after she had divorced a young musician by the name of Legrand White, she married Harrison Fiske, editor of the *New York Dramatic Mirror,* and left the Frohman syndicate. When she returned to the stage, in 1893, it was under her husband's management so that she could choose her own roles. Although she appeared in many comedies and musicals, she won critical acclaim for her dramatizations of Thackeray's *Becky,* Hardy's

Tess, and above all for her roles in plays by Ibsen. Her performances established her as one of the greatest interpreters of the intellectual drama of her time.

This young woman, whom George and many another theatergoer idolized, not only acted but also sang. George would never forget the radical understatement with which she sang "In the gloaming, oh my darling," as she gazed not at the audience but into the gas-log fireplace in one of the scenes of *Caprice.* Although she was not tall, she carried herself with an almost regal presence. As Frank Griffith, one of her biographers, observed, "Everyone was captivated and smitten with her masses of glorious red hair, her deep blue eyes, and her magnetic luminous intensity." Perhaps only a perfectionist like James Montgomery Flagg would have caviled at the fleshiness of her nose.

She was born on December 19, 1865, in New Orleans, into a family of actors. She made her stage debut at age three in Little Rock as the child Duke of York in Shakespeare's *Richard III* and later played several other boys' roles—among them, the Gamin in *Under the Gaslight* (1869), Little Fritz in *Our German Cousin* (1870), and Paul in *The Octoroon,* for which the undated Lafayette Opera House playbill (probably 1874 or 1875) listed her as "Little Miss Minnie." When she was eleven years old she gave scores of performances as Little Eva in the dramatization of *Uncle Tom's Cabin.* In 1878 and 1879 she appeared as Ralph Rackstraw in Gilbert and Sullivan's *H.M.S. Pinafore.* In 1880 she played the ingenue in four musical romances: *The Honeymoon* and *René's Daughter* (a double bill), *In Spite of All,* and an early version of *Caprice,* for which the Lafayette bill headlined her as "The Young American Artiste." By 1881, just before she started touring the country with the musical comedy *Fogg's Ferry,* she had made at least a dozen appearances in Lafayette.

Of course in 1881 George was aware of only those accomplishments of Miss Maddern's that any other member of the audience knew of, although he was no doubt more perceptive than any other spectator his age. What he had witnessed of her achievement convinced him that she was something special and that she could not help having an even more brilliant future. He was so impressed—and she was, after all, close to his own age—he decided to consult her about his play *Old Dominion.* Although she was his senior by only a year, he "respectfully solicited" her "candid reactions and suggestions."

In a two-page letter, the lady informed me [McCutcheon later reports with self-deprecating wit] that there was really a great deal to my play. In fact, she went so far as to say that there was more to it than any other play she had ever seen. The first act alone, she wrote, would run (if permitted) from eight o'clock in the evening until nearly six the next morning.

Miss Maddern was characteristically generous. She did not say that the first act would consume "two weeks' playing-time," as brother John teased in his version of the anecdote. And she no doubt would have taken the time to respond to George even if she had not accepted the hospitality of the McCutcheons at one of their after-theater suppers. Her aesthetic rule of parsimony, quite sound of course, later prompted her to write one-act plays herself—among them, "The Rose," "Not Guilty," "A Light from St. Agnes," and "The Eyes of the Heart"—and to cut or tighten the three-act and four-act plays, except Ibsen's, which she and Harry Fiske produced once she left the Frohman syndicate. Anyway, even though she had in effect said, "Give it up, George," and plunged him into a two weeks' depression, the young McCutcheon persisted in writing plays. He managed also to stay abreast of the studying required in the college-preparatory program at Ford School.

Extant rosters of Ford graduates do not include the name of George Barr McCutcheon because by 1882, at the age of sixteen, he was enrolled in the Purdue Preparatory Academy. Despite the solid foundations he received at Ford, or could have received had he remained with their Class of 1883, he could not be admitted to Purdue University without preparing, at the Academy, for the rigorous University entrance examinations about which President Emerson White was adamant.

President White presided over the required chapel services daily at 10:30 a.m. and listed himself in the catalogue's roster of faculty as professor of philosophy and psychology. Other members of the faculty listed in Purdue's Ninth Annual Register (1882-1883) included John Maxwell, professor of English and history; Annie Peck, instructor in Latin and foreign languages; and the celebrated Harvey Wiley, M.D., professor of chemistry and physics. Dr. Wiley was also the baseball coach. The same register lists among the "irregular" (i.e., non-degree) students "George Barr McCutcheon, Elston."

As for the curriculum, according to the First Annual Register:

Students in any of the [programs] except Agriculture and Industrial Design are required to spend five terms in the study of French and seven terms in the study of German Language and Literature. . . . The time given by the student in English, French, and German . . . affords a general knowledge, which must prove of practical advantage in any pursuit.

Latin was apparently not required but was offered as an elective by Miss Annie Peck, who was (according to Purdue historians Hepburn and Sears) "remembered for her excellence in Latin." With her, George almost surely read Plautus's *Menaechmi (The Twins),* Plautus and Terence then characteristically part of beginning college Latin.

The Register for 1882 does not specify textbooks, but it does list some "Recommended Reference Books"—among them Andrews' *Latin-English Lexicon,* Allibone's *Dictionary of Authors,* Chambers' *Cyclopedia of English Literature,* and Taine's *History of English Literature.* The same Register also lists names of periodicals subscribed to by the Library—among them the *Atlantic Monthly, Harper's Weekly, Harper's Monthly, The Nation, American Naturalist, Scientific American, The Magazine of Art, The Athenaeum, The Century, North American Review,* and the *Times* of London.

Secret societies, fraternities, and sororities were not permitted, although professional clubs were encouraged. Among the most prestigious, at this time, was the Carlyle Club, devoted to the cultivation of literature and oratory. There is no evidence that George was a member. Unfortunately, while George was at Purdue, there was not yet a Harlequin Club, devoted to play production.

The whole idea of having prep students on the campus—a policy not to be abandoned until the presidency of James Smart in 1894—was regarded with contempt by the upper classmen. H. B. Knoll, a Purdue historian, writes, "Regular Univeristy students regarded the Preps as an infestation, saying that they gave Purdue the air of a high school, and assailed them with all manner of gibes and ridicule. A Prep was depicted in *The Debris* [yearbook] as a stupid and ignorant little monster who should have been made to stay at home."

George was of course not exempt from the hazing that preppies and freshmen received from the upperclassmen. Thin-skinned, he tended at times to believe himself to be the "ignorant little monster" he was ragged as. At other times, in a spirit of "I'll show them!" he would compensate by indulging in an orgy of scribbling. He wrote verse (all doggerel), essays, and plays. He wrote at least two plays and several fragments, among them a fragment play, *The Reef Bell,* and a brief tableau-like play, *A Mythological Malady.*

He wrote several short stories. Rockwell, the Purdue freshman and protagonist of George's unpublished short story "Miss Divinity," was no doubt an alter ego. Rockwell was too shy to introduce himself to the young lady he worshiped from afar, (a young lady who looked like Minnie Maddern) only to learn in the end that she wished he had taken the initiative sooner. The more aggressive male would-be lovers in George's stories and epistolary fiction of this period are patent boors, whose egotistical manners are as conspicuous as their illiterate-looking grammar and spelling. Yet McCutcheon's ideal male protagonist is allowed his dreams and ambitions, which, even if not overtly announced, are deprecated with a kind of ironic wit that became part of McCutcheon's trademark voice in all his writings regardless of genre or mode. Here, for example, is the opening sentence in "Miss Divinity": "Rockwell knew that something was needed to complete the great system of the Universe and he entered Purdue with the confident belief that he was to supply the missing mechanisms as rapidly as the world could grow accustomed to them."

One of the plays he wrote at the time, "begun on March 5th and finished March 10th, 1882," as he recorded on the first page, was *Vashti, a Play in Four Acts*. This thirty-six page melodrama, which he penciled neatly on legal-size paper, reveals some precocious insights into the feminine mystique. Vashti, a young woman in love with the dashing young Dallas, at first tries to conceal her jealous interest in him and her envy of a rival, Manon Beeson. In a heart-to-heart talk with her mother, Vashti says, "Do you think Manon is pretty?"

Vashti's Mother: Very—why do you ask, my dear?
Vashti: Nothing—only Dallas thinks she is. *(Sourly)* Of course she *is* pretty. But really, do you think men know anything about it?

Later Vashti reveals her true feelings: "I feast my eyes on his—I devour his every syllable—I drink in his smiles, and still I'm always hungry and thirsty." In his teens GBMc seems to have been obsessed with the phenomenon of female erotic hunger. Much later, in an interview with a *Boston Evening Transcript* reporter, McCutcheon volunteered—again with characteristic self-effacement—that he was never satisfied with his depictions of women.

In 1883, the year Hoosiers were buying and quoting James Whitcomb Riley's first collection, *The Old Swimmin' Hole . . .*, George passed his entrance examinations at Purdue and was admitted as a freshman. With Professor Annie Peck he read French and German, no doubt also Latin, literature. He won the position of shortstop on the varsity nine. He also won a position as part-time reporter on the *Lafayette Journal,* his assignment to report items of newsworthy interest about persons and events at the University.

As a cub reporter and student, George found it convenient to use one of the typewriters at the *Journal* office, which stayed open all night. On his way back to the campus, after midnight, he occasionally encountered a town drunk who had imbibed too much "Forty Rod" whiskey. Such encounters inspired his doggerel "Old Forty Rod," one of *Several Short Ones* he published privately, much later, for the amusement of his family.

Another of George's verses of this period was inspired by a letter to the editor, in which a local Puritan, almost like a voice out of 1642, attacked the "iniquitous presentations at the local Opera House." In defending the theater, George puns on "angels" and "wings":

> Do the cranks who insist that the stage is a snare
> From whence dire iniquity springs
> Ever credit the angels with one little pair
> While the stage has a job lot of wings?

The puns are of course jejune, and the verse a jingle, but even at seventeen McCutcheon felt embarrassed by, perhaps supercilious toward, some of his townsmen's strait-laced fundamentalism and anti-intellectualism. Many years later, in New York, he and his wife attended one of Manhattan's most liberal churches.

4

JUVENILIA;
OR, THE HILARIOUS NOVICE

As a victim of his own snobbishness George was at least temporarily obsessed with the glamor attaching to titled Englishmen, to monetary fortunes, and to heirs and heiresses, as reflected in his comedy/melodrama *Buck & Gagg,* one of several he wrote about this time.

In this play, set in the London of 1883, Buck Pendragon, a young reporter, rooms with a Cockney his age, one Cassius Gagg. Buck and his cousin Macready Pendragon are rivals for a deceased uncle's fortune and for the affections of Miss Merriby, a young American actress, née Miss Valency, of Brooklyn. Miss Merriby is as informed with integrity and grace as the real-life actress Miss Maddern but is otherwise as indigent as the other characters who live in the run-down boarding house in the opening scene. Macready, depicted as more depraved than any of the other villains (there are at least three), is at one time believed to be the heir to the Pendragon fortune. In the surprise ending, however, the rightful heir turns out to be Cash Gagg. In fact, it turns out that he had been left in a foundlings' home by his mother, Sister Francesca—formerly Lady Pendragon!

Aside from the preposterous plot, the piece is full of aliases, disguises, duals, duels, and the innocent use of manqué language, which McCutcheon himself would later parody in his more sophisticated melodramas. But a certain amount of junk is inevitable in an early prolific outpouring. McCutcheon was indeed prolific; he was continually writing plays and producing them at home with the help of neighbors. But his juvenile attempts also reveal flashes of inventiveness, creative bravura, hilarious recklessness.

The most ambitious of his juvenilia, *Midthorne, a Play in Five Acts,* reflects, in addition, his interest in and knowledge of Colonial American history. No doubt, this interest had been stimulated by the story-telling Barr, whose family roots went deep into Colonial Virginia. GBMc's respect for that material is reflected in the meticulous neatness of the manuscript (unlike the careless scrawl in his fragmentary play *The Reef Bell*). The dramatis personae (McCutcheon's phrase) in *Midthorne* includes, besides Sir William Berkeley and Nathaniel Bacon, Berkeley's best friend, Stephen Burgoyne; Burgoyne's children, Basil and Ruth; Philip Midthorne, the Jamestown gunsmith and hero of the play; Midthorne's sister, Juliet; and Tippler Bailey, "an eccentric old man."

Here are McCutcheon's "In Substance" and his notes on "The Scenes."

In Substance—In the years 1676 and 1677 Nathaniel Bacon and a small company of oppressed Virginians rebelled against the administration of Sir William Berkeley, Governor of the young state. Bacon's famous rebellion was of short duration but it was waged with terrible determination. Several reasons were given for the revolt but in the main it was over Indian affairs. Bacon was overthrown and soon died, leaving Berkeley in power, fully hated by all Virginia.

The Scenes—The play begins in and about Jamestown during September, 1677, when the Rebellion was at its height. In the first act the homes of Midthorne and Burgoyne are shown; the second displays its incidents in the quaint old cabin occupied by Tippler Bailey just outside of Jamestown; the events of the third transpire in the Governor's home, Jamestown; the first scene of the fourth act is in the forest near the village, and the second is laid in the streets of Jamestown; act five shows Midthorne's home in London one year after the events occurring in the previous acts.

The dialogue reverberates with echoes of Shakespeare and the King James Bible:

"I hied myself to Berkeley's house."
· ·
"By what right dost call me out to greet the sunrise before the sun himself hath warmed the earth?"
· ·
"'Twere not well if we be looked upon as spies."

Two shorter pieces, *The Reef Bell* and *A Mythological Malady,* reveal an easy familiarity with the literature and language he encountered during this phase of his education. With its barrage of ablative absolutes Caesar's *Commentaries on the Gallic War,* for example, left scars on his early prose—especially on the syntax of *The Reef Bell.* The prefatory "argument" in which he blocks out the acts contains more than a few such constructions. One specimen: "In Act Fourth, Ruby is nursing Dick back to life, *he having been almost dead for several months.*"

Like many another early McCutcheon, *The Reef Bell* abounds with villains foiled and heiresses fulfilled; unlike most of his other plays *The Reef Bell* is tinged with a maritime nostalgia, reminiscent of Longfellow's poem "The Wreck of the Hesperus." The setting is the lighthouse "Old Dominion" in "Rocky View," a small town on the coast of Virginia. The lighthouse keeper, Old Joe Darrel, has brought up as his wards Miss May and Miss Ruby, heiresses of Edward Clifford, lost at sea. May's fiancé is Jack Line of the clipper *Storm-Cloud.* Ruby's fiancé is Richard Savage (quite a noble one). Ed Clifford's brother, Captain Harry, has survived the shipwreck and, in search of his nieces, employs Detective Silence (a character to be recycled in McCutcheon's melodrama *Judith Verne*).

One feature of *The Reef Bell* that facilitates its placement among McCutcheon's juvenilia is that he abandons some of his own blocking. In "Act the First," instead of meeting the characters promised in the synoptic Argument, one meets Evelyn, Violet, and Smykes. One does meet Richard, but his amorous repartee is exchanged with a Dulcie Ford, not with Ruby. The opening also "discovers" Evelyn suggesting to her friends that they "get up a party and go to a romantic resort in the region of the Lackawanna Lakes."

So much for *The Reef Bell* except for one more note. On the second page of the manuscript McCutcheon doodled some scrawls reminiscent of the Palmer method of penmanship. Beside his own name there appear a "C. Callahan" and a "Geo. M. Clifton." The latter proved to be prophetically close to "George M. Clifford," the pseudonym GBMc would use in his ill-fated (cliffhanger?) road show the next year. "Callahan" likely referred to the playwright Charles Callahan, author of the musical comedy *Juanita,* starring Minnie Madern. As mentioned above, George, along with many another male theatergoer, had a crush on Minnie. He must have regarded Callahan as a formidable rival since *Juanita,* which played at the Opera House, had been "written expressly for Miss Maddern," as the playbill said. What Miss Maddern would be keeping secret for two years was that during a subsequent tour with the musical comedy *Fogg's Ferry* she would marry the drummer in that show's orchestra.

As for McCutcheon's poetic drama *A Mythological Malady*, it reflects not only his familiarity with, but also his authentic feeling for, Homer's *Iliad* and for the tales of Troy and Greece. The place is Troy during the Trojan War, and allusions to Menelaus, Helen, Paris, Hector, and Achilles abound. The set is "a garden in Troy the day before the ending of the siege." The chief characters are Grottus, beloved of Yetive, and Grottus' sister Oveda, beloved of Deutonius. Yetive* is impatient for the war to end so that she can marry Grottus ("Oh, that Menelaus had back his Helen, that Paris had never been born!"). She tries at first to persuade Grottus to defect, but his decision against doing so ("Stay back? No! Grottus, thy adorer, will stride with Hector, his friend in battle. Is not that an honor?") echoes the theme "I could not love thee, dear, so much, loved I not honor more." Yetive's cousin Deutonius tries out on her a long ode he has written "To Oveda" ("No mortal being knows more queenly grace / nor borne the sex of Venus."). During the reading Grottus eavesdrops and at first mistakes Deutonius as his rival for the love of Yetive. The early McCutcheon mixture of bravura and corn that helps place *A Mythological Malady* among his juvenilia is exemplified in such lines as these:

Grottus: Thou art sweeter, dearer, better, lovelier, nobler, more delicious—
Yetive: Trust a man for synonyms.

In *Judith Verne* (1885) one of the most hilarious scenes satirizes dueling—not just the convention itself but also some of its stereotyped maneuvers on and off the stage. Here GBMc uncannily anticipates the Monty Python type of British music-hall humor. (Python has burlesqued the dueling in Shakespeare's plays.) Moreover, in the act after Judith Verne's Dallas has been wounded in the *chest* he appears with a blood-soaked bandage around his *head.* GBMc would be satirizing dueling even more farcically in *George Washington's Last Duel* (1892), his dramatization of, and improvement upon, Thomas Nelson Page's story of the same name.

---

*Yetive's name was to be recycled for the princess in *Graustark.* In real life Yetive was a daughter of Lieutenant Abner Pickering, head of military training at Purdue.

5

THE GEORGE M. CLIFFORD INTERLUDE

Young McCutcheon was an avid reader of the news. He knew the names and backgrounds of people elected to office nationally, regionally, and locally. As reflected in the allusions in his melodrama *Judith Verne,* George even knew the name of an obscure postmaster general (William Villas) appointed by President Grover Cleveland. Cleveland was one of McCutcheon's few heroes among public officeholders. Living in an area predominantly Republican, the Barr McCutcheon family had nevertheless remained Democrats. In fact, George, along with brother John, participated in the hurly-burly of the Cleveland-Blaine campaign of 1884. They worked actively for the Cleveland headquarters in Lafayette and, on behalf of their candidate, wrote some of the campaign copy that appeared in the *Elston News* and the *Lafayette Morning Call,* the paper for which their friend George Ade would later be working as a reporter.

All this activity, however, George regarded as marking time—at best as experience that might some day come in handy in his career as playwright and actor. In his autobiographical essay "How I Retired from the Stage" he refers to the years 1882-1884 as "dormant" except for drafts of "several plays" he managed to write:

For some reason—if I remember rightly it had something to do with the college curriculum—I remained dormant for the next three years as far as ambition was concerned. Between examinations in my freshman and sophomore years I wrote several new plays for myself and other stars. ...Miss Julia Marlowe and the then *Miss* Minnie Maddern, stars in their teens and very lovely to behold, were among the actresses selected to support me in my upward rush to fame.

30

At eighteen George was two years younger than most of his sophomore classmates. But George's sophomore year was his last at Purdue. He failed his final examinations—no doubt because he had devoted most of his time to unassigned writing. Partly to allay the pains of his embarrassment and humiliation, he joined his cousin Charles Homrig in a traveling theatrical company. This interlude should be relished in McCutcheon's own words and self-deprecating humor. His own account follows almost in its entirety:

During my eighteenth summer I achieved a great deal. In the first place I had my first dress suit. To live up to it I cultivated in a painstaking way what I was pleased to call a mustache, a nobby sort of ornament that nobody seemed to notice unless they caught me in the act of trying to twirl it. Also, I completed my college education by failing to keep ahead of the incoming freshmen and went out into the cold, unfeeling world totally unprepared to meet any of the adventures of life.

This brings me to the beginning of my career as an actor. I had a cousin [Charles Homrig] a few years older than myself who also wanted to be an actor. He was the victim of a delusion. Falling into a snug little fortune in the photography business, he decided that the best way to increase it was to organize, finance, and lead a "show." He wasn't fixed in his mind whether it should be a circus or a theatrical enterprise. At any rate he had an unchangeable longing to appear under canvas and to be transported from place to place in conveyances common to old-fashioned but glorious road-shows . . . I have neglected to state that my father was a man of means, that my home was ideal, that my mother adored me, and that my younger brothers and sister were quite satisfactory. There was absolutely no reason why I shouldn't have stayed at home and had something to eat every day instead of entering upon a career as an actor.

My cousin was definitely committed to show business. The latter half of the previous winter, he purchased a "main top" capable of seating two thousand people, numerous canvas wagons, starter-and-pole wagons, propswagons, cook- and horse-tents, a ticket-wagon of glittering gold . . . and a portable stage with three sets of scenery and accessories. My versatile cousin painted the scenery himself . . . The route the show was to take had to be so arranged that the "jumps" were no farther apart than fifteen or twenty miles, for the entire "aggregation" (as it was emblazoned on the billboards) was to be transported by wagon.

Of course I was in a tremendous state of unrest. It wasn't by any means certain whether my parents would permit me to go with the show—indeed, it was almost a foregone conclusion that they would refuse. Prematurely I was cast for one of the comedy parts. As I look back on it now, there were nothing but comedy parts. . . . The funniest part in the play was that of the young hero who returned to his native heath and sang a heart-rending ballad over his mother's grave.

I had done a great deal of work on behalf of the production. Quite humbly I confess to rewriting a play of Tom Taylor's [*The Fool's Revenge,* 1859]. If Mr. Taylor could have lived forty years longer than he did and could have managed to visit any one of a number of small Indiana towns during the summer of 1884 he might have seen a play that would have given him the . . . pleasure of laughing himself to death. But fortunately he was already dead and buried in England. [He had died in 1880.]

In fear and trembling I broached the subject to my father and mother. I was forced to tell them that unless I played the part of "Policy Newcomb" the play would be a failure and that Charlie would lose all his money. My father expressed himself very succinctly. He said it would serve the blamed fool right. My mother was a little more indefinite. She asked me if there were to be any women in the company. I had to say yes. After that she wasn't quite so amenable to reason as I had hoped. I had counted on her good offices. She was my best friend, and if she were to go back on me—well, I was a long time in even half-way convincing her that none but the very finest women in the country would be tolerated by the management: They were to come from Chicago.

Realizing the importance of having me in the cast if not on the payroll, my cousin—who happened to be a favorite of my mother—decided that the only thing for him to do was to go up to the house and talk it over with her. In the process of perfecting himself in the triple role of proprietor, manager, and star, he had acquired a plug hat and gold-braided ebony cane. Supported by these symbols of respectability, he approached my mother. She surrendered. She said she would take the matter up with my father and no doubt he would consent to let me go.

Long afterwards she confessed to me all she remembered of her conversation with my father. . . . I would have been doubly pained had I known at the outset of my career as an actor that it was to strike my father as a joke. . . . At any rate, in consenting, he assured my mother that I would be home in a couple of months if not sooner and that it was just as well to let me get the nonsense out of my system while I was still young enough to recover from the shock. What a wise, far-seeing man he was!

Well, the company was engaged, and also the teamsters, the canvasmen, the musicians, the cooks, and everyone else. The ladies of the "aggregation" came from Chicago, secured through a Clark Theatrical Agency. My leading woman, a dashing brunette, arrived in town accompanied by her small brother. She announced that unless he were allowed to travel with her she would have to give up the job. Unexpected symptoms of thrift manifested themselves in my cousin. . . . As long as he had to be inflicted with this boy, he would make use of him. So I was instructed to introduce a boy's part into Mr. Taylor's already unrecognizable play. I couldn't think of a thing better than a sort of tableau at the end of the last act, in which Ernest (that was the pest's name) was revealed in a somewhat strained endeavor to be an angel. . . . I can't remember what connection that had with the story. . . . Before Ernest had been with us for two days, he was hated by everyone in the aggregation.

It was necessary for me to provide myself with two changes of costume, also a wig and a trunk. The trunk alone deserves mention here. Firmly convinced that the name McCutcheon would not look well on the program . . . I elected to call myself Clifford. I bought a nice little trunk for two dollars and a half and had it marked with bold black letters . . . "George M. Clifford, COMMEDIAN." You will observe that the trunk dealer was either an uneducated man or one of those unhappy people who cannot let well enough alone. It was fortunate that I had decided not to be a "traggedian."

The main top was first erected on a farm owned by my aunt, some ten miles out in the country, and there we rehearsed. The troupe ate her out of house and home. There were a dozen of us, and we were always hungry. I promptly fell in love with the girl who played the character old-woman part. I shall not mention her name here, for of all that motley crew she alone in later years became a conspicuous figure on the American stage.

We opened in the village of Green Hill on a rainy night. . . . The tent was crowded. My cousin's neighbors and acquaintances flocked to our premiere.

My attack of stage fright must have been serious. . . . A sort of stupor set in about an hour before the gaily painted curtain made its spasmodic ascension and did not pass till . . . the end of the last act. My fellow players are authority for the statement that I made my entrances and exits and spoke my lines, but they went further and complained that I didn't say 'em at the right time. Nor was it any easier to get me off the stage than it was to get me on. The only thing I can remember is looking down into the orchestra and catching the troubled eye of Bob Knopf, the cellist, a red-faced little man who seemed to be as unconscious as I. For as I afterward learned, he had finished playing nearly half the selection intended for the second act while the rest of the musicians were playing the overture. I shall never forget the look he gave me. It seemed to say, "Oh, my God!" . . . It appears, however, that I had made a favorable impression. The boss canvas-man, who was in a position to hear, told me later that no less than fifty people declared, as they went out, that if it hadn't been for me they wouldn't have had a single chance to laugh.

McCutcheon goes on to relate that the standing-room-only house and the three-hundred-dollar receipts put the troupe into high but treacherous confidence. That first night, at Green Hill, Indiana, proved to be the only successful night of the entire tour. There followed rain, mud, half-empty tents, and continual losses. The canvas-men cursed the weather and drank a good deal of whiskey "as an antidote for water." The constant rain and the soggy food and bedding seem also to have melted George's manly facade into little-boy homesickness:

How I longed for home, sweet home, and for mother! I didn't long for father, for he did not represent fried chicken and gravy, griddle cakes and mashed potatoes, nor nice clean beds, nor a gargle for the sore throat I had developed, nor a sympathetic hug and a soft voice that said, "Now drink that and try to go to sleep, there's a good boy."
... The management decided to lay up for a week or two and let the rain have its way. Eight or ten towns were "canceled," the advance agent was called back for instructions, and we settled down to wait and watch.
Presently the sun shone, and with a great rattle of wagons we were off again. For three days we traveled to reach the town in which we were to re-open. Those were happy days. We were all very jolly.... My love affair progressed nicely, notwithstanding the fact that the young lady was totally unaware of its existence.... She possessed two of the heaviest suitcases I had ever had the joy of carrying. She was very sweet about it, always talking about what a strong powerful fellow I was and how helpless she'd be if I ever took it into my head to grab her in my arms and try to kiss her. Being a very courtly young gentleman, I begged her not to be afraid that I would. Alas! If only she had begged *me* not to be afraid!
Strange as it may seem, the good weather did not bring us prosperity. Town after town failed to come up to our expectations. To brace up the performances, we introduced a number of songs and some haphazard dances. Poor old Tom Taylor!
By this time I was a chastened comedian. Owing to the fact that blood runs thicker than water, I failed to receive any pay for my services. My salary was to have been twenty dollars a month, food and lodging thrown in.... I longed for the resumption of my career as a writer.... I was as good a writer at that time as I was a comedian.
With the uncanny sense of homing-pigeons, we began to work homeward instead of into the far reaches below the Ohio River. My cousin's fortune was practically wiped out.... The show was on its last legs, and the stage was about to lose two of its most promising comedians.... We "busted" early in August.... There was almost enough money left to buy railroad tickets to Chicago for the women of the company. The difference was made up by the men, who proved to be more gallant than the circumstances called for, and one day we said goodbye at the station to the half-dozen frazzled but plucky young women who had weathered the summer with our ill-fated expedition. My lady love promised to write to me and I promised to look her up if ever I went to Chicago. Neither of those promises was redeemed. But she [probably Annie Pixley] came to our town a few years later with a company ... doing *East Lynne*. The morning after the performance I called at her hotel to see her, but she was just on the point of leaving for the railway

station. I knew she was glad to see me, for her suitcases now seemed even heavier than in the old days.

I reached home after a pilgrimage of about one hundred miles. Footsore and weary, greasy and unkempt through occasional association with freight trains, hungry and ashamed, I slunk up the back stairs and entered our house through the kitchen. . . . I carried the remains of my wardrobe in a piece of brown wrapping-paper. (The trunk that had cost $2.50 had since succumbed to the inclement weather.) . . . From the dining room came the sound of many voices, high and low. It suddenly dawned on me that this was Sunday and the big noonday feast was in progress, a goodly company of relations at our board. That meant chicken or turkey and other things in plenty, and . . . I had not had anything to eat since the day before. . . .

Before I could intercept [the maid] she bounced back into the dining room and blurted out the disquieting news that the prodigal had re-turned. My mother hurried out to the kitchen. . . .

Presently I found myself in the dining room, shaking hands with my uncles and aunts and trying to look important. My father did not laugh at me. He made a place for me beside him and asked me to draw up a chair. I had a little pride left. Although I was perishing for want of food, I managed to say that I had had my dinner and wasn't the least bit hungry. My mother read me like a book. . . . She suggested that I run up to my room and tidy up a bit and she would come up a little later. . . . When she joined me a few minutes later, she threw her arms around me and said, "Don't cry, little boy." Then we went downstairs into the deserted dining room. Even my excited brothers and my little sister had disappeared.

"Little sister" was Jessie; and according to brother John, that Sunday dinner was actually in honor of her birthday:

The meal proceeded under the mask of assumed naturalness, and the prodigal son looked on. At times he was offered favorite dishes but stolidly refused them. It was not until dinner was nearly over that Mother induced him to take a cup of coffee because it was Jessie's birthday. The wall of resistance, once breached, crumbled away, and from that moment I never saw a human being eat so ravenously. I'm sure he never ate so much again, although passing years [his late fifties] and comfortable living gave him a rounded amplitude of form.

Before long, George got his reporting job back again at the *Journal.* Working there only part time gave him opportunities for writing-projects of his own. He was never sure about how much those projects were in-formed by the disciplines of journalism. "I don't think newspaper writing helps in creative work," he said many years later to a reporter for the *Boston Evening Transcript,* in its time Boston's most literary newspaper.

"What newspaper work does for you is to train the mind to think quickly, to skip non-essentials, and to make the most of important details." When asked to amplify on those two writing-techniques (tightening and rendering), he said that although indispensable they do not in themselves make masterpieces and that the "trick is to know when to tighten, when to render." In the same interview he did acknowledge his indebtedness to journalism for certain other benefits:

Newspaper work in a town like Lafayette was then, with its two hospitals, two orphan asylums, County Courthouse, schools, churches, University ... a splendid training for a young man no matter what he was to do later in life. At the time, reporters who were just leg-men were virtually unknown. The telephone was just beginning to become popular. We went out and got our stories, and we came back to the office and wrote them. Every man was responsible for his own stories. We rose or fell by what we did. We were allowed a pretty free hand, too ... we could write our stories pretty much as we chose. But we were obliged to write a pretty good story if we wanted to see it in print.

In November, 1885, Barr enjoyed more popularity than ever and, despite remaining a Democrat, was elected Sheriff of the County for the 1885-1887 term. The family moved back to the Sheriff's residence adjoining the County Jail on Fourth Street. Nobody rejoiced more than George, for aside from a respite from proximity to cattle and hogs, he would now be within walking distance of the *Journal* offices, the Opera House, the Lafayette Dramatic Club, and—even if only as an ex officio student—the Purdue Library.

Stimulated by the move back to town, he scribbled several verses, among them "Perunius Skinner, the Hog-Buyer's Son." Here are three of its ballad stanzas:

> Perunius Skinner was a hog-buyer's son
> And he drove into market the swine.
> The punching of hogs was the everyday fun
> of his "summer of roses and wine."
>
> He swore by the down of his budding mustache
> that when he reached twenty-one,
> no more would he eat of the hog-buyer's hash—
> his work as a hoggist [would] be done.

On the glorious stage he would dally his days,
would spend his terrestrial life.
He'd love all the girls in the different plays
and hanker for one as his wife.

We can only speculate on who that "one" might have been, but we would not be far from the mark if we guessed Minnie Maddern.

6

JUDITH VERNE
AND GEORGE WASHINGTON'S LAST DUEL

Except for the Clifford interlude (and briefly, in 1904, his honeymoon in Canada and Europe) George's yearning to travel—to emulate Thackeray's *Wanderjahre*—was never consummated. He consoled himself with the rationalization that Shakespeare, too, was not a world traveler. But no matter how stifling GBMc found Lafayette, at times, he enjoyed the sweetness and light of his parents' household. He loved Barr, adored Clara, admired John, and idolized Ben and Jessie. "To Mother" he dedicated many an opus, even if most of them remained in unpublished manuscripts.

It is not known how many of his plays, if any, were produced by the Lafayette Dramatic Club, in which he participated as an actor in several major and many minor roles. With understandable ambition both the Lafayette and the Purdue dramatic societies seemed to prefer more celebrated playwrights. As for most of the short stories he tried to have published during the 1880s, he was collecting only rejection slips. "He wrote reams of stories that rebounded with depressing inevitability," wrote John. "We, the family, looked on with wonder that he could weather these discouragements without complete and crushing despair, and for fear of touching on a painful nerve, we hesitated to ask embarrassing questions about his literary activities." How elated George must have been when *The Waverly,* a Boston literary magazine, accepted his short story "My First Party" even though it would be two years (1887) before that story appeared in print. Even more ironic in wit than "Miss Divinity," "My First Party" is a hilarious account of a bashful, mud-bespattered, country boy at a sweet-sixteen party of a neighbor girl he has secretly admired. Another decade would elapse before his short stories would be appearing in such widely circulated magazines as *McClure's, Munsey's,* the *Delineator, Good Housekeeping,* and the *Saturday Evening Post.*

Of all his writing projects during 1885, his priority must have been for the comedy *Judith Verne,* the first of his melodramas containing unmistakably intended parody. Reading it between the lines, one realizes that its author must have had a lot of fun writing it, as will thespians producing it in the parodist spirit. Good parody (as Gilbert Highet, Dwight Macdonald, and other collectors have observed) captures something of the spirit of the original piece even while introducing a slight variation. Judged by that criterion, *Judith Verne* is indeed a parody. McCutcheon, perversely inspired by the melodramas he had been seeing at the Opera House since he was twelve, retains most of the settings—the Deep South, old England, the effete Continent. In a cat-and-mouse game he toys with the conventions and the clichés, now aping, now lampooning them: the pristine if not always naive heroine; the villain lusting after inheritance and girl in that order; the stereotyped plot, which he inflates with extra uncertainty over who is going to get whom. McCutcheon invests Judith with more coquettishness than naiveté. He involves her handsome Dallas (that name recycled from GBMc's earlier melodrama *Vashti*) in extravagant heroics, and the villain Fordham (a caricature of the villain in conventional melodrama) in delicious dastardliness.

In the 1880s when melodramas were deadly serious—"had not a spark of humor," as Daniel Frohman conceded—McCutcheon's injections of humor were indeed innovative, as was his parody of duels. (Credit for poking fun at duels in *George Washington's Last Duel,* 1892, would of course have to be shared with Thomas Nelson Page.) In *Judith Verne,* in the scene following the one in which Dallas has been run through the chest with apparent finality yet survives with a bandage around his head, as mentioned above, the clowning may seem abortive. But McCutcheon's triumph, in this play, remains his parody of the highfalutin sentiments and diction of melodrama in the late 1800s. Here, for example, are Judith and Dallas.

Judith: I wish Dallas would condescend to let me pin a buttonhole bouquet in his coat. I never saw anyone like him; he's so inexorable—so distant. I cannot make the slightest impression on his imperturbable mind.
Dallas: (Aside): I can't undergo another day of this suspense. I will know my fate before I leave. But pshaw, she can care nothing for a poor artist,

when her rich cousin is her suitor for her hand. *(Aloud)* Judith—Miss Verne—you undoubtedly think I am the most cold-hearted person you have ever known—you think my heart is incapable of containing the softer feelings of nature—impregnable to the supplications of love and esteem.

Somewhat less subtly McCutcheon parodies his contemporaries' stock reliance on enhancing the hero's image of humaneness by investing him with kindness to animals (e.g., patting the dog). Not content with eliciting hisses in response to the villain's behavior, moreover, GBMc now involves the audience in the dubious pleasure of groaning at the hero's pun-loaded lines.

Dallas (Aside): I watch her every motion with the keenness of an infatuated *eagle*. Like an enchanted *dog* I follow in her footsteps. I cannot *bear* her from my sight.

McCutcheon also demonstrates adolescent virtuosity, probably influenced by Mark Twain, by putting absurdly irrational observations in the mouths of green provincials like George Verdant: "I hear they tried to rob the king's palace. A man must be hard up when he'll rob a king."

Thus *Judith Verne* remains one of GBMc's best juvenilia. True, audiences are expected to grant generous suspension of disbelief—especially toward the coincidence of the entire cast converging first in Italy, then in England. The first act contains too much talk—parody though that talk is—and not enough action. But an imaginative director would know which lines to cut, which to tighten. As for action and business, the play might well open with Fordham and his henchmen kidnapping Lady Verne. The audience once hooked with some such business would be more receptive to Fordham's exposition with which the long-winded original script opens. In short, with the right director and cast, a hilarious production is possible. Surely McCutcheon's intentions should achieve fuller realization once they are interpreted orally.

As a reporter for the *Journal,* later as City Editor of the *Courier,* as a practicing if unproduced playwright, and as a member of a family that occasionally entertained celebrated actors, George continued to attend many of the Opera House offerings. To keep close to the stage (although with decreasing aspirations, perhaps, as an actor) he occasionally played walk-on roles. During 1885, he accommodated the producers of the play *A German Volunteer* by serving as one of the walk-on soldiers. Unlike the rest of the soldiers, he actually had one line, as brother John teased:

"Water, water! For God's sake, water!" Throughout the 1880s George also took parts in plays of the Lafayette Dramatic Club and the Purdue Dramatic Society. He also acted in a musical drama, a few years later, at the Opera House.

The Opera House provided him with theater as curriculum. A perusal of the Opera House playbills of this period reveals that some of the most memorable plays and players held the boards in Lafayette. Of the hundreds of productions at the Opera House between 1886 and 1900, the following are a few that George may well have attended. Most of these were Frohman productions unless otherwise indicated. Even some of the Belasco productions were under the sub rosa financial aegis of the Frohman syndicate but were not billed as such since the Frohman brothers, sensitive to the tastes of their stockholders, avoided overtly sponsoring socially controversial or erotically risky plays. The following list omits return engagements of melodramas already mentioned above.

1886: *As You Like It* and *Romeo and Juliet* with Sothern and Marlowe in return engagements; *The Mikado; The Pirates of Penzance;* and *H. M. S. Pinafore,* with Minnie Maddern as Rackstraw

1887: Sir Rider Haggard's *She* and a Belasco production of Molière's *Les Précieuses Ridicules*

1888: The Belasco production of the comedy *Featherbrain,* starring Miss Maddern

1889: *Shenandoah,* starring William Gillette; Sardou's *La Tosca* (source of Puccini's opera)

1890: The Belasco dramatization of Mark Twain's *The Prince and the Pauper;* Belasco's *Men and Women,* starring Maude Adams; Augustus Thomas's *The Burglar,* starring Maurice Barrymore

1891: The Belasco production of *Helvetia,* which provided the debut for the celebrated Mrs. Leslie Carter, a divorcee too risky for a "Charles Frohman presents"

1892: Clyde Fitch's *The Masked Ball,* with Maude Adams and John Drew

1893: The perennial favorite *Charley's Aunt;* also Belasco's *The Girl I Left Behind Me* and his production of Wilde's *Lady Windermere's Fan* (Wilde, like Shaw, was on the Frohman no-no list)

1894: *Camille,* starring Eleanora Duse, whom Frohman had imported from Italy; her performance evoked Modjeska's

1895: Augustin Daly's musical comedy *Frou-Frou,* with the latest Frohman import from England, Olga Nethersole, replacing the estranged Minnie Maddern; Belasco productions of *The Importance of Being Earnest* and *The Important Young,* starring John Drew and Drew's niece, Ethel Barrymore

1896: *Rosemary,* starring Maude Adams; Sardou's *Divorçons,* starring Minnie Maddern Fiske again

1897: Mrs. Fiske as Tess; Barrie's *The Little Minister,* with Charles Frohman "presenting Miss Maude Adams"; Fitch's *Barbara Frietchie,* starring Julia Marlowe

1898: Mrs. Fiske back in *Divorçons; Ingomar,* starring Marlowe and Sothern; *Salt of the Earth* "direct from Wallach's Theatre in New York" (Wallach would soon join the syndicate); and *Zaza,* a Belasco production starring Mrs. Carter

1899: Mrs. Fiske as Becky Sharp; Augustus Thomas's *Arizona;* Belasco adaptations of *Madame Butterfly,* Dickens's *A Tale of Two Cities,* and Doyle's *Sherlock Holmes; The Conquerors,* an expurgation of *Mademoiselle Fifi,* imported from the Grand Guignol

1900: Rostand's *L'Aiglon,* starring Maude Adams, the American favorite of Charles Frohman (although they were not married); a dramatization of *When Knighthood Was in Flower* by Charles Major

Charles Major, a lawyer and novelist from Shelbyville, Indiana, who was to serve on the Purdue Board of Trustees from 1902 until his death in 1913, sold the dramatization rights to his popular romance *When Knighthood Was in Flower* to Julia Marlowe. The Lafayette and Indianapolis productions preceded the New York production by a month. Whether McCutcheon saw the Lafayette or the Indianapolis production, he could hardly have helped being impressed, as reflected in his subsequent romance *Graustark.*

He would have to wait until he was twenty-one before being promoted to full-time work at the Lafayette *Journal.* Meanwhile he had permission to use the office for typing work of his own when he was not on duty. Ordinarily he penciled most of his pieces in a neat and legible longhand (he was left-handed), destroying most of the superseded drafts, and keeping only those with very few revisions. Both prolific and methodical, he set himself a goal of a thousand words a day and usually met that quota. Even during his Lafayette years, he was serious enough about his writing to hire a competent typist, Henry Guyer, to type final drafts of certain pieces. Much later, in his affluent forties, as a commercially successful novelist, GBMc employed a secretary, Miss Matthews, to transcribe his penciled manuscripts into typewritten drafts. He also carefully recorded the composition dates of most of his pieces, precise dates of "beguns" and "completeds."

He did this even for the verses in his privately printed collection *Several Short Ones* (1904). He tags as "1886," for example, a light verse about an abandoned umbrella in the *Journal* office ("In the corner stands an object . . .") and as "1886/87" several light verses about office romances: ("I purloined a kiss/from an opportune Miss/as we passed in the hallway last e'en." and "The little god of Love one day / passed near my careless heart . . . and slyly brought me face to face with you.") Obviously no Cole Porter.

Taking advantage of the office typewriters, and not inclined to let well enough alone, even after Minnie Maddern had gently advised him to forget about his play *Old Dominion,* George typed (or employed Henry Guyer to type) two copies anyway and sent them to the Copyright Office in Washington, D.C., thus unwittingly relegating that play to ultimate public-domain status. He did not try to compose first drafts at the office. For those he needed the privacy of his room at home. "After a day at the newspaper," John T. said, "George would go home and write far into the night."

In 1887, when Barr was elected City Treasurer, the McCutcheons moved to a large house on Sixth Street, a few blocks south of the Opera House and the *Journal* offices. In that same year George, now twenty-one, was promoted to full-fledged reporter on the *Journal*. The promotion had little to do with his age. Rather, he earned it on the strength of his news scoop about a train wreck of national prominence.

On the evening of August 10, after leaving a party for young people in Elston, George walked to the Junction, where there stood at that time a hotel and the Wabash Railroad Depot. While waiting there for the train to Lafayette, he heard the telegraph beginning to click. The telegrapher exclaimed, "Will you listen to that! The train bound for Niagara Falls has gone through the Chatsworth, Illinois, bridge and many excursionists have been killed!" As soon as George reached Lafayette, and before he went home, he stopped at the *Journal* office, typed up the story and handed it to a morning editor. The *Journal* and only one other news-paper were the first to inform the nation of the Chatsworth train wreck. Because of this scoop, and for other reasons, James French, the publisher of the *Journal,* became one of George's admirers and hired him as a full-time reporter.

The real-life train full of excursionists bound for upstate New York resorts stuck in the consciousness—perhaps also in the subconscious—of McCutcheon, playwright. In his play *The Flyers* (of which more, later) he has a train full of excursionists, including two pairs of elopers, delayed and frustrated by a washed-out bridge. That image became one of the dominant symbols in his writing—and in his life, a self-fulfilling prophecy against which he would struggle.

George was an avid reader and buyer of books. Early in 1892 he was reading, among other things, Thomas Nelson Page's *Elsket* (1891), a collection of short stories that included "George Washington's Last Duel." McCutcheon was apparently taken with the possibilities of dramatizing that story. When he did, he prefaced his manuscript with the following apology:

This play was made from Thomas Nelson Page's story "George Washington's Last Duel" without his consent and for the education of the unfledged dramatist, George Barr McCutcheon. It was written in 1892 shortly after the book appeared.

McCutcheon's acknowledgment was more honest and gracious than the acknowledgments he would be seeing—if any—prefacing other writers' dramatizations of his prose works. In GBMc's dramatization, as in Page's story, George Washington is not The Father of His Country but rather an old black factotum almost as wily but not so treacherous as Babo in Herman Melville's *Benito Cereno*. Over the years, Washington has been servant in name only; actually he has taken charge of "Marse Nat," the bachelor Major and owner of a mid-nineteenth century Georgia plantation. Washington enjoys his status as major-domo, lords it over three hundred slaves, and helps himself to his master's clothes, liquor, and tobacco. The exasperated and somewhat obtuse Major has repeatedly threatened to punish Washington—paradoxically, by setting him free. Washington knows that the threat is idle, the Major being a slave to his own creature comforts for which he depends upon "his man." Almost as idle is the Major's alternative threat: to marry a shrew and thus confront Washington with a stern mistress. But as Washington well knows, the Major is by now an inveterate bachelor; in fact, a woman hater.

The only female the Major can abide is his beloved niece and ward, Margaret, who is more adroit than even Washington in manipulating people. Before her uncle knows what has happened she manages to put him in the company of a prospective wife, the widow Jemima Bridges, a Yankee from New Hampshire and an aunt of Margaret's best friend, Rose Endicott. Evading what would have been the Major's veto, Margaret on her own initiative invites Rose and Mrs. Bridges as guests to the plantation.

Whereas in Page's story Mrs. Bridges is a widow, McCutcheon makes her a wife who has been deserted by an exasperated husband after their first year of a wretched marriage. McCutcheon also heightens her calculating nature as she sets her cap for the cantankerous Major and unwittingly exacerbates his misogyny. (Rendering the battle of the sexes through repartee and stage business was to remain one of McCutcheon's virtuosities in most of his plays.) McCutcheon also exploits the characterization of Mrs. Bridges not only as a strong-minded woman but also as an aggressive Abolitionist with offensive insensitivity to her status as a guest.

As in Page's story, Margaret's beloved is Jeff Lewis, and the man that Rose is to become engaged to is Pick Lawrence. However, McCutcheon makes Pick a much younger man than he is in Page's story. (In the latter, Pickering Lawrence is closer to the Major's age, having been his classmate in college.) With the four young people closer in age, McCutcheon heightens the cross-flirtations, jealousies, misunderstandings, and general suspense before sorting the couples out for their true destinies and hearts' desires. McCutcheon devotes several more scenes than does Page, indeed, to the young lovers—although fewer scenes to Washington's intrigues against the Major. The added scenes occur in such McCutcheon sets as the ballroom, the veranda, and the conservatory. The cotillion is the center of much of act 2, wherein the audience meets in person Judge and Mrs. Carrington, characters only alluded to by Page.

In both Page's story and McCutcheon's play the chief misunderstanding —Rose's over-conscientious coaching of the shy Jeff in how to propose to Margaret—leads to Pick's challenging Jeff to a duel. The Major encourages this affair of honor by offering his set of matched pistols and a grassy plot next to the family graveyard. He also offers to act as a second for Pick and *manipulates Washington,* for a change, into acting as a second for Jeff. The Major conceals a number of ulterior motives concerning not only Washington but also the young men. He terrifies the latter with preparations for gravedigging, with the display of a wooden coffin, and with gory details of mutilations in recent pistol duels. McCutcheon revises Page on the fatality in which the Major and Washington (Washington's *first* duel) had finished off one of the Major's rivals, Judge Carrington; McCutcheon changes that victim's fatality to a near-miss (both shots fired in the sky) and resurrects Carrington as one of the plantation guests.

When both Jeff and Pick fail to show up at the appointed time and place, the Major insists that he himself and Washington adhere to the Code, which prescribes that seconds carry out the duel. This unbargainedfor turn of events sends Washington packing for good. When Jeff and Pick show up and—in sight of their fiancées, whom the Major has tipped off—take up the duel, it is with pistols the Major has loaded with blanks. In any event, there would have been no fatalities, since both young men shoot into the ground. Everybody is reconciled, and all's well that ends well.

McCutcheon makes Washington cleverer and more diabolical than did Page and emphasizes the black man as a foil to the obtuse white Major. But McCutcheon reproduces almost verbatim the black dialect Page used— indeed the stereotyped "de," "dey," "dem," "dat," "dis," and "dose" prevalent in literature of the period. And McCutcheon, although not consciously racist, tends to fall into his contemporaries' supercilious attitudes toward blacks.

As for the ethics of dramatizing another's work, it is well known that Shakespeare, for example, dramatized, in some instances copied verbatim from, several of his predecessors. Dramatizations—among them, McCutcheon's—can be justified to the extent that they transmute their sources, originally designed to be *read*, into more vivid mimicry of life through the medium of the stage: sets, props, business, and dialogue—dialogue interpreted by living, emoting persons. A dramatization like McCutcheon's heightens, for the audience, such elements as suspense, humor, and dramatic irony.

But excellent as were some of the dramas GBMc would be writing— especially *Brood House, One Score & Ten,* and *The Man Who Loved Children*—none would surpass in poignancy and hilarity some of the episodes in his own life.

7

GEORGE ADE, THE *JOURNAL*,
AND "THE WADDLETON MAIL"

During his sophomore year at Purdue, George had met a freshman by the name of George Ade, a young man from Newton County, Indiana. Friends though they remained throughout their lives, Ade was ultimately to gravitate closer to John T. McCutcheon and Booth Tarkington, like Ade himself Purdue undergraduates and Sigma Chi Fraternity men. After graduation and a two years' stint as a reporter in Lafayette, Ade joined John as his roommate in Chicago, where both were to make their reputations as journalists and writers. For brief periods in Lafayette, Ade and GBMc experimented with earning their livings in occupations other than journalism: McCutcheon, in the photography business with and without his cousin Charles Homrig; Ade, with the Home Remedy Company. But these interludes served only to confirm what these young men knew in their hearts: They would devote their lives to writing.

During 1888 and 1889 George McCutcheon and George Ade shared a closer friendship, in Lafayette, than they would ever share again. Both were for the most part reporters, Ade working for the *Morning Call*, McCutcheon for the *Journal*. Both were bachelors. They often went out together on double dates, occasionally with blue-blooded young women introduced to them by Booth Tarkington of Indianapolis. The North Indianapolis debutantes no doubt overawed one of the Georges. GBMc was always shy, and among Indianapolis debutantes he was painfully self-conscious of his provincialism, although he was by no means the boor he caricatured in "The Waddleton Mail."

In contrast to the left-handed GBMc, Booth Tarkington was quite suave. He had just won the position of Art Editor of the Purdue yearbook,

The Debris. And like the sophisticated young men in GBMc's comedy *The Double Doctor,* Tarkington would be finishing his education at Princeton. Tarkington's family and Indianapolis friends, denizens of the fashionable North Side, typified the upper middle-class society that inspired *The Double Doctor* even though GBMc made a Chicago suburb the fictive setting of that play, no doubt as a disclaimer against possible recriminations.

On Indianapolis dates with Tark, John, and Ade, GBMc was the least lively. He was in fact embarrassed by Ade's persiflage and practical jokes, even though the young women did not regard them as offensive. The tall gaunt Ade capitalized on his deadpan face and vaudeville timing. With hilarious finesse he often played the role of *eiron,* deflating GBMc's or John's *alazon.* One of his stunts that "brought down the house," said John, "was the one in which I'd start a serious [recitation] with my hands clasped behind my back while Ade, stooping behind me with his arms through mine, made requisite gestures, such as pulling out my watch, blowing my nose, picking my teeth."

With their local dates—the Ruger sisters Flora and Lizzie—the two Georges went boating and picnicking on Sunday afternoons and, on an occasional weekday evening, attended one or another of the popular attractions at the Opera House. Before taking their dates home, they would stop at a nearby ice-cream parlor or at the soda fountain of the Wells-Yeager Pharmacy, for sarsaparillas or rootbeer floats. McCutcheon and Ade were fond of good plays, as well as of the techniques of good theater, but also weak in resisting what GBMc called lowbrow. He was no spoilsport, but he teased Ade for being too vulnerable to such attractions as Buffalo Bill's Wild West Shows, custard-pie comedians, and burnt-cork endmen—"the vaudeville of the Truckmuck Family and the minstrel shows of Willis Sweatman."

In the reviews McCutcheon wrote for the Lafayette *Journal,* he castigated ephemeral productions. In reviewing the play *A Barrel of Money,* for example, he wrote, "The troupe should be satisfied that they made expenses. It was another instance of the clap-trap shows that are an imposition on the public and that should be denied admission to the Opera House." In the *Courier,* a few years later, in a mini-review of a play called *Blue Jeans,* he quipped that that piece "had the appearance of being much worn . . . more or less out at knees and elbows. There is a lot of dramatic rot in *Blue Jeans,* and it was given striking emphasis in last night's performance." About this time GBMc also came down hard on the musical comedy *Out in the Streets:*

N. S. Woods, who attempted to star in the presentation *Out in the Streets* at the Opera House, last night, at one time wrote blood-curdling stories for the Beadle's dime library and in this way secured the funds for his stage career. When he first became a playwright he presented the drama-tization of his own stories, himself the hero who killed all but the heroine. It was food for the gallery gods, most of whom had read his stories and were excellent critics. . . . In *Out in the Streets* Mr. Woods attempts a better class of play. . . . But the acting could be termed a poor grade of ranting. The singing was miserable, one girl having a voice that sounded like the croaking of a pond frog.

On the other hand, he did not stint in his praise of good plays and good performers. Most of the *Journal* and the *Courier* accolades for Minnie Maddern came almost certainly from GBMc, as did the following typical praise for Julia Marlowe: "Miss Marlowe has a charming stage presence. . . . She read her lines well, and her modesty added to the beauty of the character *[Viola* in *Twelfth Night]*. . . . An audience admires and praises Modjeska; it loves and glories in Marlowe."

A few years later, his reviews began to reflect his firsthand encounters with playwriting as a craft. Here, for example, is an excerpt from his review of Augustus Thomas's play *Arizona:*

The audience that saw and enjoyed *Arizona* last night was not half as large as it should have been. . . . *Arizona* is faultlessly constructed—at no point is there a scene overdrawn. Mr. Thomas is a past master in the art. . . . There is a plausible reason for every movement of the characters and there is scarcely a line that does not have some bearing on the central idea.

McCutcheon's praise for *Arizona* extended to its cast, especially to Vincent Serrano, a Mexican-American originally cast as Tony the Vaquero. "Mr. Thomas considers Serrano the ideal Mexican," GBMc said, and he added, "By the way, Serrano was born in this country and is one of the best young actors now before the American public." It is noteworthy that GBMc could be generous in praise of an actor from a minority group that was then unpopular in Indiana.

McCutcheon and Ade compared notes on the fun they were having in their reporting and also in their writing of "colyums." McCutcheon's apprenticeship in column writing paralleled less that of Ade, however, than that of William Makepeace Thackeray. Just as the young Thackeray's apprenticeship in journalism developed into his writing epistolary fic-tion, so, too, did McCutcheon's. Just as the young Thackeray's *The*

Yellowplush Correspondence (1837) depicted a bumptious illiterate bent on telling about his experiences in society, so, too, the young McCutcheon's "The Waddleton Mail," which (much later) Ade would imitate.

Waddleton was a fictive town in Kentucky, and the "Letters to the Editor" were represented as coming from a "Mr. William Gunn, Esquire." Gunn's malapropisms, his spelling and syntax, and his use of "esquire" along with "Mr." dramatized risible illiteracy. McCutcheon's fictive correspondent did not discuss political issues but rather affairs of the heart and, in general, manners ("ettikett") and morals. Here are two of Gunn's letters:

Dear Seer: I arove in this city yesterday morning after passin threw 1 of the most awfullest train rex you ever heerd tell of. Did you heer about it? . . . I got a invitashion just after arrivin in town to go to a picknick. I swore off on picknicks onct, but a reel purty girl with long black hare asked me and I coodnt refuse. I am going to take her in a horse and buggy from the livery stable. I was goin to take her in a bote but I kant roe and I hate like blazes to ask her to. I want to ask you a few questions on ettikett. Is it proper to ask your girl to roe a bote wen you cant? (some fellow tole me that I oughter ask her to do it cause it was the stile nowadays). . . . Also is it stile to eet with a nife wen you aint got no fork at your place? . . . Also to go to bed with your stockins on or not? You see I have got in with some awful stilish crowds an I don't hardly know wat to do for fear of bein lafft at by the fokes. . . . I am in offal hot water an if you don't rite purty soon I will be just rediklus made fun of.
Yours with respex to all & etc.

Mr. William Gunn, Esq.

Waddleton (wich is in Kentuck)
P.S. My girl's name is Miss Susie Blake.

Dear Seer: Your letter of the other instinct was recieved with mutch plesure. . . . I was so bumfuzzled about the stockins that I forgot to take my pants off the other nighte wen I went to bed. . . . You no I tole you I waz goin to a picknick. Well, I went. Suzy an me went in a nice buggy about sicks mile up the river. . . . Close by on a stump hung a pair of womans hoops made of wire. It was a deliteful sene. I dont no how them hoops got there, but the girls all kinder laffed when I got smart and was ashowin off. . . . After I had bandaged my eye, I perposed dinner. So they all got out there vittles wich they had brung along in baskits, buckets and other vehickles. Being of an accomodatin natchoor, I sot about to help 'em. So did Bill Waring. I don't like that feller. . . . [Bill Waring ultimately steals away William Gunn's Susie Blake.]

"The Waddleton Mail" was imitated—and improved upon—by George Ade in some of the Chicago newspaper columns he later selected for his *Fables in Slang* (1900). In turn, some of the gentle Ade's satirical letters were imitated with a vengeance by the more cynical Ring Lardner in his South Bend newspaper columns later collected in *You Know Me Al: A Busher's Letters* (1916). Earlier, just before the turn of the century, Finley Peter Dunne had popularized epistolary social criticism in his "Mr. Dooley" columns in two Chicago newspapers. But Dunne's Mr. Dooley was shrewder and more political than either Lardner's half-literate baseball rookie Jack Keefe or McCutcheon's illiterate William Gunn.

In the Waddleton letters McCutcheon demonstrated a keen ear for the language of Appalachians. But in Gunn, he was probably shooting down the yokel in himself—the yokel he suspected was the source of most of his rejection slips. He could not help feeling, perhaps, that his rejectors were unjustly associating him with his fellow provincials. So he, too, soon came to look down his nose at provincials, just as Ring Lardner would a couple of decades later. In GBMc's story "The Scaffold" the narrator, a young newspaperman on the side of the angels, cries "Damn them— but what could anyone expect of a jury composed of farmers and hayseeds?" And in the stage directions of his play *One Score & Ten,* set in Rumney, Indiana, the wallpaper is "gaudy and typically rural."

At seven o'clock in the morning on Sunday, July 22, 1888, Barr died at the age of sixty. His death released him from the intermittent pain he had been suffering without complaint ever since he was wounded during the War between the States. At ten o'clock in the morning of Tuesday, July 24, the funeral procession from the McCutcheon home on Sixth Street to the family plot in the Spring Vale Cemetery was one of the longest and most memorable in Lafayette's history. The casket was draped with the Union flag. Behind the hearse rode Clara, a widow at forty-seven; George, now twenty-two; John T., eighteen; Ben, thirteen; and Jessie, five years old. Next marched a block-long contingent of uniformed war veterans, the Light Infantry men who had assembled an hour earlier at the Grand Army Hall. Bringing up the rear, a stream of vehicles carrying Barr's friends stretched for almost a mile. Some of Barr's friends walked beside the hearse. Two clergymen conducted the services. One of the eulogies that hit the mark perhaps more truly than others, and certainly more succinctly, appeared on the first page of the *Lafayette Journal:*

Captain McCutcheon was popular as a soldier, as a citizen, and as a public officer. He was humble and conscientious. . . . .Among his other qualities, was a whole-souled generosity which was greatly admired, and often abused . . . his demise a severe loss to the community.

During the elaborate funeral arrangements GBMc, as the new head of the family, found little time to think about his loss. But after Barr was buried, George broke down, ill with grief for several days. He now realized how much he had loved and admired his father. George also imagined that Barr took with him to the grave a great deal of disappointment in his oldest son.

In the following weeks and months, GBMc indulged in an orgy of writing. No doubt, he resolved anew that he would perpetuate with honor the McCutcheon name by breaking into print with a canon of memorable works. He was not now aware that one of these works, *Graustark,* would give the name of McCutcheon a dubious memorability.

On the evening of Monday, July 23, the Lafayette City Council appointed GBMc as the new City Treasurer to fill out Barr's term. That appointment apparently represented a concession in honor of Barr and Clara. Clara needed most of the remainder of Barr's $3,600 salary for funeral expenses, an extortionate amount that no doubt inspired GBMc's lifelong suspicion of, and antipathy toward, undertakers. The Council also appointed a Deputy Treasurer—a man named Collin Blackmer—who would perform the basic functions of the office, George knowing little or nothing about them. Although there is no record of any complaints, George devoted very little time "to treasuring," as he said. He was now concentrating on writing that pertained only fictively to matters fiscal. He was working on "The Waddleton Mail," and he was maintaining with a vengeance his self-imposed schedule of writing at least one thousand words a day.

He persisted in that schedule for several months but elicited only rejection slips. He could not resist a little vanity publishing—probably an early version of *Several Short Ones*—as reflected in some doggerel he dated 1889, a ditty entitled "In the Midst of Life We're in Debt":

> I don't owe the baker, the butcher, or such
> And most certainly feel that I'm clear;
> If I've forgotten an item, I'm sure it's not much.
> There is still one bill that I fear.
> Unmarried and happy—but what's this? Oh!
> Here's something I must not forget:
> I'm in debt to the printer for printing this trash.
> Ah, in the midst of life, we're in debt.

The first series of Waddleton letters now began to appear in the *Lafayette Sunday Leader.* They ran from August to December, 1889. A second series ran in the same newspaper the next year, from June 8 to August 24. These dates were recorded in his own hand and initialed "Mc" on copy he had clipped and pasted up.

For almost a year, now, John T., Purdue Class of 1889, was settled in Chicago, working as a promising cartoonist on the *Daily News.* In June, 1890, Ade left the *Lafayette Morning Call* for Chicago, where he obtained a job as a reporter on the *News,* no doubt on John T.'s recommendation.

When Ade left Lafayette, the *Journal* took note of his departure as a kind of milestone in his career: "George Ade, one of the brightest graduates of Purdue, has had some valuable experience in newspaper work and is well equipped to achieve greatness. The *Journal* wishes him unlimited success." There can be little doubt that this send-off was written by GBMc.

GBMc was now of two minds about seeking his own fortune in the world of Chicago journalism. With more experience than that of his brother and George Ade, GBMc would not need to ask for their recommendation, but it would be fun living with them. After some deliberation, however, GBMc decided to stay behind, looking after Clara and Jessie, and continuing his writing in Lafayette.

At the Opera House, on November 21, 1890, McCutcheon performed in the musical drama *Queen Esther,* based on Racine's perennially popular melodrama. George played the role of Hegai, Keeper of the Women in the palace of the Persian King Ahasuerus and Queen Vashti. What was it in George's personality that prompted the director to cast him in that role? Was that casting a practical joke or an unwitting irony? At age twenty-four, although not a womanizer, George was not a eunuch either. As reflected in his light verses he was involved in some office romances—including a brief relationship with Annabelle Baldwin—that were not mere fantasies. Later, in his late thirties, he became an idealized keeper of his women—mother Clara, sister Jessie, and spouse Marie.

He devoted the early 1890s to the writing of plays, among them *The Double Doctor* and *George Washington's Last Duel.* But he published very little more than what he wrote for his newspaper. His daily attendance at the *Journal* is reflected in another office-inspired ditty dated August 25, 1891:

> *Wanted: An Owner*
> The person who owns the black kitten
> That has come to our office to live
> Must think that the maxim is written
> "More curst to receive than to give."

One detects in that flatulent piece a McCutcheon considerably bored with office routine. In fact, as the months rolled by, the routine became deadening and he began to look for an exit.

8

THE *COURIER, THE DOUBLE DOCTOR,* AND GEORGE RAMOR

In Chicago, during 1893, the World's Columbian Exposition, which opened in May, brought the two Georges and John T. together for several visits. The Exposition provided lavish exhibits of progress in science, technology, and the arts. It also provided forums for cultural, ethnic, and religious congresses and, through the Literary Congress, for literary cliques. During the opening ceremonies Harriet Monroe read an ode she had composed for the occasion. She praised the anomalous Hall of Transportation designed by Louis Sullivan; most of the Exposition buildings were Grecian or Romanesque. Except for this praise of functionalism (but what were the Grecian columns if not romanticism incarnate?) she kept diplomatically aloof from the current controversies between romanticists and realists.

Two leading realists, William Dean Howells and Hamlin Garland, had been under attack by Eugene Field in his *Morning Record* feature "Sharps & Flats." At one meeting of the Literary Congress, romanticism was defended by Charles Dudley Warner. Although he had collaborated two decades earlier with the realist Mark Twain on *The Gilded Age,* Warner now and for the rest of his life embraced romantic idealism. He stuck for example to his idealist conviction against the hunting of wildlife. In this conviction he unwittingly sided with Minnie Maddern Fiske and George Barr McCutcheon (about which, more later).

The two Georges and John T. as a trio visited the Westinghouse dynamo and observed, on the Midway, a human dynamo known as "Little Egypt." For the *Chicago Record* Ade and John T. created "All Roads

Lead to the Fair," a daily column of Ade's interviews and John's sketches. Ade interviewed among others his favorite entertainer, Buffalo Bill, introduced him to the McCutcheons, and judged in "All Roads" that the Wild West Show deserved its popularity. (Ade's acquaintance with Bill Cody grew into a friendship, a few years later in Rome, Italy, where Cody's show was a sensation, as Julian Street recalled in his *Saturday Evening Post* article "When We Were Rather Young.") The McCutcheon brothers, including nonchalant Ben on one of the visits, did not share Ade's enthusiasm for Buffalo Bill's presentations.

Whether or not Ade and John T. tried to persuade GBMc to join them as a Chicago resident, it would be several years before the Lafayette journalist was to "burn his bridges," as he said, "over the Wabash." What he did leave, at long last, was the *Lafayette Journal* for a better-paying position on the *Courier;* in fact, for the position of City Editor. A *Courier* letterhead in his memorabilia shows him settled as early as March 23, 1893 in "The *Courier* Building, 42 & 44 South Third Street, La Fayette." On this letterhead a curious note reflects his preoccupation with "Some Girls in the Office," a kind of inventory that included one Annabelle Baldwin underscored and preceded with an asterisk. With Miss Baldwin, who seems to have transferred with George from the *Journal,* he formed no lasting relationship, although she may have been the "dear" he addressed in his romantic verses beginning "You call me fickle, dear." Miss Baldwin's name is conspicuously absent from the invitation lists prepared by Jessie for parties and other socials. Apparently Annabelle was somebody who caught George's attention like a nova glowing briefly then fading out of sight. Minnie Maddern, whom he saw only intermittently on the distant stage of the Opera House, generated in him a stronger after-image.

Sparklers and fireworks, parades and picnics characterized Fourth of July celebrations in Lafayette much as in most other Midwestern towns. But since Lafayette was, among other things, a railroad town, the Fourth of July of 1894 took on added excitement in the news that the two months' strike against the Pullman Company was practically ended. The strike was in fact broken by President Cleveland, for whom the McCutcheon brothers had campaigned. And the leader of the striking railway union, Eugene Debs of Terre Haute, was jailed. About Debs, GBMc would be hearing much more, several years later, from the pulpit of a prominent church in New York City.

As for his writing, in 1894, aside from some small-talk correspondence with Ade and John T., GBMc tried his hand on another play, *The Bachelor*

Lamb. He wrote most of the first three acts, which he then abandoned. He knew enough to quit when he did, on this play, for it is embarrassingly banal. It deserves no discussion here other than the observations that it opens in a railroad depot, one of GBMc's escape images; and that in the character of Campion, GBMc (the son of an honest sheriff) vents his contempt for big-city policemen of the 1890s. Campion is "a greedy, unscrupulous, uncivil, impudent, totally derelict thief." As reflected in *The Bachelor Lamb,* among other pieces, GBMc seemed not to have forgotten the heated editorialized dispatches of 1886 about "the good cops" (killed) and "the bad cops" (killers) in Chicago's Haymarket Riots. (Three of the jailed anarchists had recently been pardoned by Governor Altgeld largely on the strength of a petition circulated by William Dean Howells, whose halo was to lose its luster for GBMc before the turn of the century.)

GBMc now tried his hand at satirical farce and the archetypal comedy of mistaken identities. *The Double Doctor,* a one-act play, centers in the characters' confusion about the appropriate masks to wear during a visit by a Dr. Thomas Brown, physician, and a Dr. Thomas Brown, clergyman, to the suburban home of their former Princeton classmate Jack Murgatroyd. While the play uses, sometimes parodies, the convention of mistaken identities, it emphasizes satire. It satirizes hypocrisies and other foibles of the bourgeoisie.

The play is set in the drawing room of Mrs. Jack Murgatroyd, a model of middle-class respectability, or so it would seem. Surreptitiously and guiltily, however, Mrs. Murgatroyd indulges in what she believes to be "delicious little" vices—alcohol, cigarettes, and vulgar sheet music. Much worse, she resists being disabused of her notion that all clergymen are puritans.

Dick Matternot, a friend of Jack's, is visiting with his fiancée, Marie Jerrold, and is embarrassed when at the Murgatroyds' he runs into an old flame, the flirtatious widow Bessie Farrington. The situation and characters afford zany repartee, which McCutcheon exploits with finesse.

As the play opens, Mrs. Murgatroyd, expecting the clergyman, starts hiding cocktail glasses and ashtrays, and covers profane sheet-music with sacred hymns. Matternot, who has just arrived, offers to help her.

Matternot: I'll put your pictures of [the naked] Psyche here, Gertrude, beneath this pile of music. The top piece is "The Gaiety Girl"—
Mrs. Murgatroyd: Don't leave that one there . . . stick it farther down in the pile—put another on top—

Matternot: The next is . . . "My Pearl Is a Bowery Girl"—
Mrs. Murgatroyd: Put them all behind the piano, Dicky—I won't have him [Pastor Brown] see those for the world!
Matternot: Ah, here is one—"Abide with Me"—let's see *(reads)* "Come live with me, my darling, In my cot down by the sea. There's room for two, my darling. But there is no room for three." *That* won't do! Here they all go! *(places them behind the piano.)* I'm ashamed to learn that Jack allows you to sing such stuff.
Mrs. Murgatroyd: It's the only kind of music he cares for.
Matternot: That's because they're familiar to him. He went wild at the Olympia, last night, when Jennie Nabob came out and sang—
Mrs. Murgatroyd: Last night! Why, last night he attended a meeting of the directors!
Matternot: I know it—Why, er, they met at the Olympia, and I bought the tickets—
Mrs. Murgatroyd: Richard Matternot, I don't believe you.
Matternot: I knew you wouldn't. Nobody believes the truth anymore. If I had said some other woman's husband had gone there, you would swear it was true.

Early in the play one of Jack Murgatroyd's former Princeton room-mates says, "I hope Jack hasn't gone and married a crank on religion. Is it possible that Christianity has got a foothold out here [in the Middle West]?" But the theme of Eastern prejudice soon takes second place to that of more universal hypocrisy, particularly hypocritical attitudes toward clergymen. These attitudes are consistently expressed by Mrs. Murgatroyd and Dick Matternot. When Matternot says, "Brown is a hypocrite. . . . No good preacher would talk football, bet, swear, and spoon like he does," Dick unwittingly describes the behavior of physician Brown. But the audience, aware of something Dick is not aware of, learns of *Dick's* hypocritical prejudices about what clergymen should and should not do. As this farce unfolds, it gets increasingly satirical, the absurdities always close to truths and realities. On that acid test, postulated by Dion Boucicault, among others, McCutcheon deserves praise for *The Double Doctor.*

After the death of Barr, and especially in the 1890s, the Lafayette McCutcheons—Clara, Jessie, George, and Ben—made several changes of residence both in town and in West Lafayette ("Snoddy Town"). Early in 1896 they settled into a large house in town at 118 South Street. Ben was now a senior at Purdue and a member of Sigma Chi, so that he spent more time on campus than at home. Raven-haired Jessie was en-rolled in a private academy in Illinois, but she came home during school holidays. She and Clara opened the house to young people, once to a party of sixty, duly written up in the *Courier*. As recorded in Jessie's memorabilia—her flowered registers of party guests, her leather-bound autograph books, her printed invitations—these parties invariably included, for the benefit of brother George, one or two older sisters of Jessie's teenage friends, especially Louise Van Natta and Bessie Coffroth. To Jessie's chagrin, George would manage to be out. He would be either working late at the *Courier* or attending with Ben a dance at the Sigma Chi House, even though George was not enthusiastic about dancing.

Jessie was becoming concerned about George's single status. He was by now over thirty years old. She did not intend to be subtle when she hummed, within earshot of George, one or another of the current popular love songs. (By 1899 the staple became "Oh, the moonlight's fair tonight along the Wabash.") How delighted she must have been, during her school's spring recess of 1896, when the opportunity arose for her and Clara to leave George completely unchaperoned in Lafayette! For the two McCutcheon women were summoned to Chicago to help John T. and George Ade decorate their new apartment—or, rather, an old one they had newly acquired.

But if Jessie was worried about what she imagined was GBMc's need for a wife, Clara was not. Clara was thinking of the happiness she had known with Barr, her late husband. Had she not married a man considerably older than herself, older than any of her other admirers? Besides, she believed, her children's careers should come first. There would be time enough to marry later. (A few years later, in 1900, she felt that Ben was marrying too soon before realizing his potential for achievement.) For now she was content that George's mind was much more bent on publishing than on marrying. She knew that John, too, was sensible enough to land on his feet, although he waited until he was forty-seven, a year after Clara's death. As for her "other son," George Ade, Clara probably sensed that he would live and die a bachelor.

GBMc seems to have settled in as an impervious bachelor, or so he thought at this time. His state of singleness had nothing to do with scanty income, however, for he now felt almost affluent in his new job as City Editor of the *Courier*. Nor was he by any means a woman hater, as reflected in his light verse theatrically titled "An Aside":

> You call me fickle, dear,
> Because I seem to see

In every pretty face a charm
That breathes of love to me.

followed by this "Toast":

Here's to a woman's smile,
To that sparkle of bliss
Which the eye may kiss
Where it stops for the briefest while.

At least the first of these verses was very likely inspired by Annabelle Baldwin.

In October 1896, his short story "The Ante-Mortem Condition of George Ramor" appeared in the *National Magazine*. The "ante" foreshadows Ramor's death, which is self-induced. Ramor, although admired by young women as an eligible, turns out to be a failure and a fraud. McCutcheon may well have identified with Ramor as an alter ego. Although not a fraud, McCutcheon was by objective standards a failure as far as self-realization was concerned. At age thirty he had not published more than a few of the scores of stories he had written, and he had not succeeded in getting even one of his plays produced except perhaps by amateurs.

Still, he continued to write. And regardless of the genre he chose to write in, he continued to poke fun at certain social and literary conventions. In *Judith Verne* he had parodied highfalutin diction between hero and heroine. In *The Double Doctor* he not only parodied the convention of mistaken identities but also satirized hypocritical attitudes of certain middle-class citizens towards their pastors. In one of his best comedies, *One Score & Ten,* he would lampoon mob irrationalities and would poke fun at the well-made plot. And in his short story "The Ante-Mortem Condition of George Ramor" he has the narrator assume the droll persona of a Laurence Sterne and intervene with these obiter dicta:

Why should a writer render his heroine? Is there any more satisfaction in knowing that she is tall dark willowy . . . than in knowing that she is only beautiful—beautiful as each of us sees beauty in our especial ideals? Tall dark willowy women are as common as the birds of the air; slight golden-haired rosy-mouthed dimple-cheeked women are miserable in their abundance. Women with tiger eyes, women with blue-black hair, women with perfect teeth are just as common as women with red hair and crossed eyes.

In moments like these McCutcheon demonstrates the kind of fin-de-siècle wit one associates with Oscar Wilde. One is also reminded of Lessing's observations in his *Hamburgische Dramaturgie* that wit is inseparable from its intellectual roots.

Ironically, however, George Barr McCutcheon had become too intellectual (perhaps even too stuffy) for the popular magazines of his day and perhaps too bumptious for the proper Bostonian *Atlantic*. But if he "couldn't make 'em laugh," he decided one day in the autumn of 1896 that he would try to "make 'em cry"—a decision that resulted in his writing "Pootoo's Gods." A tale of romance and savagery on a South Sea island, it was probably influenced too much by Melville's *Typee* (1846). In any event it elicited only rejection slips. (A few years later McCutcheon recast "Pootoo" with more humor into the best-selling novel *Nedra*.) In the 1890s he seemed to be "getting nowhere."

During the late 1890s, when continual rejections aggravated his feelings of frustration, what outlets did he seek? He did not take up with loose women (Annabelle Baldwin was not a loose woman) and he did not engage in competitive sports except for an occasional baseball game at picnics. Ever since his baseball days at Purdue, he had enjoyed as a spectator some of the campus and municipal baseball games. He also walked several miles a week, especially on weekends. And in warm weather he swam in the Wea Creek and canoed on the Wabash. Canoes and rowboats were available for rent at a popular wharf near the foot of State Street on the west bank.

On occasional Sundays Ade came down from Chicago for an outing with GBMc and the as yet unmarried Ruger sisters. If the outing extended into the evening, Ade would involve the foursome in singing Sigma Chi songs and the inevitable "On the Banks of the Wabash." On GBMc's visits to Chicago, he took up golfing with Ade.

My first game of golf, [GBMc tells us in "The Winning Shot," an autobiographical essay] was played with George Ade on the links of the Exmoor Club at Highland Park [near Chicago] . . . just before the Spanish War. Ade had been playing the game for about two months and was no mean antagonist even for a beginner. . . . [McCutcheon goes on to tell how he borrowed—and broke—two of Ade's golf clubs.]

In the course of a very few months, my game was such that I was almost unable to tell which was my favorite shot. As a matter of fact, I've been more than twenty years trying to make up my mind. It is not distance with me so much as precision, accuracy. . . . Address the ball as if it were an old friend . . . let it know that you have the utmost confidence in it.

If there is anything resembling a moral here . . . it should be this: Your favorite shot should be the one you are just going to make and not the one you have already made.

By "shot" he of course had in mind attempts not just in golf but in writing. His decision to try for more of the enthusiastic reception his newspaper serial "The Waddleton Mail" had won a few years ago came early in the summer of 1897. As City Editor of the *Lafayette Daily Courier*, now, he had the inside track, as he said, for publication of occasional installments of a long, allegorical "summer story, The Wired End." This "History of a Two Weeks' Vacation [at Otherside on the Squeegee River] with Its Pleasures, Its Frivolities, and a Few of Its Sensations," as its subtitle announced, appeared as fourteen serial chapters twice a week, beginning Wednesday, July 21, and ending on Saturday, September 4, 1897. It was never published as a book.

"Otherside" suggested escape for both the author and his fellow vacationers or escapists. But the significance of "Squeegee," somewhat more private, was no doubt related to the author's feeling of being stifled by his native (i.e., Wabash River) habitat. The story begins:

Standing on the railroad bridge which spans the Squeegee, one may look north or south, east or west, up and down, and see the whole world. . . . Three or four times a day trains hurry across the bridge, stop at the station if flagged, then *fly from the sequestered spot as if seeking the breath of life, which seems to have forsaken the lonely community*. [Emphasis added]

Aside from abounding in names, locutions, and rhythms of life along the Wabash, this story represents one of several intimations that McCutcheon yearned to escape from his routine journalism in Lafayette. "At the *Courier* George worked ten hours a day, six days a week," said John Raleigh (many years later) "to help support the family after my grandfather's [Barr's] death. My mother [Jessie] told me that at home George would work half the night. He would emerge from the bathroom clutching handfuls of toilet paper, every sheet covered with his scrawl. . . . A trunk of his manuscripts sat around for years."

At the end of 1897 McCutcheon published another story, "The Maid and the Blade," in the Christmas Supplement of the *Lafayette Courier*. Appearing in the same issue was brother Ben's story "A Check for Twenty Dollars." Ben's story, about a young man's decision to marry, foreshadowed a similar decision Ben himself was to make shortly. More significantly, the publication of that story testifies to some forgivable nepotism—to the older brother's love and respect for Ben, since GBMc almost surely had some say about what went into the issue.

Walking between the *Courier* offices and the McCutcheon residence, GBMc must have caused many a young woman's heart to flutter. He was a handsome man. Although only five feet, eleven, he appeared more like six feet tall because of the ramrod erectness with which he carried himself. He had a boyish ruddy complexion and abundant curly dark hair. His broad shoulders suggested the athlete to anyone not seeing him dressed in his golfing knickers and woolen over-the-calf socks. His legs failed to match the stoutness of his shoulders. He himself was keenly aware of that incongruity in his body's architecture:

Early in life [he wrote in his essay "How I Retired from the Stage"] I abandoned the hope of being a Romeo. It was a matter of legs. The more I studied them the firmer became the conviction that as a Romeo I should have nothing to stand on. You can't be a Romeo without a pair of legs. It doesn't matter how well developed your shoulders and back may be. You've got to have something that will take the wrinkles out of a suit of red tights.

9

CHICAGO
Graustark, Brewster's Millions, and The Sherrods

McCutcheon would long remember 1898 as the year brother John, a correspondent in the Spanish American War, covered the Battle of Manila as an eye witness. GBMc would also remember 1898 as the year in which his story "The Maid and the Blade" achieved reprinting in the prestigious *Short Stories* magazine. Like his play *Midthorne* "The Maid and the Blade" is set in Virginia at the time of Bacon's Rebellion. That story is one of GBMc's few short pieces which resonate (like his longer Graustarkian novels) with the romanticism of the long ago, the far away, and the erotic reach exceeding the grasp except at the very end.

A few months after the publication of "The Maid and the Blade," GBMc's latent passion for things romantic was reawakened when he read Purduvian Charles Major's swashbuckling *When Knighthood Was in Flower* (1898), a romance that would be dramatized by Julia Marlowe. For at least a year before Marlowe produced her dramatization, GBMc was hard at work on a romantic novel of his own—*Graustark*—completing a draft before the end of 1899. As is well known, this romance is set in the mythical Alpine principality of Graustark (literally "hoary-strong"), whose Princess Yetive falls in love with and becomes the bride of the young American Grenfall Lorry.

At the turn of the century, when booksellers were hailing the publication of George Ade's *Fables in Slang* and were not even aware of Dreiser's *Sister Carrie* (because a squeamish publisher had withdrawn it from the market), GBMc was accumulating rejection slips on his much more marketable *Graustark* manuscript. Anti-romance editors like William Dean Howells and his emulators rejected it out of hand. GBMc did receive from the H. S. Stone Publishing Company in Chicago an offer to buy the manuscript for five hundred dollars outright—no royalties. He consulted Ade for advice.

Go ahead and accept [Ade advised]. If the publisher gets your book for a small figure, he will advertise it . . . for the profits of the sale will accrue to him. If the book is a success, you can get more money for your next ones. The important thing is to break into print . . . get your name on a good book issued by a first-class publisher and make yourself known to the public. But don't sign up for any future books. Keep yourself free and get your important returns on books that come later.

The Stone Company proved to be quite reputable, and Ade's advice, which McCutcheon took, proved to be quite sound. "Important returns" did indeed materialize on books that came later, and even for *Graustark* the Stone company voluntarily paid him a generous supplement.

On June 5, 1900, GBMc escorted Jessie on the train down to Kentucky to attend Ben's wedding to Anna Barnes of Covington. Clara did not attend. Ever since the death of Barr, she seemed to have taken an increasingly dim view of marriage for any of her sons. George served as best man. Ben had met Anna at a Fourth-of-July party in Lafayette, and that encounter proved to be love at first sight. Anna was a daughter of the Colonel Barnes who raised thoroughbred horses on a Louisville farm that ultimately became associated with Churchill Downs. Although she could not help being called a Southern belle, she rejected that stereotyped role and was in fact quite shy and retiring. Ben had recently been promoted to the position of Commercial Editor on the Chicago *Record,* and the newlyweds' first home was in Chicago, at 630 La Salle Street. They later shared an apartment with GBMc, and with no friction. Anna was just as considerate as Ben. Ben was the perfect brother—his presence gentle, wise, unobtrusive. Before long, under the pseudonym of Benjamin Brace, he would be publishing what he called "some negligible novels" of his own, among them *Sunrise Acres* (1905) and *The Seventh Person* (1906). Soon these two brothers would be comparing notes, sharing reactions to each other's writing.

From Chicago, with his *Graustark* contract in hand (puny though that contract seemed) George returned temporarily to Lafayette. Before moving from Lafayette, he would wait to see what happened with sales of *Graustark* and he would have to have at least one novel, preferably two follow-up novels, ready in the event that commercial success came at last.

Even aside from the acceptance of *Graustark* he was understandably motivated to concentrate, now, on the writing of fiction. Playwriting he would set aside for a few years. Plays and playwrights were not so important, these days, or so it would seem. "The player was now the thing," he rationalized. As the bells rang in the new century, Minnie Maddern and her leading man Maurice Barrymore, for example, were picking their own readings almost at random. Audiences flocked to see Julia Marlowe and E. H. Sothern much more than to soak up Shakespeare. Even Shaw playwright was to be overshadowed by Ellen Terry actress, within the next few years, in *Captain Brassbound's Conversion,* the only Shaw play the New York syndicate dared to present.

In 1900, all the extant McCutcheons except George were living in Chicago. Even Clara and Jessie had moved there; they were living on Bellevue Place. Just as George was about to announce to the family the good news about the sale of *Graustark,* he learned that John T. had come down with pneumonia on December 20—had in fact come down also with malaria on December 30—and was not expected to live. But miraculously, he survived. (Somebody, not Dr. Keyes, theorized that the malaria had burned off the pneumonia.) To help John recuprerate he was sent on February 25, 1901 to a sanatorium in Asheville, North Carolina. George still said nothing about *Graustark,* which was beginning to be distributed in so-called prepublication copies to selected bookstores. Understandably GBMc was not talking very much about the terms of his contract with the Stone Publishing Company. (The better the book sold, the more embarrassing that contract would appear.)

The train between Chicago and North Carolina stopped regularly in Lafayette, Indiana. On a trip back from North Carolina to Chicago, on February 28, 1901, a party consisting of Clara, Jessie, Ben, Anna, and George Ade stopped in Lafayette to report on John's rapid recovery and to congratulate George. By now it was no secret that prepublication copies of *Graustark* (official publication date was to be March 16, 1901) were selling thousands of copies a week.

GBMc, although unable to join the train party down to North Carolina, did visit John as often as possible. On April 5, 1901, GBMc shared with John the news that Jeanette Gilder, one of the Frohman syndicate's dramatizers, was negotiating with Stone for the dramatization rights to *Graustark.* This news struck John as exciting. He probably did not understand George's lack of enthusiasm—no doubt, attributed it to show-off modesty. Actually GBMc felt that he was the one who should do the dramatizing but he knew that he stood little or no chance for this with the Frohman syndicate. Had he not sold all the rights to Stone? To the syndicate he would now be just one more of those entities Charles Frohman called nugatory. Still in 1901—the year New York playgoers enjoyed Richard Mansfield in the dramatization of Tarkington's *Monsieur Beaucaire,* the year David Graham Phillips published his muckraking novel *The Great God Success*—George Barr McCutcheon's novel *Graustark* launched him to fame and fortune, though not to literary distinction. The first copy of *Graustark* the author received he inscribed for Clara:

March 20, 1901

Dear Mother—
I'd rather have you enjoy this story and feel it is one half as good as the standard set by John—although you must not say so—than to have the plaudits of all the critics in the land.

—George

"The standard set by John" suggests that George had been feeling overshadowed. But during the succeeding months, when *Graustark* sold hundreds of thousands of copies, and became the national best seller of 1901, nobody was prouder of George than John. In fact, John felt embarrassed when people kept referring to George as "John's brother." "From now on," John said, "*I'll* be referred to as the brother of George Barr McCutcheon." For many years, however, with characteristic self-effacement, George kept referring to himself as "brother of the Chicago cartoonist and war correspondent."

With the success of *Graustark,* GBMc was considered, at least in Indiana, important enough to be included in the Benjamin Harrison Benefit readings at English's Opera House in Indianapolis. On May 30 and 31, 1902, he appeared there with George Ade, Booth Tarkington, Lew Wallace, Charles Major, James Whitcomb Riley, and other Indiana writers. According to reports in the Indianapolis newspapers the Benjamin Harrison fund-raising show consisted of "a brilliant program of readings, one of the most notable literary and social events in the history of this city of writers. There was a capacity crowd, occupying even the orchestra pit and applause came spontaneously." Lew Wallace read excerpts from *Ben-Hur.* Charles Major read a passage from *When Knighthood Was in Flower.* Riley read "When the Frost Is on the Punkin" and "That Old Sweetheart of Mine" and was applauded tumultuously. George Ade read, from *Fables in Slang,* "The Night the Men Came to the Women's Club."

Tarkington read a short piece called "Dance Music." McCutcheon read an excerpt from *Graustark*. The *Sentinel* reporter was as much taken as the audience:

George Barr McCutcheon, the first reader of the evening, is a natural, unassuming gentleman. His reading of the first chapter of "Graustark" was warmly applauded, especially Mr. Grenfall Lorry's courtship of the sweet young woman he met on the train enroute from the West to the East. McCutcheon was recalled and for an encore simply remarked, "They were later married."

Well before the vogue of unmarried couples living together without benefit of clergy, the more conventional arrangement undergirding the conventional happy ending, about which McCutcheon assured the audience, apparently pleased them. But his patronizing attitude toward his own book, or parts of it, and toward those in the audience who liked it, is revealed in a remark he let slip to the *Sentinel* reporter: "I read that chapter," he said as he returned from the footlights, "because it is the shortest and as a matter of fact the worst in the book." GBMc would later make similar derogations about certain parts of *Graustark* sequels, most of which he knew were potboilers, as he admitted to Montrose Moses, a drama critic for the *New York Times*. Still, here in Indianapolis he had experienced stage fright—"a considerable degree of trepidation," he confessed to a reporter from the *Indianapolis News*. Although "Mr. Riley and Mr. Major were patting Mr. McCutcheon on the back encouragingly, he intimated that if he knew the way out of the theatre by some back door, he might disappear."

McCutcheon and Ade enjoyed the two days immensely. They seized the opportunity to resume the sophomoric bantering of their Lafayette days. The two writers, now in their thirties, were staying in adjoining rooms at the Hotel English. A reporter for the *Indianapolis Journal* interviewed them.

This was at 12:30 o'clock this morning in Mr. Ade's room. . . . Mr. McCutcheon, who occupied an adjoining room, had come in to make a visit. Ade and McCutcheon are fast friends, having been students together at Purdue. . . . "This is Mr. Ade—the gentleman with his head protruding from beneath the covers," remarked Mr. McCutcheon. Having performed the function of introducing his friend, the author of "Graustark" put a coat on over his suit of pyjamas, and lighting a fresh cigar, prepared to make himself comfortable in an easy chair. The young man in the bed, who has perhaps amused more people than any other newspaper writer in the country, threw down the covers, slowly drew himself up to a sitting posture and prepared to make himself agreeable. . . . "Ade has been roasting me from the time I appeared on the stage until you came in," remarked the author of "Graustark."

"Not so," declared Ade. "I enjoyed your appearance immensely. You see, it was this way. We who are to appear tomorrow night all sat in a box. They had us sit there as a sort of guarantee of good faith. . . . Tell him your hard luck story, George."

The hard luck story concerned a news scoop that had eluded McCutcheon's paper, the *Courier,* and had fallen inadvertently into the hands of an editor on Ade's old paper, the rival *Lafayette Call.* The body of a missing Purdue coed by the name of Carrie Stengelmeier, who had left suicide notes, was found in the Wabash River. The news went to the *Call* and was somehow withheld from the *Courier* until after it had gone to press. Ade liked to exploit the accommodating McCutcheon, who was always willing to confess in amusing ways his own blunders and short-comings.

Shortly before the Indianapolis readings, McCutcheon's novel *Castle Craneycrow,* a sequel to *Graustark,* was accepted by Stone. GBMc decided the time was now ripe for his exit from Lafayette. George Ade and John T. were making it in Chicago. (John, who had been working for the *Record-Herald,* was in fact offered a more lucrative position on the *Tribune* and moved there early the next year, into its magnificent new building built of Bedford limestone.) GBMc would resign from the *Courier* on June 1, 1902. His departure was announced early in April. The *Courier* Editor gave him a well-intentioned but mealy-mouthed send-off—"bid goodby to our faithful and reliable attaché . . . deeply regretful of his early departure . . . reap more largely the rewards to which he is entitled."

In GBMc's honor several farewell parties were given, mostly by his unmarried friends. Strategically, the invited men exceeded the invited women. One of the first of these parties, written up in the Social Events page of the *Courier,* was given by Louise Van Natta and Bessie Coffroth, daughter of the McCutcheon family's attorney, at the Coffroths' brick town-house on South Street. Apparently, Annabelle Baldwin of the *Courier* was not invited. (Nor does her name—unlike the names of the Coffroth and the Van Natta girls—appear in any of the sign-in guest books in Jessie's memorabilia.) Bessie and Louise, the older sisters of Jessie's best friends, almost surely had matrimonial designs on George, so that they must have been friendly adversaries ("If anyone in Lafayette is going to get him, let it be one of *us!*"). They had turned up, by invitation, at all of Jessie's parties in which George, when present, would have been the only male compatible in age with that of the prospective fiancées.

At the farewell party in the Coffroth home, besides the progressive card games, including euchre, a new diversion was introduced—table tennis. A few of the avant-garde young men and women—those whose denominations did not forbid it—engaged in dancing. They waltzed to disc music on the Ediphone—such hits as "In the Good Old Summertime" and "She's My Sweetheart, I'm Her Beau." Later when Bessie played ragtime on the piano, some couples two-stepped to "Hello, Central" and Scott Joplin's "Maple Leaf Rag." GBMc had to be coaxed into dancing; he was, he protested without false modesty, too clumsy. But he felt quite at ease with the groups that surrounded him at the non-alcoholic punch bowl.

Farewell parties accelerated in frequency during the rest of April and May, but for one day in April GBMc's announcements about *Castle Craneycrow* and his forthcoming exodus to Chicago were overshadowed. On Thursday, April 24, George Ade's musical comedy *The Sultan of Sulu,* for which John T. had designed the costumes and sets, played in the Opera House to an enthusiastic audience, including a whole gallery of Purdue students. GBMc judged this quasi roadshow an improvement over the version he had seen previously at the Studebaker Theater in Chicago, and he gave it a fulsome write-up in the *Courier.* For him to do anything less would after all have been unthinkable. If he felt pangs of envy or if he detected flaws in the play he tried to conceal all these in his review. ("Ade's book a masterpiece . . . clever bit of satire.")

Still, nothing in the review said what the play satirized or why GBMc judged it a masterpiece, so that one suspects the use of that epithet was purely honorific. Besides, most of the review dealt with matters on the outskirts of the play itself: how the Purdue boys cheered at the right moments, "putting the knockers to shame" [one wonders who the knockers were and what they were knocking] ; how Mr. Walthall's music was "good"; how the women in the chorus were "pretty and could sing"; how Ade and John T. gave command speeches after the second act, Ade saying he was glad to be home, John saying somewhat chauvinistically that he had not followed the Sulu costume styles too closely, "preferring not to shock the ladies"; how the entire company enjoyed an after-show supper at the Lahr Hotel and took a special train back to Chicago at 1:30 in the morning.

June the first, resignation day, could not seem to come too soon for GBMc. When that day arrived, and he was cleaning out his desk at the office, he discovered an old pistol, probably not his, which accidentally went off. Bang! One of GBMc's colleagues thought that an anarchist had set off a bomb. The first moment of terrified silence was followed by pandemonium, including a stenographer's scream. Fortunately, nobody was hurt—at least not by the bullet. But the *Courier*'s rival newspaper, the *Lafayette Call*, lost no time in calling attention, on the front page of its June 2, 1902, issue, to McCutcheon's valedictory:

MR. McCUTCHEON DID NOT KNOW
THE GUN WAS LOADED

Tragedy Narrowly Averted
in Courier Office

The genial former City Editor was ransacking his desk of old papers, picking here and there a valuable clipping. All passed well and the waste basket had been unloaded several times of its contents. . . . Good wishes were being given the author of "Graustark" and "Castle Craneycrow." When the final load to the basket was consigned, Mr. McCutcheon opened another drawer, and his eye espied an old revolver that had been stowed there since his days of scoops [a reference not only to the train wreck but also, no doubt, to the Stengelmeier suicide, about which *The Call* had scooped the *Courier*]. He drew it quickly from its place of forgotten concealment and was just upon the eve of making his mind for its final disposition when a loud report disturbed the quiet of the Editorial Room. Luckily no one was hurt, the ball going wide of its mark. The report caused some confusion from the floor of the composing room to the flooring beneath the trembling feet in the counting room. In the Editorial Sanctum there was general paleness. The hair of the Managing Editor made a desperate attempt to stand on end but failed through natural causes.

The next day *The Call* carried a large cartoon of the incident along with the caption "Parting Shot." GBMc was of course teased about "going out with a bang," an expression that had become a cliché even before T. S. Eliot used it a couple of decades later.

The *Courier*'s version of the incident "Consternation in the Editorial Room" (Monday, June 2, 1902) mentioned that when the retiring City Editor was cleaning out his desk of personal effects—

the accumulation of years—sweetly perfumed notes marked "personal"— mementoes of a local career in journalism and society, he came across an old and rusty revolver. . . . He picked it up gingerly, then caressed it in a manner which suggested that a man with courage enough to go to Chicago to live shouldn't be afraid of a gun. . . . He cocked the revolver and pulled the trigger. There was a sound as of the explosion of a ton of dynamite. . . . For a moment the *Courier*'s force was palsied. Then the employees looked at George. He may have had stage fright when he went on at the authors' readings in Indianapolis, but he didn't tremble there as he trembled here, and he will never be paler than when he realized what might have happened.

By August GBMc was living in Chicago "in an apartment presided over by a widow," according to Jessie. (The widow was not Marie Fay but may have been Carrie Jacobs Bond.) Writing to George years later, Jessie said:

Dear George, to put your mind at ease, for I am sure you are losing sleep 😌 trying to recall the rooms I decorated. The place, Michigan Avenue, an apartment presided over by a widow in black crepe weeds. Ben lived there too, and I was visiting him when I took the liberty of fixing up your room during your absence. Can you imagine anything more audacious? Well, How young I was!

When Jessie wrote that letter she was nineteen, a tall brunette beauty. She was always more enthusiastic than any other McCutcheon about Chicago. In 1902 it afforded scenes like those described by Dreiser's Drouet to sister Carrie: "It's a second New York . . . theaters, crowds, fine houses, Lincoln Park, and Michigan Boulevard. They are putting up fine buildings." (Lincoln Park had been created largely through the efforts of Lawrence Proudfoot, whose daughter Marie would one day become the wife of George Barr McCutcheon.) George was now within walking distance of great libraries and museums, among them the Newberry and the Art Institute. Unlike the horsedrawn streetcars of Lafayette, Chicago's electric trolleys and the new elevated railway around the Loop made much more noise than he had been used to. The crowds and the noise seemed to excite people around him, but George's superlatives were reserved for other places, other times.

Although he could no doubt have obtained a position on one or another of the Chicago newspapers, given his credentials and experience, he was now determined to devote all his time to freelance writing. And devote himself he did. He allowed himself very few diversions from his rigorous schedule, except for evenings and weekends. John and Ben, along with Anna, respected that schedule as a rule. All of them did celebrate, however, the evening George Ade's comedy *The Sultan of Sulu* reopened at the Studebaker Theater. They were also celebrating the publication of GBMc's novel *Castle Craneycrow* and, in *McClure's* magazine, his story "The Advocate's First Plea."

Actually, neither of those two pieces deserved celebration as far as any literary values were concerned. No doubt, Hamlin Garland, then an editor at *McClure's,* had accepted "The Advocate's First Plea" because he was in search of human interest stories, even if this particular piece did not quite add up to a story. The impassioned plea made to the court by the young lawyer Edward Gray on behalf of his honest but impetuous young brother Frank would at best make a climactic scene in a play. As for the Luxembourg castle, the setting of *Craneycrow,* it is here that another Grenfall Lorry type meets and marries a boyhood sweetheart but not before he rescues her from a murderous prince to whom she is temporarily betrothed.

Much more accomplished than any of McCutcheon's other fiction— no doubt his best novel—was *The Sherrods* (1903), the first of forty-two of his books to be published by Dodd, Mead. *The Sherrods* is set in Chicago and in the fictive Indiana village of Proctor's Falls in the late 1800s. The protagonist, Jud Sherrod, son of a deceased physician, is a farmer by reluctant vocation. He gets through two years at the state university before his father dies but now yearns to study art in Chicago. His sweetheart from childhood, Miss Justine Van, daughter of a deceased sheriff, is the youngest teacher in the county. Although her salary is a pittance, her inheritance of a farm from a grandparent enables her and Jud to marry. On a Sunday afternoon, a few days after the wedding, when Jud is painting her portrait against the background of the Falls, the beautiful Celeste Wood and her mother, on an excursion from Chicago, come to the newlyweds' outdoor studio. Actually the Woods have wandered over while waiting for repairs on their train, whose engine has broken down. Celeste admires and praises Jud's work—he does have talent, not just ambition—and persuades him and his "sweetheart" (the Sherrods do not mention that they are married) to sell the painting. Celeste thrusts several large bills into Jud's hand, and when Justine asks her name obliges with a card, then leaves.

A few weeks later Justine persuades Jud to seek his fortune, with his drawings, in Chicago. The understanding is that as soon as he can, he will send for her. In Chicago Jud finds Celeste along with influential friends of hers who help advance his career. He and Celeste fall in love, and Jud lets her go on thinking that Justine is only a friend. "Jud Sherrod convinced himself that he loved two women honestly, purely, and with his whole soul. He loved unreservedly and equally Justine his wife and Celeste his friend." Once married to Celeste, Jud cannot reach a decision, however hard he tries, to reveal the bigamy, let alone resolve it. As Jud and Celeste leave for a honeymoon in Europe, Celeste exclaims "We are at sea! We are at sea!" And Jud says "slowly" and with heart-breaking guilt, "Yes, we are at sea."

Jud also embarks on conjugal visits, ingeniously dividing his time between the two wives. But since the Wood family is of high society, the news of Celeste's marriage appears in Chicago newspapers. During Jud's sojourns in Chicago, Justine in Indiana has to fight off Gene Crawley, a boorish and truculent farmer who is fiercely protective of and hopelessly in love with her. She makes him keep a respectable distance until news of Sherrod's marriage to Celeste Wood arrives in Proctor's Falls. Even then Justine allows Crawley to become only a hired hand on her farm. Besides, she has just given birth to Jud Junior.

Justine persists in believing that the Dudley Sherrods' marriage cannot have referred to her Dudley, her Jud, but goes to Chicago to find out for herself. At the Wood mansion, where Jud and Celeste reside, Justine arrives one day with her baby. When Jud sees that the jig is up, he commits suicide. In a Hardyesque conclusion, the two widows become friends. But Gene Crawley, who should have at last won his beloved Justine—if the President of the Immortals had allowed it—remains rejected and "sobs as though his heart would break."

The four major characters are drawn with believable motivation and behavior. And although this novel suffers from some of the overwriting that characterizes GBMc's juvenilia (the kind of overwriting that Dreiser, for example, never overcame), *The Sherrods* was a harbinger of the psychological realism McCutcheon later achieved in his play *Brood House*. Among the reviewers who noticed *The Sherrods,* the verdicts were favorable: "Carries the conviction of its reality on every page"; "far above the usual run of novels . . . a far better book from all points of the compass than his 'Graustark.'"

Sales of *The Sherrods,* while respectable, disappointed Dodd, Mead because what they regarded as their chief competition of the year—*Brewster's Millions,* published by Stone—exploded from the start into bestsellerdom. It ultimately sold over five million copies. Nevertheless, the larger and more visible New York company continued to publish most of the rest of McCutcheon's books, and his relations with the Dodd brothers continued to the end most cordial.

The idea for *Brewster's Millions* GBMc owed to his brother Ben, who had given it to him during the months George was living at Ben and Anna's apartment. The novel first appeared under the by-line of "Richard Greaves." The reasons GBMc chose to use a pseudonym are as interesting as the reasons for his use of that particular pseudonym, which suggests "grieves." Perhaps he wished to see what effect, if any, the use of a pseudonym would have upon sales. Above all, he wished to protect his Chicago publisher, Stone, along with his New York publishers against problems of marketing connected with the simultaneous publication of competing McCutcheon fiction.

Brewster's Millions relates the history of Monty Brewster, a conservative young man, age twenty-five, to whom his grandfather has bequeathed one million dollars. One of the grandfather's enemies, Monty's Uncle James Sedgwick, also bequeaths to him the sum of seven million dollars provided that Monty proves to be penniless at age twenty-six. In other words, Sedgwick perversely wishes Monty to divest himself of Grandpa Brewster's million—to maintain the integrity of an uncontaminated Sedgwick legacy. Monty rises to the challenge. He works hard to unload his grandfather's million within one year.

Monty's female acquaintances include Barbara Drew, a banker's daughter (probably inspired by one of the Indianapolis debutantes introduced to GBMc by Booth Tarkington) and Peggy Gray, an indigent but admirable young woman whose mother's rooming house had served as Monty's residence before he became a millionaire. Monty and Barbara pursue each other between on-again, off-again engagements, but Monty ultimately realizes that Peggy is his true love. We are introduced to Monty in the opening paragraphs of the novel:

He was tall and straight and smooth-shaven. People called him "clean looking." Older women were interested in him because his father and mother had made a romantic runaway match, which was the talk of the town in the seventies. Worldly women were interested in him because he was the only grandson of Peter Brewster, millionaire, and Monty was certain to be his heir—barring an absent-minded gift to charity. Younger women were interested for a much more obvious and simple reason: They liked him. Men also took to Monty because he was a good sportsman, had a decent respect for himself and no great aversion to work.

There could be no story, of course, if Uncle James had not prohibited Monty from giving Grandpa Peter's money away in one fell swoop to charities. Sedgwick stipulates that Monty must actually spend the million within the year. This proviso takes Monty and company through a tour de force of yacht trips to the Mediterranean and banquets for hordes of people Monty hardly knows, so that only a tenuous distinction remains between "spending" and "giving away." Certain crises do help Monty and his faithful adviser, Nopper Harrison, to sort out true friends from mercenary sycophants. And the ingenious ways Monty devises to spend money no doubt fascinated readers whose ingenuities were tested in opposite directions—to earn enough for subsistence.

Brewster's Millions was dramatized, a few years later, by Winchell Smith, a rival of the Frohman syndicate. Why wasn't McCutcheon asked to do the dramatizing? A perusal of Smith's play, published by Samuel French, reveals no major changes in plot, characterization, and dialogue. The play even retains the yacht scene (Act 3), although there is now an orchestra instructed to furnish an obbligato—"Give My Regards to Broadway." The play does telescope some of the novel's exposition, of course, into the kind of dialogue and stage business for which McCutcheon had long ago proved himself competent. In addition, Peggy's mother and several other minor characters—instead of being used as stage walk-ons —are simply referred to by the major characters, an economical device GBMc himself used in several of his plays. In short, nobody can argue convincingly that McCutcheon could not have successfully dramatized *Brewster's Millions* himself. Whatever militated against his being asked to do so was no doubt rooted in the realities of commerce. With no successfully produced play to his credit, he was probably regarded as too much of a risk. Besides, theater people at this time shared the idée fixe that since playwriting and novel writing are two disparate arts, novelists could not also be playwrights. Still, in whatever genre, *Brewster's Millions* remains the creation of George and Ben McCutcheon, and nobody can ever take that much away from them.

Winchell Smith was a brilliant entrepreneur. His most famous accomplishment, writes James Hart, was "his introduction of the plays of George Bernard Shaw to the United States." Smith's dramatization of *Brewster's Millions* enjoyed a long run on Broadway at the New Amsterdam Theater but was curiously unsuccessful in London. "It did not do well there," according to the dubious theory advanced by a competing spokesman, "because the severely logical British mind took it all as a business proposition, an illogical and impossible proposition." If that theory was right, English audiences at that time were apparently unwilling to suspend disbelief, unwilling to make that concession without which a comedy, or a romance, or a melodrama fails. One hastens to reject, therefore, that indictment of English audiences as too much of a sweeping generalization.

As for the royalties from *Brewster's Millions*, the embryo of McCutcheon's nest egg, GBMc shared them with Ben for fifteen years, even though Ben had only suggested the plot—had done none of the actual writing. And with *Brewster's Millions* selling thousands of copies a week, GBMc now started refurbishing manuscripts from his trunk of rejections. One of these, a slight novel about a lawyer, his beautiful client, and her unscrupulous brother-in-law, was to appear within the next few months as a Dodd, Mead publication, *The Day of the Dog*, but not before it appeared in condensed form as a short story in *McClure's* in two installments, August and September, 1903. The short story was reprinted by Scribner's in 1916 in a book entitled *The Day of the Dog & Other Stories*. Significantly, the protagonist falls in love with an attractive widow. It is not known whether this aspect of the story represented coincidence or autobiography reflecting the female company GBMc was now keeping. One suspects autobiography, given the characteristics of this widow, the lawyer's client. According to James Kopka, the initial action of the story—the lawyer and his client kept at bay by her brother-in-law's ferocious bulldog—came to GBMc in a dream, as did the resolution: throwing the dog a substitute offering, an appetizing vest.

All in all, 1903 proved to be one of GBMc's happiest years, as it was indeed for the other two members of the Hoosier triumvirate in Chicago. This was reflected in the appearance, in bookstores, not only of GBMc's novels but also of John's *Cartoons by McCutcheon* "With a Foreword by George Ade." However, this otherwise happy year ended on a gruesome note. On December 30 over six hundred people lost their lives in a fire at the Iroquois, one of the Chicago theaters that Ade and the McCutcheons occasionally patronized. ("The asbestos curtains in all our theaters today are the reminders," writes Daniel Blum in his *Pictorial History of the American Theater*.)

When "dormant in dramaturgy," as he put it, McCutcheon characteristically returned to writing fiction or to submitting batches of it for prospective publication. "Anderson Crow, Detective," his first publication in the *Saturday Evening Post,* appeared in two installments on April 16 and 23, 1904. This story he later expanded into the novel *Anderson Crow.* (Crow was a small-town marshal with all the virtues and accomplishments of GBMc's father, Captain Barr.) In fact, before *Anderson Crow* appeared GBMc published the *Daughter of Anderson Crow* (in which the protagonist, Rosalie, is the marshal's adopted daughter). The daughter novel received brief favorable notices in New York and London, but GBMc's detective Crow was not destined to win the popularity later won by the detective Nero Wolfe, created by another Hoosier, Rex Stout. The *Saturday Evening Post* had contributed scores of rejection slips to McCutcheon's collection. But his acceptance now, in 1904, was explained in part in the by-line, "By the author of *Graustark* and *Brewster's Millions.*"

There also appeared, in 1904, two more of his novels, *Day of the Dog,* expanded from the short story of the same name, and *Beverly of Graustark* (in which the protagonist, Beverly, the daughter of Major Calhoun of the South Carolina Calhouns, lives next door to Grenfall Lorry and his princess). GBMc would be inscribing a copy of that *Graustark* sequel in Montreal, Canada, on September 29, to the most important woman in his life.

10

MARIE VAN ANTWERP FAY

With the commercial success of *Brewster's Millions* and *Graustark*, among other popular pieces, McCutcheon now began to be lionized by, and invited to speak at, social and literary circles. At one or another of these societies, which tended to be dominated by wealthy women, he may well have met his wife-to-be. Most of these women were in their thirties and forties. Unlike John T., who gravitated toward women in their twenties, GBMc was far from supercilious toward women his own age—in fact, he actually preferred them, Minnie Maddern a case in point.

In September, 1904, when George Ade's comedy *The College Widow* was going into production, George Barr McCutcheon, at the age of thirty-eight, married a non-collegiate widow by the name of Marie Van Antwerp Fay. Mrs. Fay was a year younger than GBMc, but she was much more experienced in matters matrimonial: This was her third marriage. On Thursday, September 24, the first page of the *Chicago Tribune* announced

G. B. McCUTCHEON WEDDING
TO MRS. MARIE FAY A SURPRISE

and, on the third page, continued:

While friends were wondering if the rumor of their engagement was true, George Barr McCutcheon, the author, and Mrs. Marie Van Antwerp Fay were married last night. The ceremony performed by a pastor of the Highland Park Presbyterian Church was a closely guarded secret, less than a score of persons, all relatives, witnessing. . . . Shortly after the wedding Mr. and Mrs. McCutcheon started on a tour that will include Quebec and other Canadian cities. They will sail later for an indefinite stay in Europe.

Born Marie Proudfoot in 1867, she was the daughter of Lawrence and Elizabeth Proudfoot, who had moved to Chicago from New York in the early 1860s shortly after Lawrence received his degree in law. Mr. Proudfoot, born in 1828, was elected Alderman of the Thirteenth District of Chicago for the 1865-1867 term, and for several years during the 1870s served on the City Parks Commission. As mentioned above, it was he who advocated, and was the prime mover in, the development of Lake Park.

Marie probably attended one of the public schools near their home on Belden Avenue in 1880, but as her father became more successful in his law practice, she was sent to private schools. At a convent school in Paris she learned to speak French fluently and to cultivate the Gallic tastes that remained with her for life. Somewhat shorter than Minnie Maddern, Marie carried herself with Minnie's stateliness and grace. Marie's hair, not so red as Minnie's, nonetheless generated an auburn glow. According to Marie's niece Theodora McCutcheon, Marie, "a petite beauty with luxuriant auburn hair, fancied Paris fashions and knew how to dress strikingly." Theodora's recollections are corroborated by John Raleigh, Jessie's son. He adds that in New York City "Aunt Marie and Uncle George lived in a succession of Gotham hotels and apartments under French management, where Gallic customs prevailed and French was the common language. Such arrangements pleased Marie and were quite acceptable to George."

Marie's two hobbies were clothes designing and interior decorating. Her one (minor) vice was chain smoking. (In that respect she was a kindred spirit of the McCutcheons' friend Booth Tarkington, who—according to Julian Street—"smoked as steadily as Vesuvius.") Marie's smoking was the subject of one of the family anecdotes:

In the youngish minds of those days [writes John Raleigh] women's smoking elicited automatic opprobrium. Hence the first time I saw Aunt Marie light up, in one of the New York McCutcheon apartments, I admonished gravely, "Aunt Marie, ladies don't smoke!" There followed some uncomfortable laughter, and I was hustled out of the room but not punished. Mother [Jessie] explained that there were exceptions to what I had assumed incontrovertible. Later there was a brief discussion at home on the matter, during which Aunt Marie's French education and her years in Paris were mentioned in extenuating terms.

When Marie was nineteen she married, perhaps against the advice of her parents, a young man who lived in their neighborhood, a bank clerk by the name of Daniel Antwerp. (The "Van" seems to have been added by Marie herself.) No official record of a divorce has yet been found, but one of the McCutcheons remembers vaguely an annulment. A second young man, Richard Fay, was a year younger than Marie. He seems to have followed the Proudfoot family as neighbor or (according to the Cook County Bureau of Vital Statistics and the U. S. Census Schedules of 1880 and 1890) as "roomer" on Belden Avenue, on Fullerton Avenue, and on Rush Street. A clerk employed by the Merchants Loan and Trust Company of Evanston, he became Marie's second husband in 1892. He and Marie became the parents, the next year, of a son—William Pickman Fay, or Willie, as he was affectionately called. Apparently this second marriage proved not much happier than the first, as reflected in the separate residences of Marie and Richard, starting a few months after the birth of Willie—Richard living at 310 South Oakley, and Marie with her father at the Plaza Hotel.

Richard Fay died prematurely in 1902. In 1904 the attractive widow Marie Van Antwerp Fay took as her third husband the bachelor George Barr McCutcheon. Marie's third marriage was to endure, for she and George grew in their devotion to each other for the rest of their lives.

Before meeting GBMc, Marie had acquired the nickname of "Daisy," a name he apparently resisted for a long time. Gradually he hazarded trying it on the family and among close friends like George Ade and Hamlin Garland. Later, in Maine, Marie became "Daisy" to Booth Tarkington and Monty Flagg. This was long before the appearance of F. Scott Fitzgerald's *The Great Gatsby* (with its flirtatious Daisy). But GBMc rarely if ever used Marie's intimate name with publishers, or in correspondence outside the family, or even in the books he inscribed for her.

As an affluent novelist and a handsome man still in his thirties McCutcheon could probably have won the affection of a younger woman. Indeed, some of his male friends (no doubt Clara and Jessie too) could not understand why he chose to marry a thirty-seven-year-old widow. Perhaps only his brothers John and Ben understood why.

To his brothers, GBMc was constantly quoting Thackeray or talking about him, sometimes in a didactic manner, always with enthusiasm. The mature Thackeray, more so than the mature Dickens, would probably have hooted at McCutcheon's *Graustark* romances. But the young Thackeray and the young McCutcheon, in their apprenticeships as journalists and writers of epistolary satire, were virtually identical twins—what Thackeray in his Weimar days (when he was paying homage to the author of *Wilhelm Meister's Apprenticeship*) would have called *Doppelgängers*. In McCutcheon's *Renowned Collection of First Editions of Charles Dickens and William Makepeace Thackeray* GBMc listed *Henry Esmond* as "Thackeray's masterpiece." Perhaps only John and Ben sensed that George, who was given to fantasizing, fancied himself a kind of Henry Esmond in love with Lady Castlewood. It will be remembered that in marrying that widow, Henry gained a son, Frank, by her previous marriage. By marrying Mrs. Fay, GBMc also gained a son, William, by Marie's previous marriage. (Willie Fay, eleven years old, was now attending a boarding school.)

Besides, Marie looked remarkably like Minnie Maddern and even moved like her. One wonders whether George ever slipped into calling Marie, Minnie.

George and Marie's honeymoon stay in Canada was brief: two days in Montreal and two in Quebec. They lived for the most part on the *S. S. Kingston* of the Richelieu & Ontario Navigation Company. In Quebec they stayed at the Frontenac. Since their main objective was France, they managed to be on the French Line steamer *La Lorraine* by September 30. According to Moses King's *Handbook,* the Baedeker of New Yorkers at the turn of the century, the French Line's *La Lorraine* afforded travelers between New York and Le Havre "a six days' crossing in the luxury of a first class hotel . . . commodious cabins . . . and all variety and daintiness of Parisian cuisine and wines." It is not clear where the McCutcheons boarded that ship—perhaps in Quebec but more likely in New York. But by October 7, via Le Havre, they found themselves in Paris.

To see how much French she remembered from her convent-school days, Marie at first suggested staying in one of the better pensions, but George insisted on a first class hotel. Since both of them wished to move about freely, to avoid reservations and reporters, they compromised by staying on the Île Saint-Louis at the Hotel Lambert, an obscure but charming old establishment which had once housed Voltaire.

They dined at their hotel restaurant and at least once at Maxim's but soon decided they liked the food better on the Left Bank in restaurants on the Boulevard St. Michel and its side streets. Near the Sorbonne they noticed the gendarmes strolling nonchalantly but more often in pairs than anywhere else in Paris. Were the police expecting student demonstrations?

It is not known whether Marie visited her old convent school. But she did know her way around Paris. George felt lucky and proud to have his *très belle* wife shepherd him. He had only a reading knowledge of French; and speaking that language, as Marie could, often proved de rigueur. At a Left Bank bookstall George bought some well-bound copies of Molière and a privately printed first edition of Henry Adams's *Mont-Saint-Michel and Chartres.* He also bought a landscape painting purported to be by Corot, which turned out to be just a good imitation. (Many years later GBMc would become a collector of genuine Corots and Millets.)

They spent several hours in the Louvre, admiring especially the Rembrandts, the Titians, and Leonardo's *Mona Lisa.* Outside the Louvre, in the Tuileries Gardens, the autumn had decimated the roses but also the summer crowds. They window-shopped the elegant stores along the Champs Élysées (Marie later bought a dress and some perfume) and walked all the way down to the Arc de Triomphe. They climbed the Eiffel Tower, then rested while riding the tourist boat down the Seine. One night at the Théatre Sarah Bernhardt, they saw the divine Sarah perform in Rostand's *L'Aiglon* but left after the fourth act, too weary to stay for acts 5 and 6. (What would Minnie Maddern have said about the length of *that* play!)

They visited, above all, several cathedrals—not only Notre Dame on the Ile but also, in excursions out of Paris, the cathedrals at Chartres and at Mont-Saint-Michel, about which Henry Adams had written. For the McCutcheons the Virgin seemed to symbolize almost as much matronly power as she had for Adams.

Marie steered George away from the Montmartre of Kiki, the adored Bohemian artist and entertainer. He seems to have known about her only vicariously through Leonard Merrick's *While Paris Laughed,* for which he wrote the introduction a few years later. Still, in that introduction GBMc speaks nostalgically of Paris as "that youngest of old cities . . . whose denizens do not bother themselves about our virtues any more than we trouble ourselves about their morals."

After a week and a half in France, the McCutcheons crossed the Channel and spent a week in England. They made London their base of operations for tours out of the City. But since they would not be staying in London itself for more than a day or two, they checked into a nondescript hotel in Russell Square, close to the Underground and the British Museum. At the Museum George looked into the genealogy of the McCutchens (without the "o"). They visited Westminster Abbey, Windsor Castle, and the Cathedral at Canterbury. On the way back from Canterbury their tour bus stopped at Gadshill, the country home of Charles Dickens.

From London, the next day, they took the Flying Scotsman up to Edinburgh to see Queen Mary's Castle. The author of *Castle Craneycrow* grew wearier of castles and cathedrals than did his energetic wife. He preferred to browse in the bookstores, especially Blackwell's in Oxford. At the Bodleian Library he enjoyed the aura and the treasures, but he grew more and more eager to enjoy the book treasures he had mailed to Chicago and to get on with his writing.

On November 7 they were back in New York, having crossed the Atlantic on the Cunard liner *Lucania* in little more than five days. By November 9, they were back in Chicago and settled at 57 Cedar Street. (Later that month they moved to an apartment on Schiller Street.) Marie set about writing thank-you notes to the relatives and friends who had given them wedding gifts. Several late-arriving gifts had been stored in the care of Ben and Anna. George decided to give—but only to relatives—combination thank-you and Christmas thoughts in the form of a slim book of his light verses. Most of these, which he had been writing since he was sixteen, he now had privately printed in a very small edition. He did not give copies of this book, *Several Short Ones,* to any of his friends and acquaintances—not to Ade or Hamlin Garland, for example, nor to James Whitcomb Riley, whom he very much admired at this time. GBMc was well aware that his collection contributed nothing to literature, and (according to Jacob Blanck) later burned the remaining copies in his possession. He inscribed the first copy "To my wife, who has put romance instead of poetry into my career." But the roseate glow must have been short-lived. Although Marie did not complain—she had after all provided her son with a loving and lovable foster father—all too soon after the honeymoon George's literary career re-emerged as his first love. On November 26, 1904, in a letter from 300 Schiller Street to James Whitcomb Riley in Indianapolis, GBMc said, "I'm getting used to being married." He added:

I'm sending you my picture. You may hang it in your den, your bedchamber, your hall tree or . . . in a tree outside and shoot at it, but *yours* will be hung in a place conspicuous for honor if you will fire one back at me. I want to hang all Indiana authors in a bunch. Someone in the disordered East, I think, said or promised we should be hung or hanged. . . .

Ade's *College Widow* is the hit of many seasons in New York . . . you'll be glad to hear. Let me wish you a merry Christmas.

The following months brought favorable notices of GBMc's novels from reviewers in the newspapers, *The Bookman,* and the *Saturday Review* of London but no notice by any reputable critic. But GBMc was lionized in high society and in literary clubs, among them the exclusive Little Room:

There were friendly groups of artists in Chicago at this time [wrote Harriet Monroe in her autobiography] and they were less divided by cliques than in certain other cities. The Little Room was an informal association of workers in all the arts. We used to meet on Friday afternoons in [artist] Ralph Clarkson's fine two-story studio to talk and drink tea around the samovar, sometimes with a dash of rum. . . . On Twelfth Night and perhaps another date or two each season we would have a hilarious play or costume party. There was no lack of wit in the club for concoction of parodies.

The Little Room, informal enough but perhaps more socially elite than Miss Monroe averred, emulated the Bloomsbury Group of London, at least in aesthetic intercourse. (At this time the Little Roomers were almost surely unaware of the Bloomsberries' assorted sexual preferences, which would be revealed in such twentieth century biographies as Michael Holroyd's *Lytton Strachey,* Quentin Bell's *Virginia Woolf,* and Leon Edel's *Bloomsbury.* . . .) The Little Room counted among its charter members—besides Miss Monroe, who was to become the editor of a celebrated magazine of verse—the publisher Herbert Stone, the novelist Henry Fuller, the architect Louis Sullivan, the avant-garde sculptor Lorado Taft, and Hamlin Garland along with his new bride Zulime (née Taft). Unlike the Bloomsberries, who gravitated together almost spontaneously, the Little Roomers nominated and elected new members.

Not long after returning to Chicago from abroad, GBMc received this invitation dated "XIX Januarii, MCMV" from Wallace Rice, secretary of the Little Room:

Dear Mr. McCutcheon: I am glad to inform you that you and John T. have been elected members of The Little Room, and we shall be glad to meet you at tea Friday afternoon from four to six in Mr. Clarkson's studio in the Fine Arts Building.

Mr. Rice and his confrères (Harriet Monroe's epithet) must have taken for granted that the McCutcheon brothers (sans Ben) would accept the invitation. For the Little Roomers had been secretly rehearsing Rice's "Revelry in Graustark," a well-intentioned masque in honor of the newly-weds George and Marie. Tipped into GBMc's copy of the novel *Beverly of Graustark* is Rice's set of commemorative verses, overflowing with puns on the cast's names, exonerating the novelist ("It wasn't a blot on the McCutcheon") and giving, somewhat niggardly, "a cheer for Mrs. George." The playbill was dated January 21, 1905, and the cast included Wallace Rice as prompter, Marjorie Cooke as Beverly, Fanny Bloomfield as Princess Let-live (a pun on Yetive), and Herbert Stone as Baldy-the-Goat. Harriet Monroe and the Garlands apparently did not participate as members of the cast but may well have helped with the props.

After this divertissement Marie helped her new husband evade the more negligible social and fraternal distractions. GBMc resisted accompanying George Ade and John T. to the Whitechapel Club, for example, notorious for its macabre practical jokes and arrested adolescence, as Walter Blair and Hamlin Hill describe it in *America's Humor:*

A slightly younger generation of journalists—including George Ade, cartoonist John T. McCutcheon . . . and [humorist] Finley Peter Dunne— collected . . . at the Whitechapel Club in Chicago, a rendezvous for boozing, taunting one another's works, and playing practical jokes. . . . [A commentator] writes of this gathering place: "The atmosphere of the club was Bohemian, Rabelaisian, and macabre." Trophies of famous crimes, murder weapons, a coffin-shaped table, and a stuffed owl hanging by a string from the ceiling were parts of the furnishings, and the club itself was named for the area of London where Jack the Ripper currently inspected the innards of his victims. When one of the members, a man named Collins, committed suicide, it was reported that the Whitechaplers smuggled his body to Indiana, cremated it on the shores of Lake Michigan, and brought back the skull to decorate the club room. However much of a tall tale that one might be, the Whitechapel Club was a convivial group of malcontents. George Ade later remembered that "the club was in session almost every evening. . . ."

During 1905, except for attending the founders' initial meeting of the Indiana Society of Chicago, GBMc devoted himself, in a prodigious burst of energy, to literary production. Besides writing several short stories, among them "Her Weight in Gold" ("begun November 20th; finished November 23rd"), he published two more novels: *The Purple Parasol* (working title, *The Red Umbrella*) and *Nedra,* the latter a recasting of his earlier, abortive "Pootoo's Gods." He also published the story "Mr.

Hamshaw's Love Affair" in the April 1 issue of the *Saturday Evening Post.*

In *The Purple Parasol* the owner of that artifact is shadowed by a young lawyer in search of evidence for a divorce case against the unfaithful wife of a senile husband. The pursuit turns into a romance when the young lady appears to have been a victim of mistaken identity. She turns out to be not only unattached but also attainable. A *Bookman* review rightfully dismissed that slight novel with the observation "has the merit of lightness and brevity."

More imaginative, and more informed in its sense of humor, *Nedra* delineates the elopement of Hugh Ridgeway and Grace Vernon of Chicago, traveling as brother and sister to the Philippines via New York and London. Their British steamer, completely off course, founders in the South Seas near the fictive island of Nedra. (Nedra is an anagram of Arden.) By mistake—or so it would seem—instead of rescuing his fiancée, Hugh rescues the more mature and more charming Lady Tennys. These two derelicts find themselves in a kind of Typee Valley, which, like Melville, they soon tire of and manage to leave for a more cosmopolitan environment. Meanwhile, Grace, who has been rescued too, believing Hugh to have been lost at sea, attaches herself to another fiancé, the outcome quite predictable. *Nedra* became another of GBMc's best sellers, and a typical review observed "He has given us another of the kind of story Americans like—daring, delightful, and a little absurd."

Given the title "Mr. Hamshaw's Love Affair," the leading feature in the April 1, 1905, issue of the *Saturday Evening Post,* one could easily jump to the conclusion that that short story is another of McCutcheon's light romances. In actuality, it satirizes the prejudices of caste and class in American society during the early 1900s. It deflates, for example, the snobbish Mr. Hamshaw's presumption that he can distinguish one class from another, at least among second-generation Americans. Wealthy old Hamshaw, along with his valet and his cook, occupies an entire floor of a posh Central Park apartment building. Ellen the cook speaks with an Irish brogue that suggests her recent arrival here. Sago the valet, when not lapsing into fractured Japanese-American, affects Oxonian locutions Hamshaw has coaxed out of him. Ellen, who remains adamantly herself, constantly feuds with Sago, and both of them outwit the obtuse Hamshaw in his fire-rehire tantrums. When new tenants, a socially prominent family with two debutante daughters and two maids, move into the floor below Hamshaw, he mistakes the attractive young American maids for the debutantes. Although infatuated with both maids, whom he meets on the elevator and in the park, he settles on one of them, Louise, as a prospective bride, before he discovers his "mistake." He finally regards himself rescued when Louise elopes with Sago. But one suspects that the lesson will have no lasting effect; that Hamshaw will not be disabused of his prejudices.

Early in 1905 McCutcheon gave David Belasco and Oscar Eagle permission to dramatize *Beverly of Graustark,* which was first produced on April 10 at the Plainfield Theater in New Jersey. GBMc may well have regarded this modest sale to Belasco as a kind of stepping stone like the one George Ade had once suggested. Perhaps Belasco would consider McCutcheon's other, more serious, pieces—perhaps even a McCutcheon play—if *Beverly of Graustark* did well. Unfortunately, *Beverly* on stage did not do as well as *Beverly* between hard covers; the dramatization folded after a few performances. The playbill made no mention of, not even a "based on the novel by," George Barr McCutcheon. He nevertheless pasted a copy of the playbill in his copy of the novel, the edition illustrated by Harrison Fisher, whose Beverly, in the frontispiece, wears a Gibson Girl hairdo and a turn-of-the-century headscarf suggesting she is about to hazard a spin about town in an open Oldsmobile.

In 1906 GBMc published two novels, *Jane Cable* and *Cowardice Court,* and the short story, "The Green Ruby." In *Cowardice Court,* a slight but "decidedly readable and engagingly romantic" novel, a young native of upstate New York refuses to sell five hundred acres of Adirondack woodlands to Lady Penelope Baslehurst until he falls in love with her. In *Jane Cable,* another slight novel, the course of true love is temporarily blocked because of unfounded ugly rumors about the circumstances of Jane's birth and about the reputation of her fiancé's father. Among the rumor mongers is the lawyer Elias Droom, probably influenced by Dickens's Uriah Heep. A reviewer in *The Bookman* said of *Jane Cable* "As a good melodrama should, the story takes hold from its first pages." He added, "It is interesting to record from personal observation that readers of *Jane Cable* seem to evince the same absorption, the same oblivion of time and space, which a few years ago marked the readers of *Beverly of Graustark.*"

In short, like many of GBMc's novels both published and to be published, *Jane Cable* and *Cowardice Court* would remain primarily time killers. However, his short story "The Green Ruby," which appeared in the May, 1906, issue of *The Reader* magazine, demonstrates greater artistry. This story anticipates in part Lord Dunsany's one-act play *A Night At An Inn* (1914) but embroidered with McCutcheonesque values.

In Dunsany's play the coveted ruby is the goal-in-itself of the protagonist, a seaman called the Toff, whose crony Albert steals the gem in India from an idol's eye; and Dunsany's "two black devils" in pursuit are two of the idol's priests. In McCutcheon's story the two blacks are giant bodyguards sent from Patagonia by Harry Green's father-in-law to shadow Harry and ensure that he return to his Patagonian wife once he retrieves the ruby. Harry is to retrieve this gem from either Agatha Holmes or "Miss" Betty Carrithers, two of his former fiancées. Through Miss Carrithers' central intelligence McCutcheon dramatizes the story's moral values. All the characters except her reveal themselves as mere ruby-oriented materialists. Only Miss Carrithers values personal integrity above rubies and diamonds. At one time infatuated with Harry, she finally perceives him for the shallow person he has become, and she experiences a change of heart:

He was no longer an idol; her worshipful hours were ended. Instead, he was a weak, cringing being in the guise of a strong attractive man; he had not the excuse of love to offer in extenuation. Pity and loathing fought [in her] for supremacy. Something was shattered, and she felt lonely yet relieved. Strangely, she seemed content in the discovery. . . . She unclasped the chain and dropped the great jewel into his shaking hand. He turned deathly white and leaped up with a shout of incredulous joy. . . . She smiled and shook her head pityingly as Harry Green passed out of her life. . . .

A few years later GBMc would even more effectively dramatize similar humanistic values in his best play, *Brood House.*

Through the Little Room club, which met in Ralph Clarkson's studio, down the hall from John's, in the Fine Arts Building, GBMc met, and became a good friend of, Hamlin Garland. Garland, who was six years older, had been unsuccessful with his naturalistic ("veritist") novels and would not be publishing his (more popular) autobiography, *A Son of the Middle Border* until 1917. Early in the friendship Garland and GBMc hit it off because Garland, too, was an unproduced playwright. One of his short plays, *Under the Wheel,* later rewritten into a now forgotten novel *(Jason Edwards),* apparently struck GBMc as worthy of acquiring as a collector's item. ("Remember," GBMc wrote, "I'm depending on you for *Under the Wheel!*") The friendship lasted long after McCutcheon moved to New York, where he nominated Garland for membership in various clubs and invited him to be his house guest. ("Why don't you come and see me and have a look around," GBMc wrote in one letter, among several others from New York.) In Chicago Garland kept trying to get George involved in Little Room committee work, which George weaseled out of as politely as he could. ("I returned to the City today," GBMc wrote, "and found your note advising me that I am a member of the committee. I'll try to do what I can and will see you as soon as possible. ..." And on another occasion: "Sorry I couldn't get around to the luncheon the other day. John gave me your message, but I was tied up.") Still, GBMc gave generously of his time in responding to Garland's writing and in keeping up a cordial correspondence when the Garland family was out of town. ("Mapleshade! How good that sounds . . . cooler than West Salem and Chicago. We are all fine and strong here, and I hope that Mrs. Garland and the kiddies are the same.")

Unlike the teetotaler and non-smoker Hamlin Garland, GBMc was not abstemious, although he was moderate in his smoking (an occasional cigar) and in his drinking (a toast on special occasions), and was not given to invectives against the evils of alcohol and tobacco. However, in an unpublished story "The Gloaming Ghosts," GBMc castigates drunkenness with surrealistic and macabre humor. The ghost of the murdered Mrs. Gloame says to the ghost of her jealous husband, "It was not the murder I condemn so much as the condition you were in when you did it. You do not know how humiliating it is to be killed by a man who is too drunk to know where the jugular vein is located."

In "The Gloaming Ghosts," as in his play *Brood House*, one discerns more than social criticism, more than comment on the turpitudes of alcoholism and infidelity. In such stories and plays GBMc escapes from the escapism of his romantic novels into darker and more private worlds. In these nether worlds GBMc gives more faithful expression to his compulsive discordances, to his disparate mix of tenderness and acerbity. ("None of us understands himself," says Yvonne Brood of *Brood House*.) This dark side of GBMc is not evident in those of his stories—realistic or not—that magazines like *McClure's* and *Saturday Evening Post* published.

Still, since those magazines were publishing some of his stories, and since the well-known Dodd, Mead and Company had published, by 1906, seven more of his novels (never mind *Graustark* and *Brewster's Millions*), GBMc was gaining in visibility. At least at Indiana University, he was considered important enough by Professor J. A. Woodburn to be included in a compilation entitled *Men of Mark in Indiana* (1907). On February 18, 1906, Woodburn had sent him a questionnaire, to which

GBMc responded obligingly. To the question "Which sport do you enjoy most?" the answer was "Golf." To the question "What suggestions do you have for young Americans?" the answer was "Let each attend to his own business and cultivate a charitable heart." All his life GBMc practiced that precept, especially in his relations with Marie and Willie.

After living on Schiller Street for a few months, George and Marie—for some obscure reason—moved back to 57 Cedar Street, where they lived during 1906 and 1907. During the days, George settled into a rigorous writing schedule. Only in the evenings did he and Marie visit Ben and Anna or John T. and George Ade. Occasionally, to get away from the Windy City, Marie and her husband spent brief holidays in Warm Springs, Georgia. They also enjoyed brief vacations in Asheville, North Carolina, where George liked to play golf. It is not known whether Marie took up golf, but she probably did not; at this time, golf tended to be a preserve of males.

On September 11, 1907, George gave a bride away—sister Jessie, a raven-haired beauty, to Albert Raleigh. The musical backgrounds included the singing of the popular "I Love You Truly" by Carrie Jacobs Bond. Jessie did not know then that she and Carrie would later become very close friends.

On one of the nights-out-on-the-town the McCutcheons attended, at the Studebaker Theater, a performance of George Ade's comedy *The Slim Princess*. GBMc must have reacted to that performance with mixed emotions. On the one hand, he probably envied Ade's success in getting the play produced; on the other hand, he could not have helped feeling flattered that the play alluded to *Graustark*. It may also have crossed GBMc's mind that Ade's play was innocuous, safe, and non-controversial—the opposite of the plays he, McCutcheon, had been writing. But if that thought did occur to him, he would not of course have said so. Besides, the pot would have been calling the kettle black; for, with some few exceptions, was not GBMc himself deferring to convention in his novels, especially his escapist pieces, which were also innocuous, safe, and non-controversial? Although Ade's comedy was to prove popular with theater audiences for several months—audiences were then hungry for what Gelett Burgess called "the Flodden Field" of literature; that is, things romantic—Ade's dramaturgy along with his intended humor now strikes one as nugatory. Ade was rarely, if ever, as imaginative and intellectual as GBMc. In retrospect, many years later, Carl Van Doren wrote, "However amusing Ade's plays were, they were cast in molds other dramatists had furnished him." "Ade was a facile writer, who seldom revised," writes Terence Tobin. In whatever genre, Ade's use of slang elicited teasing from his best friends, including John T., Tark, and Julian ("Pete") Street. At a party Ade gave for William F. Cody in Rome, Italy, Julian Street read the following quatrain:

> Somehow I always like to think
> of GEORGEADE as a Summer Drink,
> sparkling and cool, with just a Tang
> of Pleasant Effervescent Slang.

(Street had been working on a couple of plays with Tarkington and Harry Leon Wilson on the island of Capri.) Ade's hit plays *The Slim Princess* and *The College Widow,* especially the latter, have not stood up. They now strike one as banal (as do some of the fables in slang, for that matter.) "Nobody denies nowadays that Ade's plays are banal," writes a contemporary Mark Twain scholar; "why beat a dead horse?" There is no intention here to praise George Barr McCutcheon by denigrating George Ade. But how must McCutcheon have felt about the production of Ade's plays? GBMc knew his own plays to be wittier and more incisive in their social criticism. He must have eaten his heart out with disappointment when the Frohman syndicate was producing bad Ade while rejecting good McCutcheon. Wasn't McCutcheon testing his contemporaries' conventions and assumptions? The Frohmans knew all this only too well, but they were not about to slaughter sacred cows, were not about to invest in precarious commercial risks. It was that bitter thought, no doubt, that must have dampened GBMc's enjoyment of Ade's *The Slim Princess.*

In 1908, the year in which the Hoosier David Graham Phillips' feminist play *The Worth of a Woman* was produced on Broadway, GBMc published two more novels, *The Man from Brodney's* and *The Husbands of Edith.* *The Man from Brodney's,* set in the fictive South Seas island of Japat, attempts to interest readers in two old Englishmen who, through their representative from the Brodney Agency in London, bequeath fortunes to two grandchildren, respectively, on condition that these young people marry each other or forfeit the bequests to the islanders. This all too slight novel should probably not have been published.

The Husbands of Edith (not based on anything known about the husbands of Marie) proved more urbane and successful as a novel. Young Medcroft, a London architect, arranges with Edith, his wife, to visit cousins in Vienna whom he has always wanted to meet. However, to contest a hateful upcoming parliamentary bill, even if behind the scenes, he remains in London, incognito. He persuades a friend to play the role of Edith's husband overtly only. The masquerader does not seduce Edith, although Medcroft agonizes over that possibility, but does fall in love with Edith's sister. A reviewer in the *New York Times* recognized this novel as "an uncommonly good comedy in plot and execution."

But the most absorbing and exciting hours of the icy Chicago winter of 1908 GBMc devoted to the writing of his best play, "The House of Brood," which he later retitled *Brood House*. He completed a draft on the following May 13, 1909. The likelihood that he tried, and failed, to have *Brood House* produced on Broadway has yet to be corroborated. One infers that the Frohman syndicate, at least, was even less interested in this play than in GBMc's play *The Flyers,* which Daniel Frohman saw in an out-of-town experimental production and declined.

McCutcheon's productivity had been abetted by a severe winter, which often confined Chicagoans to their homes. Some of the snow accumulated as high as six feet on the streets, to say nothing of the cutting winds and deaths from pneumonia. Self-fulfilling prophecies like "cabin fever" and "stir crazy" appearing in the newspapers did not bother GBMc as much as they did Marie. Aside from her reactions to the weather during the winter of 1908-1909 she was becoming increasingly restless in Chicago. Some of her reasons were no doubt rooted in her loving concern for her husband. Wouldn't there be more opportunities for George to have his plays produced if he and she were to move to New York? She realized by now how much a success with his plays, especially *Brood House*, meant to him. Besides, didn't he need more distance from the Little Room and from his relatives, affectionate as all of them were toward one another?

By early 1909 the last argument was to prove a rationalization. Ben and Anna were the only relatives remaining in Chicago, and they were the most unobtrusive of the entire family. Jessie and Albert Raleigh had moved to a new home near Helena, Montana. Clara, from the beginning cool toward Marie and unenthusiastic about George's marriage to her, would soon be joining Jessie and Albert. John had taken a leave of absence from the *Tribune* to go on safari in Africa.

John won his leave from the *Tribune* with the understanding that he would contribute to that paper occasional reports describing his exploits. These reports began running serially and would later be collected and published as *In Africa: Hunting Adventures in the Big Game Country.* He had started out with Mr. and Mrs. Carl Akeley, the naturalists, in search of lions. Later the Akeley-McCutcheon group joined forces with those of Colonel Theodore Roosevelt and his son Kermit in search of elephants. John revealed himself an admirer of Teddy's machismo.

John would not need to worry about his business affairs in Chicago. As the model older brother, George agreed to take care of them. George paid the rent on John's share of Ade's apartment, paid the rent on John's studio in the Fine Arts Building (then owned by Mrs. Marshall Field), paid the utility bills, paid some back bills on John's Locomobile tires and service. Writing to John on September 22, 1909, George said,

> Everything is going along nicely here. . . . Mother plans to go to Helena about October 15. . . . Jess and Albert are getting settled in good shape. Jess is expecting her baby in November. I've sent them a lot of books, and recently Daisy sent them a large box of baby clothes. *Our own increase is due late in November, and our excitement is getting to be intense. Daisy's feeling fairly well.* . . .
> Ben has finished a play and is doing some pictures for the *Tribune.* He had a story published recently in the *Blue Book Magazine.* I think he's fairly encouraged.
> *Beverly [of Graustark]* is going well, and *Truxton King* has started off with a big rush. . . .
> I have been in New York, looking for property out in the country. . . . We have not fully decided on a place. We will rent a place first and see how we like certain neighborhoods.
> I am getting bills every day for you to pay—which I am paying. Your $1200 won't carry you over, but I'll attend to that.
> Everybody misses you at the *Tribune,* and many people have discontinued the paper during your absence. That shows how you have held together vox populi.
> Your studio is occupied but the rent is being paid, so don't let that worry you. I will send the check to Mrs. Field on her return from Europe.
> We all miss you tremendously. . . . There will be many changes when you get back, not the least of which will be family matters. . . . Daisy and Bill [Fay] send love and we all pray for good luck to you.
> More anon—
your brother
George

No later than September, 1909, then, Marie had prevailed upon George for them to leave Chicago. They did not know then that they would end up in New York City. They were looking for a place in the country apparently because they were expecting a baby. But in none of Marie's extant letters of 1909 is there any mention of her pregnancy. No doubt, her joy in learning that she was in her second month of pregnancy, in April 1909, was tempered by her fear. She was after all forty-one years old, a dangerous age for giving birth. In November, Marie's ninth month, she and George learned of the death of Jessie's infant son, McCutcheon Raleigh, on the twenty-first, in Helena. George wrote the note of condolence. (Jessie's second son, John Raleigh, born October 18, 1911, was destined to become George and Marie's favorite nephew.) Marie's son, Willie Fay, now fifteen, was attending Phillips Academy in Andover, Massachusetts, and came home only on a few of the major school holidays. As much as he was loved (and generously remembered in family wills) he appears to have lived more at boarding schools than at home.

On November 30 Marie began experiencing labor pains. George rushed her to the hospital. What happened he tells poignantly in this letter to John, who was now picking up his mail in Nairobi, British East Africa.

December 5, 1909

Dear John—

Just a few lines to tell you how our baby boy came and then left us so quickly. He was born on the night of December 1 at Passavant Hospital and was as perfect a little chap as ever came into the world. A knot in the umbilical cord was responsible for asphyxiation. He lived but a few minutes after being taken away with instruments. Daisy had a dreadfully hard time of it, and for two days we felt she would not pull through. Today the doctor says she is on the fair road of recovery. It's a great deal to be thankful for. I don't know what I'd have done if she had been taken, too.

Fate seems to be against us. Jess's blow was harder than our own, for her boy lived 18 days and they had come to love him dearly. Our baby is buried in Rose Hill. I expect to take him to Lafayette in the spring.

Everybody has been so nice to us. I never knew how much we could appreciate the kindness of others. It's a new experience to me.

We're all awaiting your letters in the *Tribune*—the whole town is, in fact. I suppose you'll have had a fine warm Christmas by the time this reaches you. Let us hear from you occasionally, between hunts, and remember us to the Akeleys and Col. Roosevelt.

Mother is bearing up well under the enormous blows she's had, so I'm told. She's a real marvel.

with love from
George

Clara's "enormous blows" included news not only of the two infants' deaths but also of the suicide of one of her Glick nephews in Lafayette. Her bearing up well was no doubt assisted by the loving care she received in her long recuperative visit with Jessie and Albert Raleigh in Montana.

Because Marie was now forty-two years old, the doctors advised against her trying to have another baby and in fact recommended a hysterectomy, which she and George at first resisted but ultimately acquiesced to. The operation was successful, but for the rest of his life GBMc regretted that he and Marie could not have a child of their own. George and Marie could not bear to handle the layette they had bought for their baby. Ben and Anna were enlisted to pack and store it—to save it for *their* next baby.

Ben and Anna, who had lost their first baby, a girl, were now the parents of a boy they had christened John Barr McCutcheon II in honor of Captain Barr but who soon acquired the nickname of B. Peabody. Early in December, 1909, Ben wrote to John T: "Anna is down at George's with B. Peabody, packing away the baby things. . . . B. Peabody has outgrown all of his clothes, too. . . . Anna and B. Peabody join me in wishing you a very merry Xmas. . . . Don't take any chances with them there impala things."

Deaths in the family in December, 1909, had been preceded by some lively literary production on the part of GBMc. During the months when New York theatergoers were attending—among other attractions—the productions of two poetic dramas by the Hoosier William Vaughn Moody, *The Great Divide* and *The Faith Healers,* the indefatigable McCutcheon published two more novels, *The Alternative* and *Truxton King.* In *The Alternative,* a father and son story, the son improves upon the father's generation and ideals. A *New York Times* reviewer praised the "amusing situations and the delightful crisp dialogue."

In *Truxton King,* another Graustarkian, the protagonist Truxton ranges the earth in search of adventure. He finds his ultimate adventure, along with romance, when he jumps over the Palace wall at Graustark. That GBMc's experience in writing melodramas was informing his fiction was reflected in a *Bookman* review of *Truxton King:* "McCutcheon is a master of melodramatic ingenuity," the reviewer said, but added in a backhanded compliment, reflecting his Eastern prejudice, "McCutcheon has come up from a benighted Midwestern town." Brother Ben, writing to John about this time, observed that "George's new novel 'Truxton King' is easily the best seller in the U.S. . . . I think that if he wrote a treatise on hydraulic engineering it would sell over 300,000 copies and net him enough for a new home on the Wea road."

Amid all the adulation for GBMc, Marie graciously stepped to the rear. But she would be happier once she and George moved to New York; Chicago had furnished her, for the most part, with nightmares.

11

NEW YORK AND *BROOD HOUSE*

In the spring of 1910 George and Marie moved to New York City, closer to Dodd, Mead and the major theaters. When they arrived in the metropolis they found it even more dazzling than Chicago. There were even more imposing hotels, restaurants, theaters, department stores— more specialty shops of jewelers, furriers, florists, confectioners, haber- dashers; there were Lord and Taylor's, Altman's, Tiffany's. Temporarily they stayed at the Astor but found it too elaborate for their tastes. Their next temporary perch was at the Hotel Brevoort, on Fifth Avenue and Eighth Street, where the management and cuisine were, as Marie put it, "more sensibly French." Their furniture and books in Chicago would of course have to wait until they found a large apartment, preferably in the sixties or seventies close to Central Park.

They enjoyed walking. Early each morning before breakfast they took a brisk constitutional, GBMc's word. They took longer, more leisurely walks in the late afternoon after GBMc had written himself out. They would stake out certain sections of Manhattan to do, Marie's word, one section at a time. On one afternoon they did the old financial district, Wall Street, Trinity Church, and the Battery. A food-processing warehouse nearby constantly filled the air with the aroma of fresh-roasted coffee, George's favorite beverage. As a change from hearing the honking of taxicabs and the clanging bells of streetcars, they listened for the bleat of foghorns and the whistles of Hudson River steamers and ferries. In fact, they took the ferry to Staten Island the better to see the Statue of Liberty and the Manhattan skyline, although New York—except for its twenty-one story Flatiron (1902) and its fifty-story Metropolitan Life Building (1908)—could boast fewer skyscrapers in 1910 than could Chicago. Out in the Harbor, the ocean breezes stung with an invigorating saltiness.

On other days they walked, sometimes rode hackneys, through Central Park, starting at the Plaza Hotel, on Fifth Avenue and Fifty-ninth Street, to which they would take a cab (later one of the new double-decker buses). On still other days, they walked up Fifth Avenue past the Victorian mansions of Cornelius Vanderbilt, John Jacob Astor, the Goulds, the Whitneys, and the Huntingtons, as far as Andrew Carnegie's and Ninety-second Street. The lower end of town and Greenwich Village, where Theodore Dreiser was living, interested them only casually, although Marie enjoyed strolling past some of the brownstone mansions on Washington Square.

They explored above all, and on weekends attended, the theaters, which were beginning to cluster on and near Broadway. The old Lyceum, on Fourth Avenue at Thirty-fourth Street, provided the McCutcheons with a glimpse of the Frohman star factory. Here Minnie Maddern had captured the hearts of New York theatergoers as early as 1885 in an adaptation of Sardou's *Andrea.*

One can well imagine GBMc's feelings as he and Marie passed The Empire Theater on Broadway at Fortieth Street. For GBMc that stronghold of the Frohman syndicate must have stood as both a threat and a challenge. Here on February 15, 1894, Minnie Maddern had played Nora in Ibsen's *A Doll's House,* one of the rare occasions on which the ultraconservative Frohmans had made a concession to Ibsen. The performance, a benefit for the Hahneman Hospital, was given on a Thursday afternoon so as not to conflict with the Empire's regularly scheduled Wednesday and Saturday matinees of more popular plays. Mrs. Fiske's matinee had cracked the solid front of American opposition to Ibsen. Her subsequent triumphs, including her leading roles in *Pillars of Society, Hedda Gabler,* and *Rosmersholm,* would be under the management of Harrison Grey Fiske, whom she had married in 1890.

George and Marie often concluded their walking tours with dinner at the Brevoort or at one or another of the "temples of gastronomy" (George quoting Dreiser). Occasionally they dined at Delmonico's with or without a reservation, although reservations soon became unnecessary for George Barr McCutcheon, the popular novelist and generous tipper.

Whether at the Brevoort, or Delmonico's, or Sherry's, or any of the other sybaritic restaurants, deciding what to order could consume up to fifteen minutes, so profligate were the menus. They were organized by courses, and the diner typically chose one item from each course. Marie's knowledge of French served the McCutcheons well, for the menus were printed mostly in French albeit with a slightly incongruous admixture of English (for example, "turtle soup") no doubt as a reluctant concession to unsophisticated, if affluent, provincials. From the hors d'oeuvres (as if one needed appetizers after miles of walking) one could choose from a score of delicacies, from escargots and oysters on the half shell to pâté-de-foie-gras. The poissons course afforded a half dozen choices from lobster Newburg to salmon à la Victoria; similarly, the potages—from crème d'asperges to soupe à l'oignon gratinée. A dozen entrées included châteaubriant and pigeons aux olives. The list of twenty legumes started with pommes Lyonnaise and ended with quartiers d'artichauts. There was no salad course as such, but under the relèves (relievers?) one could order coeurs de célerie. An appropriate wine was recommended to wash down each of the above courses. The list of thirty desserts boggled one's palate: baked Alaska, cerises flambées, gâteaux assortis, fromages variés— to say nothing of the kinds of ices, parfaits, fruits, nuts, tortes, compôtes and mousses. All this would be topped off not only with coffee (demi-tasse) but also with crème de menthe or another liqueur.

After dinner Marie enjoyed shopping, especially for Paris imports. "She was a stunning lady," says her niece Theodora McCutcheon. "Her auburn hair, sea-green eyes, and delicately chiseled face reminded one of the dolls that Aunt Jessie had been hand-crafting." Marie was also doll-like in her petite figure. She could and did shop for the sample (i.e., petite) sizes of dresses and shoes. When out of doors, she liked to wear gauzy veils over her hat and face, *haute couture.*

But try as she might, Marie could not cut herself completely free of Chicago. "Clara was not pleased with George's move to New York," writes John Raleigh, "maybe rightly crediting the decision to Marie." Whether or not Marie felt guilty for having persuaded George to leave Chicago or whether she only wished that he have as much time as possible for his writing—perhaps for both reasons—she saw to informing her in-laws of "our progress." Less warmly accepted by Clara than by Jessie, Marie corresponded with Jessie. On May 25 Marie wrote, "We have fallen in love with New York, and George is more productive than ever." Marie's letters were usually brief—in fact, less letter than note but always on elegant stationery that smelled faintly of roses.

Through the influential offices of Dodd, Mead, George sometimes obtained tickets for theater premieres. Thanks to the generosity and thoughtfulness of Edward Dodd, in fact, George and Marie had been making brief excursions from Chicago to New York for several years before Marie's pregnancy of 1909. Edward Dodd (who was aware of GBMc's fondness for Minnie Maddern) had gotten the McCutcheons tickets for the opening night performance, November 17, 1908, of Edward Sheldon's melodrama *Salvation Nell,* starring Minnie as Nell. Miss Maddern was "presented," so said the playbill, by Harrison Grey Fiske, who had managed to rent the Hackett Theater on Forty-second Street. Of Minnie's performance, a reviewer wrote, "Mrs. Fiske, in the manner of a slender ribbon of pale light, brings to the part of Nell, the saved girl of the slums, a little strange face with a look of dawn upon it and a voice of spring, in this most interesting melodrama of all time."

Mrs. Fiske enjoyed a well-deserved reputation for being gracious, and open to after-performance receptions. Although no record has been found of a reunion that evening, GBMc almost surely visited her backstage, if only to introduce Marie. Since the 1880s (when they first corresponded and when George had gotten up the courage to greet Minnie backstage at the Lafayette Opera House) much water had flowed under these celebrities' bridges, GBMc having experienced more of what he considered washouts. The McCutcheons would be attending several other performances of Mrs. Fiske's—among them her *Becky Sharp* and her *Lona (Pillars of Society).* Later GBMc attended Mrs. Fiske's guest readings at the Dutch Treat Club and the Coffee House.

Marie's letter to Jessie had not been exaggerating George's productivity. For in 1910 he saw through the press two more of his novels, *The Butterfly Man* and *The Rose in the Ring. The Butterfly Man* remains a slight story about a parasitic young man who battens on the purses of his friends and the hearts of debutantes. Except for the virtue that his protagonist remains a rotter to the end (an anomaly among McCutcheon's happy endings), the novel remains one of several that McCutcheon should probably not have published.

The Rose in the Ring proved somewhat more substantial. Nevertheless, a versifier by the name of Arthur Guiterman twitted McCutcheon for that novel's romantic idealism, as if it were a disease. In "A Rhymed Review of *The Rose in the Ring*" published in the old *Life* magazine Guiterman's last stanza quipped:

> . . . Thus Right prevails:
> It always does with George McCutcheon.

And, on the whole, some "Graustark" tales
are bigger blots on his escutcheon.

Yet except for the happy ending, perhaps, there is nothing Graustarkian about *The Rose in the Ring.* The ring is not a marriage band but rather one of the sawdust pits of a three-ring American circus, which GBMc had competently researched. The story does open with another McCutcheonesque washed-out bridge which obliges certain train passengers to continue on foot, "heavy stoicism their burden." The somberness is intended, so that the novel owes nothing, unfortunately, to Thackeray's *The Rose and the Ring* (1855). Thackeray's satirical tale of Paflagonia and the wicked Gruff-a-Nuff revolves around Prince Giglio's magic ring and Prince Bulbo's magic rose, each talisman making its possessor appear ever lovable. (GBMc owned a valuable first edition of that Tolkienesque fairytale illustrated with forty-eight woodcuts by Thackeray himself—item no. 412 in GBMc's *Renowned Collection of First Editions of Dickens and Thackeray.*)

In the letter to Jessie ("We have fallen in love with New York") Marie's "we" presumed a little. For George was never as enthusiastic about Manhattan as was his mannequin-like wife. Some of his reservations are reflected in his Hawthornesque short story "The Wrath of the Dead," which centers in the prophetic destruction of Manhattan ("New Sodom") as a punishment for its iniquities:

Here was the home of Midas and the tent of Momus, the playground of Bacchus and the scented resting place of Aphrodite! Gentile and Jew, Pagan and Puritan—all, all knelt at the common shrine and lifted praise to Mammon. . . . God was forgotten; Christ was banished. . . . Men and women exchanged their eternal souls for a brief instant of power; they trafficked in the values of love, in the profits of honor, in the commodities of friendship. . . . The day of reckoning was at hand.

Back in Chicago, meanwhile, John's accounts of his African exploits had been running serially in the *Tribune.* The walls of John's studio in the Fine Arts Building bristled with the stuffed heads of wild animals, among them that of a rhinoceros, also "the tawny skin of my first lion; heads of African game; tribal shields and weapons; assorted guns and historic shell fragments."

Hunting and killing wildlife went against George's grain, and just about all his family and friends knew this. He was regarded as something of a sissy and was teased about it. Years later, John's wife, Evelyn, recounted to James Kopka the good-natured banter, on this issue, which she had overheard between her husband and her brother-in-law: "John always fussed with George," she said, "for *writing* about adventure rather than *doing* anything about it."

Conservationists will no doubt vindicate George Barr McCutcheon for *writing* about, for satirizing, in his play *Brood House*, senseless slaughter of wildlife. More significantly, *Brood House* raises one's consciousness of the wreckage resulting from one person's inhumanity toward another. In this play, the set is strewn with lion skins and elephant tusks—is bedizened with swords, pistols, knives, Buddhas, and other icons of hatred and of love. That there is only one principal set, incidentally, James Brood's large upstairs studio (except for a brief final scene in the garden at the front of Brood House), reflects not only one of the classical unities in this play but also GBMc's development as a playwright. *Brood House,* which he thought well enough of to have privately printed, surpasses all his other works. Although it may at first remind one of Ibsen and O'Neill, it is in the end indebted to neither: it is all McCutcheon. His growth was in part parallel to that of those playwrights; it did not derive from them.

James Brood, the master of Brood House in New York City, is about fifty years old, and twenty years older than his new wife, Yvonne. A veteran of several big-game expeditions in Africa and India, he is affluent enough to retain, in his mansion, the servant Ranjab, among other servants, and his old cronies Dawes and Riggs. Brood has driven away his first wife, Matilde, believing her to have been unfaithful to him with her music teacher. Brood also believes that her son, Frederic, is not his own, and treats him cruelly.

Frederic is in love with Lydia, James's secretary, but is almost seduced away from her by his stepmother. Yvonne at first behaves toward him like a Phèdre. She does this to hurt James, who soon suspects unholy intrigue. In the third act, James, pretending to mistake Frederic for a burglar, shoots (but does not kill) him with one of the otherwise decorative pistols. In horror and remorse, Yvonne then reveals to James that she is the sister of his first wife and has married him only to avenge the innocent; that Frederic is indeed James's son.

The climax of this melodrama in the third act, along with its dénouement in the fourth,* inspired McCutcheon to some good theater and

---

*_Brood House_ is now available in a three-act version.

some brilliant dialogue. But his triumph in this play remains his characterization, all his characters authentic in psychological introspection.
McCutcheon characterizes James as a man of romantic virility,
machismo chauvinism, and arrested adolescence at age fifty. The audience
first sees Brood as one whose penchant for wildlife-hunting is satirized by
Yvonne, as is his witting attractiveness to young women.

James: I saved Ranjab from death in a little village near Lahore. Ranjab
was to have been sentenced for the murder of his wife. She'd been false
to him and he slew her. He was in prison and was to be executed within
a week. One night my three friends and I stormed the little jail and rescued
him. We needed the excitement. You see, we were just getting over the
cholera.
Yvonne: Why not tell the story to Miss Followell and Miss Janey [house
guests] in the morning at breakfast—all about how you looted the temple
and made away with his worship [a Buddha, which sits prominently as
a trophy in James's studio] and were shot at by endlessly poor marksmen
through hundreds of miles of jungle and were pursued by tigers and
cobras and outraged natives until you were ready to drop for want of
water and sleep and food.
James: Sensible idea!

But less forgivable than James's escapades is his foible of chauvinist
jealousy, which persists convincingly to the end of the play. It is to
McCutcheon's credit that he does not try to romanticize this fault away
in a happy-ending 180° reformation of the protagonist's character. Among
James's redeeming traits, on the other hand, is his sense of loyalty. He
supports his former hunting-companions Dawes and Riggs, for example,
as house guests for eleven years. Although James is wrongheaded about
his first wife and at times unnecessarily gallant toward young women,
he demonstrates a sincere and disarming affection for Yvonne. All his
machismo, all his prowess as a lover, would not have broken down
Yvonne's initial satanic intentions were it not for his genuine solicitous-
ness toward her, along with a stubborn, perhaps unconscious residual
love for her sister. Yvonne intuits and respects that love.

Yvonne: You have held me in your arms and permitted, even encouraged,
your imagination to substitute another woman's never-to-be-forgotten
kisses for mine . . . Matilde is dead, but to you she is still alive. [Right
now, James does not know that Matilde was Yvonne's sister.]
James: Why—why I haven't dared admit that to myself. How should you
even guess at such—

Yvonne: I can see it in your eyes. Yes, James Brood, you are the most wonderful man I have ever known. You *have* a heart—a heart that still needs breaking before you will see that it is there.

James's heart will indeed be broken before the end of the play. And in his contrition he will turn "from flint to eiderdown," at least in his relations with Frederic. But even at the end of the play, James persists in his *Taming of the Shrew* tactics against Yvonne. He commands her to stay at home for a year while he and his friends, along with Frederic and Lydia, sojourn abroad. The understanding is that Yvonne and James will need at least a year's separation to see if they still feel like resuming their marriage in a new key. At the same time, McCutcheon wisely implies that it would take at least a year, if not longer, for James to be disabused of his insufferable chauvinism. One can well imagine the audience hissing James when he says to Yvonne "I don't intend you shall ever forget that you are bound to me—that you are my property—."

In young Frederic, McCutcheon re-creates the archetypal rejected son in search of a father's love. James Brood's secretary, Lydia, protests, "I have never known you to give Frederic a loving tender word. You don't like him, Mr. Brood. I can't see why that should be. But I will not hear you revile him, sir." Frederic attempts, but fails in, a desperate showdown reconciliation with James. Ironically, the reconciliation is at last achieved only because Frederic erroneously assumes that his stepmother is going to run away with him.

Soon after shooting Frederic on the pretense that he is a thief (in more than one sense), James learns from Yvonne who Frederic really is. The melodrama of the shooting is thus heightened by classical peripety —by the father's realization that he has shot his own flesh and blood, not an adulterer's bastard. The shooting also provides catharsis for the son. For Frederic has all along, however unconsciously, wished to be punished. And it is only this cataclysmic wound that brings with it some peace of mind.

Frederic's return to Lydia, his first love, may strike some audiences as a little too facile—depending on the Garboesque conviction with which the role of Yvonne is played. But Frederic's feelings for Yvonne have never amounted to anything more than infatuation; she had indeed mesmerized him. His love for Lydia, though latent, has always remained genuine.

The second Mrs. Brood, Yvonne, remains one of the most complex of all McCutcheon's female characters. As mentioned above, knowing that her sister Matilde, the first Mrs. Brood, was calumniated and persecuted, Yvonne sets out to hurt James Brood by seducing his son. In the first act Yvonne initiates with Frederic an amorous fishing expedition, pointing out their age discrepancies but hoping to be contradicted.

Yvonne: Then you *were* in love with her? Pah! I might have known it. You are just the sort who would be carried away by a lily-white bloodless creature such as she is. Why don't you marry her? How pretty it would be! How wonderfully respectable her kisses would be! A peck or two, that's all, and you'd think you'd been really loved! Not the warm, hungry, endless kiss of hot red lips that burn and quiver with the passion of a real, a big, an amorous love! No, no—not that kind of kiss! Only the very proper peck of a *good* girl—how nice!

Nor does Yvonne make any attempt to act discreetly with Frederic when James is present. On the contrary, she deliberately continues to hurt her husband. Yet no matter who is present, the mention of Frederic's mother's name, Matilde, instantly switches Yvonne off from her vampire role—makes her "suddenly stiffen and stare with wide fierce eyes." This silent paroxysm alarms James and elicits his tenderness. Everybody senses, however vaguely, some relationship between Yvonne and Matilde. During the first soirée, when Ranjab prepares to entertain with one of his sword tricks, the subject of unfaithful wives and avenging husbands comes up. Yvonne flinches as if she fears that Ranjab's sword is aimed at her.

James: My dear one—is it possible you have the least fear of Ranjab? If you are nervous, I'll send my poor murderer away.
Yvonne: Fear Ranjab? No, my husband. After all, he did no more than kill his *own* wife. Why should he kill yours? *It is only the faithless wife who is killed, and she by her own husband.*

Here Yvonne, momentarily blind to her own behavior, is of course needling James about *his* behavior toward Matilde.

Toward Frederic and Lydia, Yvonne soon develops a noticeable ambivalence. On the one hand, she plays the role of Lydia's rival and intended, though never consummated, seducer of Frederic. But on the other hand, despite her initial intentions, Yvonne falls in love with James. She then reforms from a would-be avenger to a loving stepmother, in the end encouraging Frederic and Lydia to patch up their earlier falling out. McCutcheon probes deeply into Yvonne's psyche and the psyches of avengers. Through the drama of good vs. evil warring within Yvonne, the playwright successfully performs a histology of the human heart.

McCutcheon makes Lydia a poignant foil to Dawes and Riggs. The old pensioners have been treated shabbily by Yvonne. Her contempt for these cronies of James's, who seem to get in her way, comes out not only in her icy stares at them but also in her acid remarks: "Is this an inebriates' asylum—a home for sentimental paupers?" But young Lydia treats Dawes and Riggs much more compassionately.

Lydia: Something has tried you dreadfully, you dear silly old children. What is it?
Dawes: James never locked anything up [referring to the liquor cabinet] when your father was alive. [Lydia's father had been one of James's hunting companions.
Lydia: Oh, that is it? Mr. Brood has at last come to realize that he must keep it under lock and key. Well, you dear old ninnies, it was the only way. Come now, cheer up! He'll unlock it tomorrow.

Despite Lydia's condescending vocatives, what she *does* for these old men—interceding on their behalf with her employer—reflects genuine affection. Dawes and Riggs, in turn, bestow on her a touching avuncular love. When she becomes exhausted from intensive manuscript work for James, the two old men "solicitously fan her and pat her shoulder." In short, McCutcheon balances not only the genders but also the ages— types of young and old.

While not overemphasizing satire—not even the satire of big-game hunting—McCutcheon takes a passing slap at the tactics of irresponsible surgeons. In the first act a dinner guest, exchanging small talk with the surgeon Dr. Hodder, says, "Hindu parents go on the same principle you American surgeons follow. When you operate to find out if there's anything the matter with one's stomach, you whack out the appendix as a matter of expediency whether it needs it or not." That acerbic slur may well reflect GBMc's ambivalent feelings about whether Marie's hysterectomy was really necessary and, perhaps even more so, his suppressed bitterness about the mismanaged delivery of their baby boy.

Brood House also contains elements of the frivolous and the ridiculous. The elder Miss Followell, another house guest, indulges in malapropisms, and she salvages an otherwise disastrous faux pas by saying "Sorry, but you were talking into my deaf ear." Another house guest, Mrs. Gunning, whose chief weapon is her mouth, complaining about how boring Dr. Hodder has been, is informed by the hostess, "But my dear, Dr. Hodding is one of the country's most famous surgeons." Mrs. Gunning says, "I've never met a famous man who wasn't stupid. Give me jackasses like my husband every time."

The departure-for-Europe scene in the last act affords another brief interlude with Dawes and Riggs, as they pack their valises. Dawes says, "Do you know, Joseph, I'm always forgetting my toothbrush." Riggs adds, "Yes, and the last time we went away, you forgot your teeth." Dawes and Riggs are in fact used for most of the comic relief. After the tenseness of the shooting scene—after James shoots Frederic—and there is talk of calling the police, Dawes and Riggs try to protect James. Each pensioner vies comically with the other to be the first to "confess" to the shooting.

Many of the lines in this play are witty: some are brilliant. McCutcheon misses few opportunities for dramatic irony, double entendres, and plays upon words. For example, when James confides to Yvonne the reason for his cruelty toward Frederic, namely the unfounded notion of Matilde's unfaithfulness ("Her lover was that ˌboy's father"), Yvonne knows that the audience senses something James does not: James himself was that lover. When Lydia goes to the picture gallery to give Frederic and Yvonne their privacy in the studio, Yvonne says, "What a nice wait she's been having with the Old Masters while the young one stops here with his head full of other things (eyeing him languorously)." On her return to the studio, Lydia glances scornfully at Yvonne. Frederic says "Confound it, Lydia, I don't understand that glance." Lydia, smiling faintly, says, "My glance is like the moth. It always seeks the flame." James regards the studio, where he works with his secretary, as a kind of private sanctum. When he and Lydia are interrupted in their work by Yvonne, he says, "We are getting on toward the end [of this manuscript]. We have just escaped captivity in Lhasa." Yvonne says, "So I perceive. You stopped, I daresay, just as you heard the tread of the vulgar world approaching the inner temple." Then, with an even more biting double entendre: "That's what *you* broke into and desecrated, wasn't it!" In another scene, when Frederic excuses himself with "I think I'll go to bed," Yvonne observes, "Bed is a sepulchre, Frederic. We bury half our lives in it."

The dialogue also contains some master strokes of paradox, especially in the last act. When Frederic observes, in the dénouement, "We all understand each other once more," Yvonne says, "That may be, but none of us understands himself." Finally, Frederic, preparing to depart for Europe without Yvonne, pleads "Hang it all, Yvonne, Lydia and I won't be happy unless you come to our wedding. It isn't too late. We can hold the boat for you."

Yvonne: You know, both of you, what I have done, what I tried to do and failed. I tried to take you away from James through the agency of hate. Hatred failed. It was because I could not hate well enough. . . . You must admit, though, that my failure was a success after all.
Frederic: [But do come with us] for my mother's sake!
Yvonne: I am no longer fighting for Matilde . . .
Lydia: You love him [James] for yourself?
Yvonne: Yes. I love that man. I love him. I don't understand myself.
Frederic: It's a shame. You don't deserve this [separation].
Yvonne: Women very seldom get what they deserve.

In short, all the elements of this play contribute to, and illuminate, the melodrama of good vs. evil. The moral imperative "We must love one another or perish"—the idealism—is dramatized with convincing realism, and if only for that excellence *Brood House* must sooner or later be recognized as a first-rate melodrama. No less a playwright and critic than George Bernard Shaw might well have applauded *Brood House* could he have seen it and measured it by his own criteria:

A really good melodrama is of first-rate literary importance [Shaw wrote] . . . simple and sincere drama of action and of feeling, kept within the vast track of passions and motives common to the philosopher and the labourer, relieved by plenty of fun, and depending for variety of human character on contrasts between types of youth and age, sympathy and selfishness, the masculine and the feminine, the serious and the frivolous, the sublime and the ridiculous. . . . The whole character of the piece must be idealistic, full of moral lessons.

As hinted in *Mr. Bingle* (much later) *Brood House* was very likely submitted to, and rejected by, the Frohmans. Surely the syndicate would have had nothing to do with any play that lampooned big-game hunting and, by implication, Theodore Roosevelt. But Minnie Maddern's husband, Harrison Fiske, if approached, would probably have produced it, Minnie herself playing the role of Yvonne Brood. GBMc could probably have persuaded Minnie on the basis of the safari-satire alone. As an avid reader of newspapers, he knew that she had been making public utterances against irresponsible hunting, thus antagonizing Theodore Roosevelt. "Roosevelt was one of those who admired her genius," wrote Carlos Griffith, "but possibly his regard had been dimmed by her attitude toward his African trip for the purpose of slaughtering wild animals." In fact, Mrs. Fiske was later to be honored in Washington, D.C., "for twenty-five years of un-swerving devotion to the Crusade for Justice to Animals." Except for Mrs. Fiske, perhaps the only other well-known anti-hunting critic during the early 1900s was Mark Twain's collaborator on *The Gilded Age,* Charles Dudley Warner. In his essay "A-Hunting of the Deer," Warner com-miserates about man's inhumanity: "It cannot be denied that we are so constituted as to feel a delight in killing a wild animal, which we do not experience in killing a tame one."

In short, GBMc stood little chance of getting *Brood House* produced unless he approached the Fiskes. But with characteristic diffidence, he did not, as far as is known, approach them. Rather, he had the play privately printed in an edition of seventy-five copies. He also alleviated some of his galling failed-playwright frustrations by rewriting the play, the next year, as a novel—*Black Is White,* that title reflecting no slight cynicism.

For the most part faithful to the play, the novel, published a few years later, elicited disappointingly mixed reviews. A *New York Times* reviewer was erroneously reminded of "the most marvelous parts of Poe's 'Ligeia'," to which neither the novel nor the play bears more than the vaguest resemblance, although the reviewer did acknowledge "several dramatic scenes." Another *Times* reviewer, more attentive than the first, recognized the novel's "convincing illusions of reality.... Mr. McCutcheon has a plausible way of presenting what is remarkable but true both in characters and in scenes." A reviewer in the *Springfield Republican* nominated *Black Is White* as McCutcheon's "strongest and best." But the *Boston Transcript* reviewer, H. T. Parker (Tark's "Hell-to-Pay Parker"), cut GBMc with the dismissal "It is the mildest form of frankness to say that *Black Is White* is worth neither the serious discussion nor the space here given it." Many another popular novelist might have shrugged off that cut, grinning all the way to the bank, but not GBMc. The wound hurt for a long time, much as Lockhart's below-the-belt attack on *Endymion* had hurt Keats. It is quite possible that Parker had not even read *Black Is White*—had jumped to the conclusion that it was just another McCutcheon potboiler. And GBMc, at this time far from cured of writing without conviction, may have started hating himself, even if only subconsciously, for having failed to resist writing Graustarkian sequels and other ephemeral crowd-pleasers.

If Parker did read *Black Is White,* he may have been outraged by the implied slurs on Roosevelt. Yet GBMc must have learned from his Dutch Treat friend Julian Street—indeed, just from reading reviews—that reviewers and editors were either pro safari or anti, pro Roosevelt or anti. The Rough Rider was now the subject of Street's little encomium *The Most Interesting American,* which apotheosized Preparedness, the Strenuous Life, and Big-Game Hunting: "The Colonel's shooting, like his vast reading, has been done in spite of exceeding near-sightedness. He is the most farsighted nearsighted man in the country." Street did not intend irony or disrespect. He added, "If the Colonel is not our greatest American, who is?" The Colonel's study at Sagamorc Hill, as Street put it, "is a small museum . . . with animal skins on the floor and mounted heads of animals on the walls."

A chilling anticlimax to all of GBMc's 1908–1910 excitement with *Brood House* occurred on January 24, 1911. On that day he and Booth Tarkington were shocked to learn that their fellow-Hoosier David Graham Phillips had been murdered by an anti-feminist. The assassin imagined that Phillips's play *The Worth of a Woman* had slandered his sister and that Phillips had "torn down the ideals of American womanhood." By coincidence McCutcheon was working on a short story with a satirical feminist theme, "When Girl Meets Girl." But the loss of a friend and the story's tone of levity now prompted him to put it aside for at least a year. Whether because of the shocking murder or because he was beginning to experience an identity crisis, perhaps for both reasons, he settled on writing *What's-His-Name,* a novel that would occupy his working days for the next six months. In that novel, set in the world of the New York theater, an actress with the dazzling brilliance of a Minnie Maddern (although she is called Nellie Duluth) is married to a self-obliterating man who is overshadowed by her and who regards himself as much more of a failure than he really is.

12

THE FLYERS
AND THE FROHMANS

McCutcheon was probably not aware that about this time a young Hoosier student at Yale had written a song in praise of melodrama:

Oh, I know it's hardly *comme il faut*
But a melodrama fills my soul with bliss.
My tastes may be plebeian
But efforts herculean
Can never change my taste for plays like this.

If Cole Porter liked melodrama—and who else but Cole would have put it that way?—he would have relished George Barr McCutcheon's melodramas with their playful bursts of comedy, parody, and satire.

Satire inspired McCutcheon not only in his plays but also in some of his fiction, excluding the Graustarkian romances. The kind of philistine and American Anglophile he poked fun at in his novel *The Flyers* (1907), he also satirized in such fiction as *The Sherrods,* "Her Weight in Gold," "When Girl Meets Girl," and *The Hollow of Her Hand.*

In "Her Weight in Gold," a money-mad suitor agrees to marry a behemoth of a girl provided her weight is reproduced pound for pound in a gold dowry. Ironically, before the marriage is consummated, the bride-to-be falls ill and loses about half of her original weight. This story was the first in a collection of the same title originally published by Bobbs-Merrill (1911) for the Chicago Indiana Society; was reissued in 1912 by Dodd, Mead; and again in 1914 by Charles Scribner's Sons.

The idea for the short story "When Girl Meets Girl," which first appeared in *Good Housekeeping* (June 1912), may have been suggested by Marie, who was anti-feminist although not anti-suffragette. (Once given the right to vote, Marie would no doubt have voted against some of the women's rights hard fought for and won since her time.) On this issue GBMc was perhaps more reasonable than Marie. Still, he could not resist poking fun at a situation that might have arisen in feminism carried to its logical (perhaps also its illogical) extremes. In this tour de force GBMc has two young Amazons kidnap an eligible wealthy bachelor on behalf of a third Amazon, who demands that he marry her. Before she has a chance to rape or shoot her captive, or both, he is rescued by a traditionally "ladylike" young woman, whom he marries.

The Hollow of Her Hand (1912), set in GBMc's contemporary New York, tells how Mrs. Challis Wrandall comes to befriend her husband's murderer, a young woman whom the philandering Mr. Wrandall had betrayed. A reviewer in the *Boston Evening Transcript* praised the novel for its "very good character painting" and added that the reader's "interest starts as soon as the story opens and never wanes." GBMc inscribed copy number 14 of *The Hollow of Her Hand* to its illustrator, James Montgomery Flagg and to Flagg's wife, Nellie. The Flaggs had by now become close friends of the McCutcheons. The congenial foursome sometimes dined together before attending plays.

Of all the plays the McCutcheons attended in 1912, they would remember the longest, no doubt, the out-of-town experimental production of GBMc's play *The Flyers*. Unlike its spin-off novel, the play, which GBMc had written several years previously, is somewhat more irreverent, although in a lighter vein than *Brood House* and not so melodramatic. The main theme of this "comedy in four acts," as GBMc subtitled it, is that true love, for which there is no substitute, gets hobbled by the ridiculous conventions society foists upon it.

The intrusions of society are embodied in Mr. and Mrs. Van Truder, especially Mrs. Van Truder. She is thoroughly myopic, whereas Horace, her husband, is only physically nearsighted. Now pathetic, now ludicrous, Horace represents only the man's shell which his once integrated self—before his marriage to Gertrude—has long ago evacuated. The yearning of all parties to escape convention—the two pairs of young lovers, Joe and Millicent, Windomshire and Anne; even the Van Truders, who attempt to escape their own boredom—is symbolized in the train trip. Although the original destinations of the elopers are Boston and Washington, D.C., respectively, their plans are changed by engine trouble. (How many of GBMc's escape trains develop heart trouble!) Everybody on the train ends up in the state of New York at a resort hotel called Omegon.

Omegon connotes not only an "agon" (or prize to be won by competing characters) but also "omega," which on a scale from alpha to omega, must mean ultimate resort. Also symbolic of the protagonists' frustration en route is the washed-out bridge, which makes it necessary for them to row across to the next stretch of train tracks.

If there is a fault to be found in this play, it is that—just as in some of the comedies of humours by Molière and by Ben Jonson—characterization is sacrificed to satire. For example, the two sets of lovers—Joseph Dauntless in love with Millicent Browne, Lord Windomshire in love with Anne Courtenay—have been "engaged" to the wrong persons because society has at first held them hostages to convention.

Among the subordinate themes of the play, the penchant of Americans to marry titled Englishmen is satirized, as is the eligible Briton's motivation: "His Lordship likes Milly because she's going to have a million some day." At least that *was* "Lord W's" initial conditioning by society. (He is later exonerated because he follows his unmercenary secret heart.) Besides satirizing the English, McCutcheon pokes fun at Americans who worship them. This is evident in the scene in which Windomshire rudely escapes the company of Mrs. Van Truder. He interrupts her attempted conversation with him. "Beg pardon!" he says, "Appointment, you know—" Responding to his behavior, Mrs. Van Truder observes, "I am quite sure I would consider that inexcusable in an American." In an Englishman, however, rudeness is to be overlooked, especially from the point of view of one currying his favor.

Other satirical brush strokes appear in the caricature of the unctuous cadaver-snatcher Hooker, an agent for a medical school's anatomy laboratory. His lugubrious livelihood is first revealed in a conversation with Brimm, the Omegon's stingy and self-aggrandized maître d'hôtel.

Hooker: I see you are in the habit of beating your wife, poor thing.
Brimm: What do you mean? My wife has been dead seven years.
Hooker: That interests me. I deal in 'em.
Brimm: Deal in 'em? Wives?
Hooker: Not especially wives. Either sex, but wives are easier to buy. Widowers have no scruples. They're looking for live ones.

The stage business includes some delightful confusions. Right from the start of the two pairs of lovers' elopements on the same train headed east, there is confusion between "Car No. 5, Section 7" and "Car No. 7, Section 5"; also between "Track 2 at 3 o'clock" and "Track 3 at 2 o'clock." Lending credibility to such confusion is the lovers' nervousness. More nervous than any others are the young men, who miss the train. When the news reaches Millicent, she believes she has been deserted. She is assured that "his [Dauntless's] baggage is aboard." "Yes," she cries, "I am his baggage—unclaimed!" But the two young men eventually show up. They are covered with coal dust, having ridden in the coal bin of a locomotive Windomshire has hired to catch up with the missed train, conveniently stalled by a washed-out bridge.

The young men have tried to conceal their identities, along with those of their companions, with silly disguises. But these prove ineffective, especially to the sharp eyes of the snooping Mrs. Van Truder. Dauntless's man Taps complains, "I've come to say, sir, that I refuse to wear this mustache any longer. Two dogs have tried to bite me, and—" Dauntless replies, "Take it off—and change those clothes. You don't need a disguise any more, you idiot. They know us."

Until a connecting train arrives from the East, all the passengers must stop at the Omegon Hotel. On the hotel's terrace at dusk the double-dinner scene generates more hilarity. Dauntless has ordered dinner for seven, and so has Mrs. Van Truder—for the same seven guests, who are too embarrassed to reveal their conflicts of interest. The resulting confusion, which the greedy Brimm could have averted but has deliberately encouraged, includes some hilarious table hopping and some missequence of courses (Mrs. Van Truder: "Here's the coffee and ice cream, and—my heavens—what's this—the roast!") The banquet is broken up by an impending thunderstorm, which sends all the diners scuttling into the hotel.

The final scene takes place in front of a country church, where the couples are to be privately married. Adjacent to this church is its cemetery. The cemetery-bound Hooker, bent on exhuming a cadaver, is mistaken for the minister. Double entendres and dramatic ironies follow about witnesses (to the marriage? to the exhuming?). But the confusion is finally resolved with the arrival of the legitimate minister, and the true lovers are at last joined in holy matrimony.

All this business, the caricatures, and the satire make this comedy of manners as pleasant as those of Plautus and Terence, and as good as the Rochester drama reviewer judged it, if not better.

In January, 1912—on the fifteenth, sixteenth, and seventeenth—*The Flyers* was produced experimentally in the Lyceum Theater, Rochester,

New York. McCutcheon attended the opening matinee performance even though he was on the verge of an appendicitis attack. In the audience, among various talent scouts, sat Daniel Frohman, brother of the omnipotent syndicate boss, Charles Frohman.

The syndicate by now owned some of the best theaters in New York City and in many of the larger cities of the United States, to say nothing of its holdings in London and Paris. The syndicate also managed the most celebrated actors and actresses, along with the road shows spinning off from Broadway hits. This powerful trust had started in the early 1890s in a series of shrewd maneuvers that culminated in the Empire Theater Stock Company, the stock pertaining less to thespian repertoires than to the portfolios of the investors.

As the powerful head of the syndicate Charles Frohman presided behind the scenes literally and symbolically, in his office in the Empire Theater, aptly named because from here he did control an empire. Among the pictures on his wall a portrait from the playwright Clyde Fitch was signed "To C. F. from c. f." Charles's brother Daniel, although a little older, played the role of executive assistant, carrying out C. F.'s suggestions, especially in matters of firing. Thus when an indiscreet actress, a divorcee, had to be fired for political reasons, Daniel wrote the order. In the case of Mrs. Leslie Carter, he wrote to stage manager David Belasco, "Dear David: The stockholders request us not to have Mrs. Carter on our stage any more."

Within a few years of its incorporation the syndicate managed to alienate several actors and actresses (among them Minnie Maddern), playwrights, managers, and directors—ultimately Belasco himself, albeit with on-again, off-again relationships. Miss Maddern was to be briefly reconciled about the same time that Belasco had a falling-out. But in 1893, shortly after her marriage, which Charles Frohman never forgave, she and her husband, Harrison Grey Fiske, tried to produce Ibsen and some playwrights of their own choosing without benefit of the syndicate's resources. That enterprise proved frustrating, for the Fiskes found syndicate stages closed to them and had to resort at first to obscure theaters, liberal churches, school auditoriums, and even barns, until their ultimate triumph on Broadway, several years later, with the Fiskes' Manhattan Company. In the fall of 1897 Fiske, Editor of the *New York Dramatic Mirror,* launched a histrionic attack against the Frohmans. A special supplement of the *Mirror* castigated them as "mercenaries," "middlemen," "illiterate managers," "theatrical throttlers," "insolent jobbers," "crooked entrepreneurs," and "greedy, narrow-minded tricksters."

As anyone might have expected, the syndicate brought suit for libel. The head of the Frohmans' legal corps, and one of the stockholders, was a Marc Klaw, whose Dickensian name McCutcheon might have invented had it been necessary to do so. The Fiskes were quite popular, whereas the Frohmans were after all acting in restraint of trade. The grand jury found in favor of the Fiskes and on March 5, 1898, the case was dismissed.

Was Charles Frohman an ogre? It would be all too easy to depict him as a tarantula in his den at the Empire Theater. It might be poetic justice to hiss and boo him, as did the Fiskes, overtly in the *New York Dramatic Mirror;* and McCutcheon, vicariously, in *Mr. Bingle* and elsewhere. But Frohman was probably less despicable than wrongheaded. Early in his career he did resort to such peccadilloes as papering the house and planting paid applauders at melodramas, along with paid laughers at comedies. He did this not just to ensure favorable reviews but also to educate the provincial audiences he shrewdly judged to be half-educated. He was a self-appointed teacher providing America with its theater curriculum, and within the frame of his didactic Victorian vision, his standards remained high.

Still, he was also something of a snob. "His policies were always pretentious; he always admired big names," said Daniel. Whenever Charles had a choice, he slighted American talent in favor of imports. He courted British playwrights and Continental actresses. Nor did he delegate to Daniel any of those imports. C. F. crossed the Atlantic himself at least once a year, until he went down with the *Lusitania* in 1915. He kowtowed to such Continental actresses as Bernhardt, Duse, and Modjeska. He bowed and scraped before Henry Arthur Jones, Sir Arthur Wing Pinero, and, above all, Sir James Barrie. (The Frohman production that catapulted Barrie along with Maude Adams to unprecedented heights was *Peter Pan,* 1904, which McCutcheon's Mr. Bingle regarded as "the greatest play ever written.") When Frohman produced Barrie's *The Admirable Crichton,* Max Beerbohm praised Barrie for "having the courage to show that the most servile slaves may become, in a place where there is free competition, the most masterly of masters." How ironic that Beerbohm was talking about Barrie's Crichton, not Barrie's Frohman! Frohman produced only one of Shaw's plays, most of which struck him as too iconoclastic. But he cultivated Shaw's friendship with sycophancy, going so far as to toss pebbles and breadcrumbs at Shaw's studio windows.

In Frohman's snobbery, which antagonized McCutcheon and infuriated the Fiskes, CF was after all a child of his milieu. His was an era in which Americans of rising mercantile families were lionizing titled British and Continentals, as Dixon Wecter observed, and were aspiring, via marriages of eligible daughters, to enhance plebeian escutcheons with royal heraldry. (Compare GBMc's playful reversal of that pattern, however, in having an American *male* marry a *Princess* Yetive of Graustark.) As long as writers of romances—the Anthony Hopes, the Charles Majors, the George Barr McCutcheons—endorsed such aspirations (never mind instigated and glorified them) the Frohman stockholders were content. But they became uneasy, regarded it as personal affronts, when such sacraments were demeaned. For example, when McCutcheon in his play *The Flyers* satirized titled British "catches" and lampooned the whole idea of long formal engagements between fiancés and fiancées these iconoclasms antagonized the Frohmans, as did certain other of McCutcheon's overt and implicit criticisms of Victorian lifestyles.

The *Rochester Union* reviewer of *The Flyers* had evidently been entertained, although he made a guarded effort to take away with one hand what he gave with the other. Had he been thinking about influences, he might have noted that the zany lovers derived in part from McCutcheon's exposure to such Gilbert and Sullivan operettas as *H.M.S. Pinafore* (1878), *The Pirates of Penzance* (1879), and *The Mikado* (1885), all of which he had seen by 1886. But the reviewer was unreservedly taken by GBMc's inventiveness in the character of Hooker: "One real novelty among the characters is that of William Hooker, whose specialty is furnishing cadavers to medical colleges . . . a source of real entertainment; and the complications arising from the misconceptions [e.g., the engaged couples' mistaking him for the minister] of what his work really is furnish the most genuine amusement." The reviewer had reservations about the character of Windomshire, or at least about whether it was appropriate for an American playwright's satire. Indeed, McCutcheon's caricature of "the silly-ass type of Englishman," unlike Sir William Gilbert's, struck the reviewer as offensive. The reviewer did emphasize, however, that the play as a whole "could be highly successful farce" contingent upon "a decided revision of the first act." He did not say that that act contained too many iconoclasms, but he did venture "it is a safe assertion that revision of the piece is already underway" since "there was a goodly representation of New York managers and producers [including Daniel Frohman] in attendance at last night's performance."

The upshot was that the Frohmans made no offer to produce *The Flyers*. Thus, GBMc must have fumed, if you were an American playwright and aspired to be produced by the syndicate, you had better be a genius like Eugene O'Neill, who happened also to be a native New York and the son of the celebrated Irish actor James O'Neill. If you were only George Barr McCutcheon, an upstart from the Waste Land, your chances were quite dim. Your chances might brighten a little if, despite Hoosier origins, you happened also to be—like Booth Tarkington or David Graham Phillips—a Princeton graduate; if you lunched at the Algonquin Round Table and cultivated David Belasco, the Bishop of Broadway.

Belasco had settled on the persona of Episcopalian priest, complete with black gabardine and white collar, even though his congenital magnetism hardly needed such overkill. Besides directing and writing, he did much of the rewriting ("A play is never written," said CF, "it is only rewritten.") Nor was Belasco's rewriting confined to tightening and otherwise improving a play technically. He often bowdlerized a script to accommodate alleged tastes of "mixed audiences." And Belasco was only one of several of the syndicate's play doctors, whom even the arrived playwrights courted. So how could a Midwestern maverick like McCutcheon, who preferred not to court Belasco and was not about to allow any play doctor to tamper with his scripts, expect to be produced by the syndicate? That McCutcheon's feelings were justified—that they were not entirely a Midwesterner's bitter-grape paranoia about a mythical Eastern conspiracy—was corroborated by the testimony of his fellow gentleman from Indiana, Booth Tarkington. Tarkington, who had adjusted more realistically to rewritings and collaborations, and who, in his triumphs within the Eastern establishment was a friend-of-the-enemy, conceded that Easterners held disparaging attitudes toward Indiana writers.

The public's reception of Tarkington's plays, written for the most part in collaboration not only with Julian Street but also with Broadway play doctors affiliated with the syndicate, is reflected in the following *Brooklyn Eagle* review of *A Man from Home* (1909):

His play is served, to be sure, in a framework of melodrama which has done duty for a century, but the threadbare plot serves well enough as a foundation for Mr. Tarkington's *message of the superiority of honest homespun American ways.* [Emphasis added.]

Tarkington was a conformist and an apologist. As John Carmody put it, "One reason for his popularity is his friendly attitude toward the basic assumptions of the American middle class."

If McCutcheon deferred to "honest homespun" middle-class values in his novels—almost meretriciously, as he himself admitted—he was not about to compromise in his plays. His adherence to integrity in his plays underscores his profound respect for, his aesthetic seriousness about, that genre.

After *The Flyers* suffered a qualified failure at the Rochester Lyceum (much as Henry James's play *Guy Domville* had in 1895 suffered a qualified failure at the London St. James's) McCutcheon did not let his wounded ego keep him from forging ahead immediately with writing more plays and novels. Moreover, like Henry James, GBMc injected into subsequent novels (especially *Black Is White, Yollop,* and *Oliver October*) certain techniques of playwriting: dramatic structure, psychologically motivated characterizations, only dialogue that moved the action forward, and only scenic properties used or experienced by the characters. Some of these elements, especially dramatic structure, were to be recognized and occasionally applauded by the more perceptive reviewers for the *New York Times* and the *Times Literary Supplement* of London.

13

THE MAN WHO LOVED CHILDREN

George Barr McCutcheon, plotsmith, was not only ingenious, as reviewers noticed, but also prolific. What he initiated as a discipline had by now grown into a habit. He kept at least one novel, often two, shaping in his daily forges. And he kept the novel-fires aglow or banked, depending on the temper of a play or short story he was forging with more intensity. The ready market for his fiction salved in part the wounds he suffered when his plays, which were more distinguished than most of his novels, were rejected.

Probably one of the wounds from which he never recovered was the snub from his once-revered James Whitcomb Riley. On April 27, 1912, in a letter headed "ONE WEST SIXTY-FOURTH STREET, NEW YORK CITY," McCutcheon wrote to Riley, who lived in Indianapolis: "I have taken the liberty of dedicating my new little book *[Her Weight in Gold...]* to you, a copy of which goes to you under separate cover.... If the title could have been '*His* Weight in Gold' the dedication would have been of some moment.... Please forgive me for hanging the book on you." Riley may have been suffering from one of his intermittent attacks of gout; or, having taken to drinking heavily, he may have been drunk; or he may simply have been too busy. Whatever the reason, he delegated to his nephew-amanuensis, Edmund Eitel, the responsibility of writing an acknowledgment. Intentional or unintentional, this coolness hurt GBMc deeply. Even three years later, he declined to attend a dinner in honor of Riley: "I fear that I shall be unable to come to Indianapolis for the Riley dinner on October 7," GBMc wrote to Eitel, "Mrs. McCutcheon's illness now looming as a possible and probable deterrent." Although Marie suffered at times from a kidney ailment, at this particular time she was in reasonably good health, if one excepts her chronic smoker's hack. All the same, when Riley died, in 1916, McCutcheon sent Eitel a telegram of condolence.

Like Riley, McCutcheon was inundated with more fan mail than he could respond to, but he tried to keep up with it, and he was always courteous in his responses. In an article GBMc wrote for *The Bookman,* he said, "An author in vogue finds himself at one end of an expansive correspondence, some of it quite foolish. Why should anyone respond, for example, to a telegram that reads 'Please send me your autograph at once by wire'?" In a business letter to his publishers Edward and Jonathan Dodd on June 24, 1912, he added as a postscript, "Marie is lovely, and we are thriving." Characteristically, GBMc caught up with his correspondence once he and Marie left the City for their Biddeford Pool cottage near Kennebunkport, Maine. Here they summered as usual from June 11 to September 6.

Kennebunkport, camouflaged as Corinth-by-the-Sea, had been the fictive setting of *Mary Midthorne,* one of McCutcheon's melodramatic novels published the previous year. Mary Midthorne, sister of Horace Blagden, the local bank president, has married the worthless Philip Midthorne (one of GBMc's recycled names) against her family's admonitions. Both Mary and Philip lead disgraceful lives, respectively as adulterer and murderer. After the deaths of these derelicts, their two children, Eric and Little Mary, become the wards of Uncle Horace and the enemies of his only child, the insufferable Chetwynd. In a favorable review in the *New York Times* McCutcheon was hailed as a "master of ingenuity in shaping and working out a plot." Still, *Mary Midthorne* remains perilously close to bad soap opera. It was soon to be surpassed by one of GBMc's more charming and successful soap operas.

Relegating other work to the back burners and not giving himself time to commiserate about the rejection of his play *The Flyers,* GBMc now devoted all his attention to forging a new play, *The Man Who Loved Children* ("begun June 15, 1912; completed June 28, 1912, Biddeford Pool, Maine").

The play contains several Dickensian touches. Mr. Bingle, the protagonist, has established a tradition of reading Dickens's *A Christmas Carol* every Christmas Eve to his large family and household staff. The play is indeed permeated with a love of large families of children. Also Dickensian in tone is GBMc's criticism of unscrupulous power and greed in individuals as well as institutions, especially the institution then known as the theater syndicate.

Mr. Bingle, because he has been kind to an eccentric uncle whose more immediate family would have nothing to do with him, finds himself no longer a lowly bookkeeper but, instead, the beneficiary of a fortune and the Vice-President of Sidney Force's Bank. With his windfall wealth Bingle, a man who loves children, adopts eleven of them (Mrs. Bingle has up until now proved unable to conceive any of their own) and employs a huge staff of servants, several with well-rendered personalities. For television viewers this play can evoke the kind of ambience and humor generated by *Upstairs, Downstairs.*

The subplot of the play furnished GBMc with an outlet for his bitterness against the Frohman syndicate. Dick Flanders, a reporter and aspiring playwright, is in love with Amy Fairweather, the Bingle family's admirable young governess, who was once an actress. Flanders has written an excellent play, which he fails at first to sell to the syndicate. Flanders resembles a younger McCutcheon, while the model for Amy Fairweather is in several transparent aspects Minnie Maddern. Like Miss Maddern, who adopted a child, Amy loves children. Like Minnie, too, Amy has acted as a child star and has later refused roles she hasn't believed in. Bingle, while still wealthy, plays angel—offers to stake Flanders to a vanity production starring Amy. When the syndicate managers learn that a millionaire has volunteered to underwrite Flanders' play, they turn dogs-in-the-manger and withdraw their original rejection.

Amy: You shall have a box on the opening night. I want you to see us.
Bingle: I expect to be behind the scenes, my dear. Isn't that where the angel sits—as Flanders would call us?
Flanders: (Hesitating): That's another thing I wanted to speak to you about, Mr. Bingle. I—I'm afraid we can't carry out our little plan. The—the syndicate refuses to let anyone else have a finger in the pie.
Bingle: You mean, they now think it's so good they can risk their own money on it?
Flanders: I suppose that's it. They notified me yesterday that I have to give them entire control or drop it altogether.

The main theme of this play (and of its later embodiment as the novel *Mr. Bingle*) concerns the social problem of abandoned children. Banker Sidney Force, who has sown many a wild oat, is unaware that his abandoned daughter Kathleen is now one of the Bingle family. But he approves compassionately of the system of placing abandoned children in private homes like the Bingles' as opposed to public orphanages. Force's wife prefers "the more scientific orphanage":

Mrs. Force: There is a scientific way of handling these children, Sidney, and I—
Force: A scientific way of handling other people's children—
Mrs. Force: Don't be sarcastic.

But the Bingle family plan, the way of love, the way Barr and Clara brought up their family, prevails as the way championed in *The Man Who Loved Children.*

A related theme concerns the hit-and-run lover, the kind of lover Amy accuses Dick Flanders of having been, at least in their earlier relationship. Although that relationship has not resulted in the birth of a child, Flanders realizes how irresponsible he has been. He also realizes that he is now more in love than ever with Amy. Having been hurt once, she is not too receptive. "We need not continue the discussion Dick," she says, "I am contented here. I am looking after children here, Dick, some of whom do not know who their fathers are. . . . The fathers of some of them are men like you, Dick, who loved as you loved, and their mothers are women who loved more deeply perhaps than you expected me to love."

It was perhaps a foregone conclusion that *The Man Who Loved Children,* given its attack on the system, would not be produced by the Frohmans—not even by rival theater managers. McCutcheon no doubt realized by now that he would sooner or later recast the play into the novel it became three years later. The novel, *Mr. Bingle*—illustrated by James Montgomery Flagg and published by Dodd, Mead—became another best seller and was eventually sold to the movies. The film appeared with the saccharine title "Daddy Dumplings" and, bearing only the faintest resemblance to *Mr. Bingle,* bypassed, of course, all discussion concerning the problems of playwrights.

Whereas the play castigates the greed of syndicate managers, the novel criticizes their blind spots in aesthetics. The theater managers, according to the novel, couldn't recognize a good play when it was staring them in the face: "A producer from the Far West [a Belasco?] concluded that there was more to Dick Flanders' play than the Wise Men of the East [the Frohmans?] were able to discern." In the novel, moreover, GBMc makes an author's mouthpiece of, and blows off steam through, the frustrated young playwright Flanders:

These [syndicate] managers are a rum lot. . . . Four-fifths of them don't know a good play from a bad one. . . . I understand it is a theory among managers that if a play is unspeakably bad they can have someone re-write it from beginning to end and make a success of it. . . . If it should happen to be a good play, they don't know what it's all about and will have nothing to do with it. . . . We don't have to ask any beastly theatrical manager to read the play.

A poignancy like the protest "Some of the best plays ever written never see the light of day" is followed by a masochistic history of McCutcheon's own wounds, in which Thomas Bingle plays the role of McCutcheon and Mrs. Bingle plays the role of devil's advocate, the role of GBMc's Socratic daimonion:

"Genius, your Granny!" she exclaimed. "Don't you suppose that these regular theater managers know genius when they see it? . . . How does anyone know that they were good plays if they were never played? Tell me that, Thomas Bingle."
"My dear, I am only repeating what history tells—"
"Well . . . what do you know about a play? Where do you get your wonderful knowledge of dramatic composition?"
"I think you will acknowledge that I know my Shakespeare pretty well."
"But Richard Flanders isn't Shakespeare. . . . He's a reporter on a daily paper. Now, for goodness' sake be sensible."

By now the McCutcheons were spending most of their winters in Arizona, with an occasional change to Warm Springs, Georgia. They apparently visited GBMc's Chicago relatives only rarely, even at Christmas. They invariably spent their summers at Biddeford Pool. Here GBMc was even more productive than he was in New York. He took only a few hours for golf in the cool of the early morning and devoted the rest of the day to writing. George and Marie hardly went near the water except on the hottest days. Neighbors Monty Flagg and Booth Tarkington dropped in occasionally, but there were seldom any house guests except for the weekend Hamlin and Zulime Garland stayed with them.

On the rocky beach below their cottage the McCutcheons entertained the Garlands with clambakes and lobster cookouts. Also, Booth Tark-ington took both the McCutcheons and the Garlands for a sail in his newly acquired old schooner, the *Regina,* piloted with the help of Julian Street and Captain Bill Trotter of the Kennebunkport Floats and Yacht Club.

George Ade kept declining invitations to Biddeford Pool, but Monty Flagg became friendly enough to call the McCutcheons "Mac and Daisy." On July 26, 1912, Flagg, along with Julian Street, delivered to the McCutcheon cottage an ode they had collaborated on in honor of GBMc's forty-sixth birthday. (A copy of that ode has yet to be found.)

In Maine, during the late summer of 1912, GBMc wrote a draft of "Prince Robin of Graustark," another slight novel which Dodd, Mead published the following year as *The Prince of Graustark*. (Prince Robin was the son of Princess Yetive and Grenfall Lorry.) Before the end of 1913 there appeared two more McCutcheon novels, *A Fool and His Money* and *Black is White* (based on *Brood House*). After the publication of *Black is White* as a book, it appeared as a whole number of *Munsey's* magazine for December, 1913. McCutcheon did not object to magazines' publishing his novels either in toto or in serial parts provided his fiction in book form reached the market first.

A Fool and His Money is the story of an affluent author who buys a castle on the Danube as a retreat where he can write. He does not realize until too late that he has also bought melodrama and mystery, including the responsibility of providing for a tenant, an enchanting refugee countess, who occupies one of the castle's wings. A *New York Times* reviewer praised "Mr. McCutcheon's sense of humor and skill leading up to the climaxes."

GBMc dedicated *A Fool and His Money* to Marie, the first such dedication in print as distinguished from handwritten inscriptions. Both the public dedication and the private inscription testify to his deepening devotion:

"To my inspiration and my spur"; "To my wife . . . who has brought this author to realize, and not to imagine, the love he writes about so feebly"; ". . . whose help and encouragement have set me a new path"; "To Marie . . . with constantly growing love"; "To Marie . . . affectionately inscribed by her greatest admirer"; "To my kindest critic, loyal advocate, and constant inspiration."

GBMc also inscribed several copies of *A Fool and His Money* to his publishers at Dodd, Mead, the "Dodd boys" "R[obert] H." "F[rank] H[oward]," "E[dward] H.," and "F[rank] C." But the first six author's copies, he inscribed in the following order: #1 for Marie, #2 for Clara, #3 for John, #4 for Jessie, #5 for Ben, and #6 for William P. Fay.

With his own money (the federal income tax would not take its first bite before 1913) GBMc was no fool. He did not lay waste his powers getting and spending in the stock market. He did invest in paintings and in rare books. He collected first editions of his favorite authors, Dickens and Thackeray; also Hardy, Kipling, Stevenson, and Mark Twain. He bought paintings by Winslow Homer, George Inness, Childe Hassam, and John Singer Sargent. He invested heavily in landscape paintings of the Barbizon School, especially those by Corot and Millet. But even from the first, he cherished these objects less as investments than as artifacts.

His independent taste in paintings now stands vindicated. Aside from masters of the modern schools, such Barbizons as the Corots and the Millets have held up, as anyone visiting major American art galleries can see. What is noteworthy is that GBMc persisted in buying these paintings despite their deprecation by an influential art dealer like Joseph Duveen. Duveen's motives, while not all mercenary (he did consult the impeccable aesthete Bernard Berenson) remain nonetheless suspect. At the same time that Duveen belittled the Barbizons, which sold in the low thousands, he extolled old Dutch and Italian masters, along with Gainsboroughs, which he sold for hundreds of thousands apiece to the denizens of the New York Gold Coast. In 1911 Duveen had built his celebrated gallery on the corner of Fifth Avenue and Fifty-sixth Street, a few blocks away from the mansions of the Fricks, the Astors, and the Vanderbilts, his target clients. He disparaged Knoedler's, where GBMc had bought some paintings, as a mere "picture-framing gallery." But McCutcheon was not to be browbeaten by self-appointed art critics any more than by syndicate play doctors. He followed his own tastes in collecting. In his unpublished inventory entitled *My Pictures* he wrote "I have gone about buying my pictures in my own way. Fortunately, I am capable of seeing them through my own eyes and not solely through the eyes of others [for example, Joseph Duveen's]." Then this reverie reflecting that his investments were not just mercenary: "I love my pictures so much that I sometimes wonder what will become of them when I am dead."

McCutcheon patronized several of the uptown art galleries besides Knoedler's on Fifth Avenue at Thirty-fourth Street: the American Art Association's on Madison Avenue, and several of the newer galleries whose reputations were yet to be made. A handsome man in his middle forties, he was himself the subject of portraits by illustrator friends, among them William Cotton and James Montgomery Flagg. In these portraits one notices GBMc's erect posture, abundant dark hair, fine straight nose, and florid complexion, the last a vestige of the rosy cheeks of his boyhood.

Photographs of him at this time show him wearing dark suits and ties, along with pince-nez glasses. He seldom wore a hat, regardless of the season or the weather. A later portrait of him, in his fifties, reveals him to be balding—also smoking a cigar, although he smoked much less frequently than Marie. To the *New York Times* drama critic Montrose Moses, McCutcheon looked "very much like Henry James." GBMc also struck that interviewer as "modest . . . generous in reference to others. . . . Mr. McCutcheon talks with a gentleness that shows him on good terms with the world."

Within the next few years, while GBMc was becoming a serious collector of paintings, his priorities began to change. Although playwriting remained at the top—to succeed in that art would remain to the end his heart's desire and frustration—the writing of novels as an end in itself began to change places with the excitement of acquiring art objects. As reflected in his elaborate inventories and journals describing his paintings, along with his annotated booklists for bibliophiles, he now seemed increasingly motivated, in his prolific production of novels, to make the money required for the purchase of fine paintings and first editions. There may also have crossed his mind the notion of some day producing one or another of his plays at his own expense. For whatever reason, the frenetic output of novels—quite a few but by no means all pot-boilers—would cost him dearly in reputation and in health. Nor can posterity extenuate his poor judgment in publishing potboilers since he himself knew when he was writing them. He admitted to Montrose Moses that *Beverly of Graustark,* for example, was "manufactured . . . artificial . . . it bored me. Only the letters from my readers forced me into it." Which was like saying "The Devil made me do it." Somebody from Lafayette twitted him, "Purdue can forgive you for everything except your boilermakers."

During the spring and the fall, while in the City, GBMc devoted his mornings to writing. One day, on a lunch break from writing, as he was browsing in a Fifth Avenue art gallery, probably Knoedler's, he was buttonholed by a *Times* reporter. "You used to write stories about princesses who fell in love with American men," the reporter said, "but in the last few years you've been writing about American girls. How would you describe the typical American girl of today?" "Health, supreme good health, is one characteristic," GBMc responded, "health in mind as well as body. She is a creature of great energy, and she's interested in sports. I don't think the New York girl is typical. To my mind she [the typical American girl] flourishes more generally in the Middle West." This reply reflected and foreshadowed the romanticized woman that would become stereotyped in too many of the rest of McCutcheon's novels.

In 1914, the year his friend Booth Tarkington published *Penrod,* McCutcheon published *The Prince of Graustark.* With a "brand-new fountain pen my brother John has just given me," GBMc inscribed a copy to James Montgomery Flagg. That celebrated illustrator was one of the founders of the Dutch Treat Club, whose luncheons McCutcheon and Tarkington had now been attending for over a year.

Actually, that club had been co-founded, in 1907, by Frank Crownin-shield, Editor of *Vanity Fair,* and by several other editors and publishers. (Frank Crowninshield was in constant demand as a master of ceremonies either because of or in spite of the fact that he was a teetotaler and non-smoker.) The founding ceremonies had taken place in Thomas Masson's office at the old *Life* magazine. The club, which was christened by George Mallon, City Editor of the *New York Sun,* met informally every Tuesday for lunch and discussion at various hotels, including the Ambassador and the fateful Martinique. Once a year this group produced a musical skit which they themselves composed and acted in. Occasionally one or another of those productions was privately filmed. During the 1930s each Yearbook of the Dutch Treat Club (a nostalgic, lavishly illustrated series) listed as members, besides those mentioned above, Booth Tarking-ton's two collaborators (Julian Street and Harry Leon Wilson, a former editor of *Puck*), Charles Scribner Jr., George Putnam, Edward and Frank Dodd (publishers of *The Bookman* and of most of McCutcheon's novels), Professor Henry Seidel Canby (of Yale and later of the *Saturday Review*), Charles Hanson Towne (an editor at *McClure's* and later at the *Delineator*), Ring Lardner, Irvin Cobb, Christopher Morley, Gelett ("Purple Cow") Burgess, Robert Benchley, Don Marquis, Rex Beach, Rupert Hughes, Franklin ("Conning Tower") Adams, Charles Dana Gibson (creator of the Gibson Girl), and the playwright George S. Kaufman. Besides Towne, Dutch Treat members Monty Flagg, Kit Morley, and Gelett Burgess remained the closest of GBMc's friends. Other clubs GBMc belonged to included the Players (founded by Edwin Booth), the Authors League, the Coffee House (a luncheon group of the most con-genial Dutch Treaters), and the Century.

Unlike the weekly and peripatetic Dutch Treat Club, the Century maintained its own well-rooted home around the clock—during GBMc's membership, at 7 West Forty-third Street. The sedate, almost austere, Century emulated the atmosphere of British clubs, after which it was modeled. Thackeray, on his visit to New York in 1852, had extolled the Century in "Mr. Brown the Elder Takes Mr. Brown the Younger to a Club." The Century brought together leading men of letters, especially those without any trace of Bohemia—for example, Frank Stockton, Paul Leicester Ford and William Dean Howells. Howells and GBMc did not seem to have much to say to each other. GBMc persuaded the Membership Committee to elect Hamlin Garland. Brander Matthews, the drama critic and Columbia professor, was a prominent member whom GBMc occasionally consulted about prospective purchases of rare books. Judging from the correspondence, one suspects that GBMc did not show any of his plays to Professor Matthews. Matthews had tried his hand at novels and plays but was best known for his books of drama history and criticism. He was little known for *Bookbindings Old and New: Notes of a Book Lover* (1895) except to bibliophiles like McCutcheon.

To the Princeton Club, on Gramercy Park, GBMc was occasionally invited by Booth Tarkington, or by Julian "Pete" Street, or by Arthur Maurice, Editor of *The Bookman*. In fact, on several visits to New York before McCutcheon moved there, he was a guest at the Princeton Club, and he described it with verisimilitude in several episodes of his novel *The Alternative* (1909), as Arthur Maurice observes in his *The New York of the Novelists.*

In 1915 the McCutcheons summered again at their beach cottage in Biddeford Pool. Booth Tarkington, who was also spending his summers in Kennebunkport, would there be building his mansion Seawood. He had recently married Susan Fletcher, of the Indianapolis Fletcher banking family, but the marriage proved unhappy and would be ending in divorce. On a Friday afternoon in June, that summer, Tarkington, dressed in a linen suit and a straw boater, drove up alone in a sleek black phaeton and proposed that GBMc accompany him on an excursion to York Harbor to call upon William Dean Howells.

GBMc was touched by Tarkington's thoughtfulness but had some reservations about accompanying him. It would be appropriate enough for Tarkington. He and his sister Mary (Mrs. Ovid Jameson) had after all been close friends of Howells since the turn of the century and had arranged for several of Howells' lectures in Indianapolis. But for GBMc, Howells remained the aloof demigod of American letters, more firmly than ever committed (as James Hart, among others, observed) to the thesis that in serving morality, literature's primary purpose should be to instruct rather than to delight. Given that conviction, there was little chance that Howells would ever notice GBMc's fiction, which was written to delight or—at best—to instruct by delighting. If GBMc looked at all into the "Editor's Easy Chair" in *Harper's,* he looked in vain for any mention, even an adverse mention, of fiction by McCutcheon. Indeed, much of Howells' adverse criticism in that monthly column tended to aim charmingly but excruciatingly overhead. Such and such a *kind* of romantic novel's virtue was its own defect, he would say, without actually naming the novel or the novelist:

The criticisms of one's books are always hard to bear if they are unfavorable. . . . It is tantamount to having it said of one that, yes, one has those virtues but one has no others. It comes also to saying that one has, of course, the defect of one's virtues [and the virtues of one's defects?].

That kind of shilly-shallying only frustrated GBMc. It also served as the easy butt of H. L. Mencken and George Jean Nathan, editors of *Smart Set,* who all too hastily dismissed Howells as "a contriver of pretty things . . . an Agnes Repplier in pantaloons."

Still, GBMc accepted Tark's invitation after all and made the trip. But Howells, as it turned out, was not at home. Except for that abortive pilgrimage to York Harbor, that summer, GBMc stuck pretty much to Biddeford Pool.

Two years later, he declined Hamlin Garland's invitation to attend a reception at Gramercy Park, New York (March 21, 1917) in honor of Howells' eightieth birthday. All the same, GBMc wrote a respectful letter which the Committee of the Literary Arts read aloud there and bound into a brochure of testimonials from leading authors: "I regret exceedingly my inability to be present in person," GBMc wrote, "but I shall be present in spirit with all those who rejoice over the good fortune that has given us William Dean Howells to look up to. . . ." GBMc also trusted—reflecting his own work ethic—that Howells "would rejoice in four score years of life, not a year of which has been wasted, nor a day."

One would have thought that by now, given GBMc's commercially successful books, he would have attained considerable self-confidence. Instead he kept turning more and more inward, becoming increasingly shy. He envied Ade's and John T.'s outgoing natures, extensive globe trotting, and exuberant letters. At the Dutch Treat Club he envied the sophisticated talk of world travelers like Tarkington and his collaborators Julian Street and Hank Wilson.

In turn, GBMc was himself envied and idolized by fans of his fiction. Marie continually warded off lionizers and interviewers. But late in July, 1917, GBMc agreed to a *New York Times* interview. The *Times* sent up Joyce Kilmer, one of its most popular young feature writers, who had three years earlier published his idealistic *Trees & Other Poems.* George and Marie shared Kilmer's sentiments ("Poems are made by fools like me / But only God can make a tree") along with similar sentiments in Charley Towne's Poem "Silences" ("I need not shout my faith. Thrice eloquent / are quiet trees and the green listening sod / —yet how they speak of God!"). The McCutcheons knew that Towne was no great shakes of a poet, but would not be swayed by the cynics who later lampooned Kilmer. Kilmer proved to be congenial, and he elicited from GBMc the kinds of sentiments readers of the Graustark romances wanted to hear:

America was born of adventure; its infancy was cradled in romance; it has grown up with thrills. . . . We are an eager, zestful, imaginative people. . . . We do two things exceedingly well: we dream and we perform.

America is essentially a romantic country, our great commercialism to the contrary notwithstanding. [Kilmer asked if there wasn't also romance in industry, a question GBMc sidestepped.]

A man who is without romance in his soul has no right to beget children, for he cannot love them as they ought to be loved.

Not long after Kilmer left, McCutcheon regretted missing the opportunity to add a word or two about the trap he found himself in—"always being typed a romanticist and, because *too long associated with another form,* not being admitted, tentatively at least, to the class of authors significantly identified as realists."

Since the journals publishing literary criticism, especially *Harper's* and the *Atlantic,* were as closed to GBMc's obiter dicta in criticism as the theaters were closed to his plays, he resorted to sending letters to the editors of the *New York Times* and the *Sun.*

Devoting himself primarily as he did to the writing of fiction and plays, GBMc would be the first to concede that he was no critic. Yet he did reply to the minor critics and major reviewers who persisted in making simplistic distinctions between romanticism and realism:

Who will dare to contend [GBMc argued] that the love story of two perfectly healthy young people is not pure realism? Why should it be relegated to 'romance'? . . . Realism and romanticism go hand in hand. . . . The Romanticist is frankly grateful to his imagination. The Realist deceives himself into thinking that imagination is not sitting at his elbow.

McCutcheon was no doubt irritated by the reviewers who pigeonholed him as a romanticist. They paid little attention to his realistic novel *The Sherrods*, and they did not of course know him as a playwright. Thus he was at best fighting a rear-guard action. But in exposing the superficiality of their assumption that romanticism and realism cannot be reconciled, he was quite sound. One hundred and fifty years before GBMc's time, Samuel Johnson had made similar protestations and had in his own writings demonstrated his rejection of critics' polarizations:

Johnson [writes Walter Jackson Bate] managed to by-pass the false dialectic with which the criticism of literature and art forces us to think in terms of polar opposites—of romanticism and classicism, realism and formalism, subjective and objective.

As reflected in the attacks McCutcheon mounted against the syndicate —for example, in *The Man Who Loved Children* and in *Mr. Bingle*—he was fighting vicariously at the side of Minnie Maddern, as he had during the Fiskes' litigation with the Frohmans. GBMc's devotion to Marie had by now cured him, no doubt, of his initial infatuation with Minnie, but he may well have carried with him to the end some vestiges of that adolescent love fantasy. With Marie, he attended most of Minnie's New York City performances, especially her interpretations of Ibsen's Nora, Hedda, and Rebecca West, which were financed and managed by her husband, Harrison Fiske. McCutcheon, so far as is known, never tried to close the social distance between himself and Minnie. In his urbane essay "How I Retired from the Stage" (1921) he refers to himself as a friend: "Miss Maddern and Miss Marlowe have come to regard me as a friend, and not as a designing intriguer."

Still, his virile output of writings remained partly a sublimation, perhaps, of his impossible-to-consummate love for Minnie, partly a compulsive drive to vindicate himself to one who in his youth and hers had gently suggested, about his playwriting, that he give it up.

Other sublimations and compensations which his writing, in whatever genres, furnished him revolved around his relations with a sterile wife and a virtually estranged mother. One infers a decided coolness between Clara and Marie, although there is no record of an overt snub. But why did George and Marie hardly ever visit Clara, if at all? And why was Clara never invited to visit George and Marie in New York? Why indeed were Clara's financial needs relegated as a responsibility of John's? During John's absence from Chicago, he saw to it that Ben—also Charles G. Dawes, less obscure then as a Chicago Trust Company officer than he would be as Vice President of the United States—would look in on Clara regularly: "See if she needs money. She might hesitate to ask for it even if she needs it. She has a vein of old-fashioned frugality that we have often struggled to overcome. She saves her new dresses until they go out of fashion."

If GBMc was disappointed about the coolness between Clara and Marie, he was even more disappointed that Marie could not bear children. After the death of their baby, Marie's physician persuaded her to undergo the operation mentioned above, which assured her permanent sterility. George never reconciled himself to that blow. Not only in his writing but also in his daily living he demonstrated that he was a man who loved children. But his affection and respect for Marie, now deeper than ever, would make unthinkable any plan for divorcing her and marrying a younger woman who could bear children. Or if such a notion did cross his mind, it got sublimated into his writing.

Bringing up Bill Fay proved all too evanescent—it consisted mainly of paying his bills at Andover and Harvard. GBMc enjoyed more, no doubt, the fond-uncle relationship he cultivated with Jessie's son John Raleigh. In letters from John Raleigh one learns that "Uncle George lavished" on this nephew not only gifts (at first, train sets; later, boys' books) but also much time, "much of himself." GBMc was apparently fonder of children than was Tarkington. Surprisingly enough, Tarkington, like James Whitcomb Riley, preferred children in literature to those in person. "The author of *Penrod,* to whom Uncle George introduced me at a luncheon," John Raleigh writes, "was not terribly fond of children." (Yet Tarkington felt grief and guilt on the death of his young daughter Laurel, as expressed in his letters to Julian Street and Hamlin Garland.) McCutcheon took young Raleigh to his first circus (Ringling Brothers, Barnum & Bailey) and regularly thereafter to the circuses and rodeos at Madison Square Garden "never mind the interrupted writing schedule." When Jessie, whose first marriage had ended in divorce in Montana, re-married in Chicago (to Andrew Wilbur Nelson) and was lying in before the birth of her son William Nelson, George and Marie invited young Raleigh to New York and took him to one of his first Broadway musical comedies.

Uncle George was also fond of his brother John's first son, whom he called "John the Second." The fondness, which was to grow mutually over the years, was initiated at the boy's birth—"or at least six weeks later," according to John T. McCutcheon Jr., now Editorial Director of the *Chicago Tribune*. On a day in December, 1917, the following letter from "112 EAST SEVENTY-FOURTH STREET, NEW YORK CITY" arrived in Chicago:

Dear John the Second:
Υou don't know it, perhaps, but the undersigned is one of your uncles —a distant relative we might say. He takes this opportunity to inform you that this is also Christmas, a fact that may have eluded your busy and preoccupied mind. Kindly accept from me the small [check] enclosed as having come from an agent of Santa Claus, and when you get old enough to do so, ask your good mother to have it cashed for you so that you may buy a railroad train or a battleship or anything you like. Give my best love to your mother and wish her a joyous Christmas and a splendid [New Year].

Your admiring Uncle George

On Sunday mornings, after reading the *Times* reviews of books and plays, the McCutcheons attended church. They walked, weather permitting, or rode down to the First Presbyterian on Fifth Avenue between Eleventh and Twelfth Streets. This graceful old brownstone had a lacy gothic steeple like those of cathedrals George and Marie had seen in Scotland. Being close to Washington Square, the First Presbyterian attracted many a denizen of that aristocratic neighborhood. The McCutcheons occasionally ran into Monty and Nell Flagg and Flagg's widowed father, Elisha; also the bachelor Charles Hanson Towne and the Princetonian Hoosiers Booth Tarkington and David Graham Phillips. After Phillips's tragic death in 1911, however, Tarkington attended only sporadically; and after 1914 not at all, having by then become a firm deist.

After church and an early Sunday dinner at Delmonico's or the Brevoort, often followed by a nap, the McCutcheons strolled through Central Park. On Sundays it seemed fairly to teem with children. How wistfully George and Marie must have gazed at them!

14

WORLD WAR I
AND *ONE SCORE & TEN*

On April 25, 1916, news came to the Gramatan Hotel, Bronxville, where George and Marie were now residing, that Clara, age seventy-five, had died. GBMc was no doubt as much stricken by guilt as by grief. During all too many years he had neglected visiting and writing her. He worked off some of his feelings in another orgy of labor. There soon emerged from his imagination foundry three more books, several short stories, and a new play. Scribner's brought out a new edition of *The Day of the Dog;* Dodd, Mead brought out *From the Housetops* and *The Light That Lies.*

The Light That Lies, which sketches all too inconsequentially how the attractive Miss Hildebrand persuades the lackadaisical Mr. Sampson to do jury service, is another of the McCutcheon novels that probably should not have been published. In *From the Housetops,* a more skillfully written novel, the calculating Anne Tresslyn breaks her engagement with young Dr. Braden Thorpe to marry his grandfather. She admits she has married the older man for his money. Several years after the marriage, Braden, who has won notoriety for advocating euthanasia, learns that his grandfather is suffering from cancer. The old man begs his grandson to put him asleep permanently. Braden finds his theories challenged with a practical test and wrestles with the dilemma. The sharply delineated characterizations and the dramatic scenes of this novel reflect its earlier incarnation as a play, *The Poinley Affair.* McCutcheon listed it in his inventory of plays but the manuscript has yet to be found. One suspects that the idea for the May-and-December marriage was suggested by the news that GBMc's brother John was now courting a woman young enough to be his daughter.

Among GBMc's new short stories, two were related to the war. "Pour la Patrie," ("Begun Friday, November 24, 1916, at the Gramatan. . . . Completed November 29") although based on an incident in the Cuban rebellion against Spain before the Spanish American War, was a contribution to Charles Towne's anthology *For France,* dedicated to the French Relief of 1916. There was some question, left unresolved, about whether McCutcheon had unwittingly pre-empted the story idea from another writer, as GBMc learned at the Lambs, where, on December 15, he was a guest of Mr. Towne's.

Within two weeks after the completion of the first story, George and Marie moved from the Gramatan in Bronxville to the Wolcott, on Fifth Avenue and Thirty-first Street. The move was apparently more important to Marie than to George. As if oblivious to the location of his writing factory, he went ahead with his short-short story "Courage" ("Begun Dec. 20, 1916, at Hotel Wolcott, NYC.; completed Dec. 23rd") to be contributed to another anthology, *Defenders of Democracy.* The story celebrates the heroism of a young soldier who rescued under fire his captain and his sergeant:

They were shooting at him from all directions. He heard the bullets, he saw the mud squirt up in little splashes, he remembered losing his helmet suddenly and mysteriously, and there was a sharp twinge in one of his legs. . . . The sergeant was next, then, after the captain. He heard men cheering. They told him afterwards that the men who shot at him cheered as he slid down into the gap of earth with the wounded sergeant on his back. . . .

As the hero convalesces in a hospital improvised from a shell-ruined chateau, he thinks about the courage it takes to be a nurse: "One must be very brave to be a nurse. The horrors they had to witness, the sufferings they had to endure in others, the mangled things they had to see and touch. He shook his head and doubted his own courage."

"Courage" foreshadowed parts of Hemingway's *A Farewell to Arms* (1929) and evokes the romantic ambience of F. Scott Fitzgerald's *All the Sad Young Men* (1916). Characteristically, the prose in GBMc's short stories, despite their compactness, is more poetically rhythmic and more sensuously rendered than that of his novels, which focus more on ingenious development of plot. The opening of "Courage" is a case in point:

He sat upon a little bench in the sunlit garden. The air was soft and clear and laden with the scent of roses. The taste of gunpowder no longer filled his throat; the close odor of freshly turned earth and the cold smell of rainwater and mud no longer filled his nostrils, . . . the twittering of birds, the drone of bees in the flower beds behind him, the voices of gentle women . . . drowning out the memory of thunder and the shriek of the thing that was not the wind.

Even though the United States was not to enter the war officially until the next year, many a young American (like Hemingway, for instance) had enlisted as a volunteer with the Allies. Marie and George felt proud that Bill Fay, upon graduation from Harvard, had joined the American Ambulance Service in France, although Marie held her breath when she first learned about it. Bill served for nine months. GBMc himself, at the age of fifty, was considered too old for military combat, but he remained on the side of the American patriots, of course, and worked for the cause.

On January 18, 1917, George and Marie took the Twentieth Century Limited to Chicago to attend the church wedding, on the twentieth, of John T. to Evelyn Shaw. At age twenty-five, Miss Shaw was twenty-two years younger than John. A brilliant graduate of Bryn Mawr, she had been working in Chicago at *Poetry* magazine as Harriet Monroe's secretary. On the evening of the nineteenth, GBMc attended the bachelor dinner given John by some members of the Indiana Society of Chicago. Before entraining from New York, George had reserved, for the newlyweds-to-be, a bridal suite at the Ritz, which he ordered filled with flowers. The newlyweds would be stopping in New York on their way to Salt Cay, a Caribbean island John had recently purchased. Unfortunately, within a few days after the honeymooners arrived at Salt Cay, John's newspaper, the *Tribune,* sent him to Europe to report on the Western Front.

The year 1917 was one of the few in which GBMc published only one novel: *Green Fancy.* That novel, essentially a situation comedy, was probably based on a play, as yet unfound. In a strangely hidden house on the border of Canada, a motley assortment of characters—two royal Europeans, an adventuring Irishman, an international thief, a bewitching young woman from New York, and some amateur actors—engage in a suspenseful international intrigue. The book became another best seller and elicited favorable reviews. A *New York Times* reviewer said "The narrative gallops along at a rapid rate with plenty of exciting situations and dramatic incidents, while the author garnishes incidents and characters with touches of humor."

McCutcheon probably did not take time to read *Susan Lenox,* the post-humous feminist novel by his and Tarkington's late friend David Graham Phillips. And there was now a temporary abatement in GBMc's writing; the ominous rumblings of war kept him and Marie contributing much of their time to various patriotic services. In February the United States broke off diplomatic relations with Germany in protest against the escalating U-boat attacks on American ships and on British ships carrying American passengers, like the *Lusitania,* which had been sunk in 1915. On April 6, 1917, the United States entered the war formally. Almost immediately Bill Fay enlisted in the Army. He was commissioned a captain, and he would be serving in France at Verdun. Before going overseas, in June, he spent a few days with his mother and his foster-father at Biddeford Pool. Monty Flagg, now a neighbor of the McCutcheons, visited too. Flagg, originator of the Uncle Sam "I want you" poster, expressed some good-natured cynicism about Bill's and other young men's enlisting:

Virile young men crave excitement and adventure the world over, and patriotism gives them a wonderful excuse to be heroes at the same time. ... Daisy McCutcheon was resentful in her sweet way about my claim that it was mostly the desire for excitement that made youngsters enlist. "Leave it to Bill," I said. Her son Bill Fay had just enlisted. I dared young Bill to be honest and tell us whether he had joined up mostly To Make the World Safe for Democracy or for the hell of it. He grinned and answered, "You said it! For the excitement—that's the truth!"

Back in the City in the fall, Marie served as a Red Cross Volunteer, and George and Marie served on Liberty Bond committees. One such committee meeting called suddenly on the evening of November 19, 1917, prompted them to give up seeing Mrs. Fiske as Madame Sand, an event for which George had obtained tickets. George was disappointed, but Marie could not have cared less. Although she was all for enfranchising women, she did not sympathize with other aspects of feminism, and she thoroughly disapproved of Madame Sand's style of life. Marie did applaud Mrs. Fiske's off-stage roles, of course, such as that of chief sponsor of and collector for the Belgian Children's Relief.

At various gatherings, among them the Coffee House meeting at which Mrs. Fiske was the guest of honor, she read Princess Troubetzkoy's moving lines, "The Belgian Children." Another of Minnie's causes, for which she gave volunteer readings, was her Committee for Stricken Animals. She buttonholed GBMc's friend Charley Towne for a $50 contribution. GBMc made similar contributions to both causes with or without Minnie's cajoling.

The initial shock of the United States' entry into the war wore off a little on the McCutcheons, but never the shock of recognition of names and numbers on casualty lists. George and Marie were particularly saddened to hear of Joyce Kilmer's death in the Battle of the Marne. GBMc continued to do what he could, not only in selling Liberty Bonds but also in contributing patriotic pep-talk editorials. Some of these editorials had appeared in New York and Connecticut newspapers as early as 1916—"Who and What Are We Americans?" "Two Kinds of Americans," "Shall They Gloat?" and "Of What Are We Thinking?" A few of these editorials he wrote in Connecticut, where he and Marie stayed when they occasionally attended tryouts of plays and musicals at the Shubert Theater in New Haven. Back in March, 1916, for example, they had enjoyed the dress rehearsal of the musical *See America First*. Marie had been captivated by Clifton Webb's nonchalant insolence. George identified with the irreverent songs written by Cole Porter, the rising young lyricist and composer from Peru, Indiana. George's energies vibrated especially to Cole's song "Something's Got To Be Done" (to be done, to be done). In fact, George continued to hum that tune when most people around him were humming or singing Irving Berlin's boot-camp song "Oh, how I hate to get up in the morning!"

Two more of GBMc's novels, *Shot with Crimson* and *City of Masks*, were published in 1918, as was Tarkington's *The Magnificent Ambersons*. *Shot with Crimson*, which deserves its desuetude, is a didactic story about the dangers of World War I spies in American homes. *City of Masks*, a more imaginative work, depicts episodes in the lives of some expatriate European aristocrats who live indigently but with dignity in a shabby home in upstate New York. They try to preserve their anonymity while treating one another with the respect due their former stations. Re-creating the hilarity of *Green Fancy*, *City of Masks*, which GBMc endowed with fewer melodramatic intrigues and more humorous characters, should now be ripe for development into a series of television sitcoms.

The Armistice of November 11, 1918, gave George and Marie much cause for rejoicing. Bill would be coming home, as would brother John along with several other relatives and friends. John for some time in danger as one of the war correspondents imprisoned behind enemy lines, had survived and was now to be released.

It was about this time, too, that GBMc staked Jessie to twenty thousand dollars so that she could manufacture the dolls she had been making as a hobby, dolls that included the statuette "The Good Fairy."

She felt there was a place and a need [according to an article in the *American Magazine*] for some lovely object that would . . . embody joy and freedom and youthful ideals, and yet would satisfy our superstition about things that bring us good fortune.

In Mrs. Raleigh's [actually, Mrs. Nelson's] studio in Chicago there were many evidences that the joyous, windblown little creature had more than fulfilled its mission. The walls of the studio were lined with the pictures of all kinds and classes of men and women . . . Judge Ben Lindsey, Helen Keller, [Carrie Jacobs Bond] . . . who had been photographed with their own little "Good Fairy" and had sent the pictures to the real fairy godmother. . . . The heads of these beautifully formed little creations were painted by students from the Chicago Art Institute. . . . In her factory several hundred persons were kept busy making "the Good Fairy" and its brothers and sisters, the dolls.

Jessie put into practice her conviction (as her son John Raleigh recalls) that dolls "should resemble children, not insult their natural appeal—should not have rolling eyes and the stiff features that were a far cry from reality." Unfortunately, a few years after the war, several European countries dumped just that sort of cheaper doll into the American markets, causing Jessie's factory to close.

Up until now GBMc, a gentle man not given to showing his feelings, had probably concealed his contempt for Julian Street's *The Most Interesting American,* which extolled—among other attributes—Colonel Roosevelt's prowess as a big-game hunter. But on April 12, 1919, at a meeting of the Dutch Treat Club in honor of Street's birthday, GBMc may well have showed his hand in his "Lines to Julian Street," Tarkington's Princetonian play collaborator. GBMc's heptameters start on a note of dubious eulogy: "What means this blare of trumpets from the crest of Mount Parnassus?", include the Delphic epithet "brazen sound of brass," and conclude with the almost insulting line "After forty years of labor Julian Street has just been born." Even if the Dutch Treat Club members occasionally roasted one another, as is evident in their Yearbooks, these verses raise questions about McCutcheon's ambivalent feelings toward, perhaps envy of, the co-author of Tarkington's successfully produced comedy *The Country Cousin.*

Later, in September, GBMc and Marie attended a performance of Tarkington's hit comedy *Clarence* at the Hudson Theater. Although the play was amusing, its ephemeral values must have bored GBMc. Of course, he would not have said so, even if the generous Tark had not given the McCutcheons a choice pair of "hold-back" tickets. After all, GBMc had himself been purveying similar values in some of his best-selling novels, albeit without conviction. He knew that Tarkington would be "massacred" (as Tark said) by critics like Alexander Woollcott and Heywood Broun and only wished that those hard-nosed critics could respond to a more momentous play like *Brood House*.

Tarkington, in letters to G. C. Tyler, his producer, and the press agent John Toohey, expressed "in deathly secret" a fear and distrust of the New York drama critics, "especially Woollcott and Broun." Tarkington even requested that his name as author of *Clarence* be withheld in favor of a nom de plume. "You may recall," he said, "that in regard to *The Man From Home* the principal criticism was to the effect that Mr. Wilson [the collaborator] and I were from the Middle West and should not expect to please New Yorkers." Alan Downer, editor of Tarkington's letters, adds that the initial request "to produce *Clarence* pseudonymously was based on the conviction that no New York critic would grant that a novelist could write a play. . . ."

Most of McCutcheon's plays and short stories do not uphold—in fact, they satirize—the values championed in Tarkington's plays. In a study of Pulitzer Prize winners, W. J. Stuckey accuses Tarkington of several deadly literary sins including "snobbery (those who have money deserve to have it and those who do not . . . ought to enjoy their poverty)." Stuckey further observes that Pulitzer jurors contemporary with Tarkington consistently chose "plays that have nothing in them to shatter conventions, drive the stock market down, or interrupt the sleep of virgins."

GBMc, chronically frustrated in his attempts to get his own plays produced, was at least temporarily assuaged when he sold to the Fox Film Corporation the movie rights to his novel *Cowardice Court*. About the same time his novel *Sherry* came out, handsome in board covers and with a frontispiece by the accomplished illustrator Allan Gilbert. *Sherry* is the story of Mr. Sherry Redpath, a social climber afflicted with a drinking problem. The novel could easily have become didactic; McCutcheon was himself not so convivial as his contemporaries in the publishing arena. Besides, he felt that the intemperate drinking of intoxicants was becoming more of a social problem than ever. Still, any episodes that might have bordered on moral lessons were tempered with much humor, a strategy the reviewers applauded.

Sherry wine, incidentally, was one of Marie's favorites. She was more disappointed than George when, on October 18, 1919, the Volstead Act passed over President Wilson's veto. By no means abstemious, George could take liquor or leave it. He had been brought up in a family of teetotalers except for Grandpa Glick, who liked Milwaukee beer. Marie regularly sipped wine at dinner, and on special occasions she took a cocktail or two. But for the rest of their lives together, George and Marie shunned the lurid speakeasies. And they only smiled at the wry humor of Cole Porter's popular song "A Toast to Volstead." (That song would be recycled in the musical *Fifty Million Frenchmen,* which Marie and Jessie attended the year after GBMc's death.) Years later, after the repeal of Prohibition, Bill Fay worked for a wholesale liquor firm in Chicago but soon became disenchanted. "I became completely fed up with that business," he said, "and everything connected with it."

The *Sherry* royalties were earmarked for the purchase of another Corot. GBMc had already acquired a Corot landscape and was now attempting to acquire one of Corot's *L'Ateliers.* The down-to-earth feeling of that workshop, in at least one of its versions, appealed to GBMc as a balance to the mistiness of the landscapes. Although Corot's landscapes created a gauzy, almost sentimental, aura, Corot himself, GBMc was pleased to learn, had remained aloof from the disputes between the classic and the romantic camps, between followers of the classic Ingres, for example, and the romantic Delacroix.

McCutcheon's chief excitement of 1919 could well have been the private printing of his superb comedy/melodrama *One Score & Ten,* albeit in a much too modest edition of thirty copies. This four-act play is set in the home of the Baxter family of "Rumney, Indiana," for the most part near the turn of the century except for the initial fortune-telling scene about thirty years before. "Rumney" is a transparent disguise for Romney, a small town south of Lafayette—also, perhaps, for Romany or gypsy.

The protagonist, Alfred Baxter Jr., labors against a gypsy's prediction that just before his thirtieth birthday (hence the title *One Score & Ten*), he will die on the gallows, unjustly accused of murder. Some time before that bad news—so the good tidings go—he will be involved romantically with "two dark women and one, two, yes three fair women." Baxter the elder, who is first to take the gypsy's oracle more seriously than do any other members of the family, vows to move to any other state where capital punishment has been outlawed. His brother-in-law, Horace Gooch, says, "That won't help any if a mob gets hold of him and lynches him. There's an awful lot of lynchin' going on in this country now [by the Ku Klux Klan, for example], and I wouldn't be surprised if it got worse."

As for the blondes and the brunettes, the Baxter family's friends manage to keep young Alfie away from all but one blonde, Edith Pompton of Boston, and one brunette, Jane Sage, daughter of a Romney preacher. (Jane's mother, Josephine, has her own dark hair bleached in London, but that is part of another episode.)

Uncannily GBMc's portrait of young Alfred's uncle and aunt, Horace and Ida Gooch, presages Grant Wood—almost as if the Gooches are pre-animations of the couple in *American Gothic*. Not a spark of humor emanates from either of the Gooches. Once Ida leaves—perhaps too conveniently by dying—Horace turns out to be the play's chief villain. He becomes an unscrupulous rival of Alfie's in the campaign for election to the state senate. Horace also instigates the public indictment of Alfie for the alleged murder of Alfred Baxter Sr., when the latter mysteriously disappears. Horace's sinister accusations seem to be supported by several bits of circumstantial evidence cleverly planted by the playwright. Later, when Alfie proves to have been innocent, Horace suppresses as long as possible the news of the senior Baxter's disincriminating return to town.

Perhaps the most comically histrionic role in this play is that of Jane's mother, Josephine, wife of the Baxter family's pastor, Herbert Sage. After abandoning Herbert and Jane for a career of acting in London theaters, Josephine returns to Rumney fifteen years later. She receives a charitable welcome and joins the chorus of commentators on the fate of her daughter's fiancé. In her sentiments she seems also to serve as one of the playwright's mouthpieces except for her bombast:

Mrs. Sage: Alfred Baxter has been haled from his house, from his simple fireside, and dragged through the streets of his beloved city, manacled and shackled, subjected to the grossest indignity, derided by a fickle public,—ah, the public! What a fickle thing the public is! No matter how long, how faithfully you serve the public, it turns upon you in time, like the adder, and stings you to death. It feeds you with praises, it fattens you with applause, it clothes you in garments of gold—and then, ah then, my friends, it strips you clean and leaves you to starve. It turns its back on you and fattens another favourite. Don't tell *me* anything about the damned public!

The bathos of that last line should delight any actress playing the role of Josephine. Not only in what Josephine Sage says but also in what the public, the mob, does (rushing down to the swamp in their itch to see the elder Baxter's body exhumed), GBMc's satire echoes the "booboisie"-baiting by H. L. Mencken and George Jean Nathan during the years they edited *Smart Set* magazine.

In *One Score & Ten* McCutcheon emphasizes the storyline and the characters, including the caricatures. This play thus remains an entertainment, not a propaganda piece, everything iconoclastic in the end subordinate or incidental. Still, he is irreverent toward organized religion, prayer, and overly idealistic preachers. The Reverend Herbert Sage, for example, is depicted as too naive in blinking the lapsarian behavior of his wife, who is after all, an adventuress. Moreover, once Josephine is also painted as a person with bleached-blonde tastes, with an obsession for all things ephemeral, McCutcheon makes her the parish's Sunday school teacher. Although McCutcheon allows the efficacy of prayer to prevail in the end, he subjects it to several irreverent trials. The well-liked skeptic Aunt Serepta Grimes says, "Poor Alfred [senior] has done nothing but pray since four o'clock this morning. . . . I went out into the hall a little while ago and told him to shut up." (Skeptical as she is, however, Serepta continues to attend prayer meetings.) The Sunday school teacher pooh-poohs prayer: "Don't go on deceiving yourself, Herbert," she says to her gullible husband, "I didn't come home because you prayed. Not a bit of it." In the last act, when Jane greets the long-missing Alfred Sr., with the joyous pronouncement "Our prayers have been answered," Joe Sikes says, "I don't believe it was prayer that brought you back." In the play as a whole, McCutcheon accords more honor to the pagans, the gypsies, than to the Christians:

First Gypsy: The stars travel through space at the rate of a million miles a minute. . . . Even as I speak to you now, my words are ancient history to the stars . . . they have witnessed all that is to transpire on this earth of ours during the next thousand years or two.
Reverend Sage: Have you the impudence, Madam, to imply that we mortals are so far behind the times as all that?
First Gypsy: I know of nothing, Reverend Sir, that proves the fact more clearly than the institution that you represent.
Reverend Sage: (admiringly): You are nobody's fool.

Of course, McCutcheon satirizes in Herbert Sage, not so much the fundamentalist as the all too liberal, wishy-washy clergyman, with whom fashionable churches were becoming infatuated. And there can be no mistake about GBMc's indictment, in *One Score & Ten,* of the mischief and immaturity of warmongering, the savage primitiveness of violence. In the first act the gypsy predicts, for the newborn Alfred, a career interrupted by war: "I see him in the classroom . . . he will be prepared for a career of great promise. Then will come the wars. He will go forth to fight for his country—in foreign lands." In the second act, Alfred Baxter Jr., age twenty-nine, has come home from the Spanish American War. Aunt Serepta, a mother-surrogate since the death of Alfred's mother shortly after his birth, muses, "How that boy must have enjoyed himself fighting out there in the Philippines with the Army—shooting and stabbing and everything without being told he oughtn't! What a joy it must have been to him to find out he was a full-grown man!" And if twisting that Swiftian rapier is not enough, McCutcheon, recycling some of his *Brood House* slaps at weapons, has Joe Sikes say:

[Alfie] got a taste of blood over there in the Philippines and—why, doggone it—don't you remember what a time we had gettin' that Mauser pistol and all them snaky-lookin' knives away from him after he came home? And them poisoned arrows and spear-heads and that head-hunter's war club he wanted to take back with him to college?

Another target of satire, in this play, is the undertaker Silas Hanks. Almost always unctuous and hushed (the stage directions suggest "hushed, lowered tones") he elicits from Joe Sikes an exasperated "Speak natural! Nobody's dead here!" Hanks exploits widows and old spinsters in his prepaid funeral plans, although he allows them to choose their own caskets. He splits referral fees with another undertaker. ("I suppose you know good old Charlie Smith over in Hopkinsville. We split us quite a little business between us. Sort of cooperate, you know.") Most vulnerable of all Silas Hanks's traits is his hovering like a low black cloud over prospective clients and situations. ("The undertaker here already? How did you get here so soon!" "The undertaker hasn't left the swamp since they started digging there [for Baxter's body] last Wednesday.") Still, Undertaker Hanks comes off somewhat better than the Reverend Herbert Sage, at least as far as a bumptious sense of humor is concerned. When the First Gypsy says, "We all come into the world by chance, we exist by chance, and we go out by chance," Hanks says, "I'd sooner have somebody tell me I'm an angel now than someone else to say I'm going to be one."

As for satire on local bureaucracies, taxpayers can identify with the plight of young Alfred Baxter, whose house and garden are ripped up by order of the grand jury. Alfie complains to Murphy, the detective and the foreman of the excavators: "Who's going to pay for restoring my property to the condition in which you and your men found it?"

Murphy: That's not my lookout. We're only engaged to dig it up. Of course, you can always sue somebody.
Alfred: Who, for instance?
Murphy: You can always make the taxpayers settle, in case we don't find what we're looking for [Baxter Sr.'s body].
Alfred: Why should the taxpayers pay for something they haven't ordered?
Murphy: For the same reason they pay for a bridge when it's washed out. They didn't order the bridge washed out, did they?

Although McCutcheon subtitled *One Score & Ten* a comedy, the play is also a melodrama and in part a self-parody of melodrama and of the well-made plot. After the first act, which is, at best, talkative exposition and which a director today would no doubt telescope or recast as flashback, the suspense builds effectively to the end. In the last act, Edith Pompton exclaims, "I am so excited! It's like a play, isn't it!" Aunt Serepta Grimes observes sourly "It ain't like a play to me." Edith qualifies her first assessment with "I don't mean a funny play. I mean a melodrama." A little later, at the climax (the scene in which Alfred Baxter Sr. returns home when Junior could be mounting the scaffold) Edith rushes to the telephone to inform the sheriff's office that "the *corpus delicti* has shown up." Josephine Sage cries:

Stop! My God, are you going to spoil a situation like this? Stop, Miss Pompton! Leave this to me! Think of the climax! Think of the stupendous effect! Don't ring in an anticlimax. I can visualize the scene now. Alfred—innocent Alfred—is actually mounting the scaffold. All hope is gone. The hangman takes his place, the noose is ready—and then we rush in with Mr. Baxter Senior: Confusion, consternation, joy—Curtain!

Actually the curtain descends on a humorous dénouement, in which the exonerated gypsy reads the palm of Melinda, a housemaid who has failed to win Alfie's notice. Says the gypsy, "I see several gentlemen. One is tall, dark, and—" Curtain.

How much does *One Score & Ten* reflect of McCutcheon's experience? The son of a dedicated sheriff he loved, GBMc makes the sheriff in *One Score & Ten* a lovable person—one who offers his own home (attached to the jail, of course) as a place where the incarcerated protagonist can marry Jane. Also reflected in this play is GBMc's disappointment with Willie Fay's progress as a student. All the money that GBMc lavished on Willie seems to have spoiled him. At Andover Willie barely squeaked through. At Harvard, where his field of concentration was government, he had achieved no distinction, although he did make the freshman crew and was popular in the cycling and the banjo clubs, of which he was president. In *One Score & Ten,* one of Alfred Baxter's friends (Edith Pompton from Boston) exclaims in awe. "You mean you went to Harvard!" Alfred replies "Yes, that's where I learned to ride a bicycle."

Perhaps the most poignant revelation in this play, if one reads between the lines, concerns how GBMc felt about some of his Indiana friends. To the report "Jane is afraid the mob will take Alfie out tonight [i.e., out of jail to lynch him]," Josephine Sage responds ironically, "Rubbish! If there was a [lynch] mob it would be made up entirely of Alfred's friends." By now, if not sooner, GBMc was beginning to feel that his Indiana friends—especially Tarkington and Ade—had let him down, had made no effort to help him get his plays produced.

Ade, especially, remained disappointingly aloof—turned down an invitation to stay with the McCutcheons at Kennebunkport, for example. He did write brief notes of congratulation upon the appearance of one or another of GBMc's novels. In response to one such note GBMc wrote a longer letter, in which he said "Thank you for your good words about Bingle" and made a special plea that Ade call, on his very next trip to New York: "Marie asks me to give you her best and to add the hope that you'll come this way." In another letter to Ade, GBMc wrote:

Marie was just saying only a night or two ago: "Why don't we ever see George Ade when he comes to town?" And I had to reply, "Damned if I know." At least, call. . . . Our number is Rhinelander 9405. It isn't in the directory . . . it's a private wire. In case you get into jail or anything like that, just remember that number.

GBMc realized that even with "Ade's help or Tark's aid," as he punned to Marie—even on the inside track to production—the McCutcheon plays would have to be toned down. Certainly few playgoers would pay to be reminded of their cherished irrationalities and irresponsibilities. But

GBMc was not about to let any play doctor tamper with his work. Tarkington was much more receptive to suggestions for revising. After he had written *The Wren,* for example, and learned that Helen Hayes would be playing the leading role, he gladly let her dictate changes in the lines—he "recast line for line," he said, "as it came naturally from her lips." Of course, he was only letting her put into her own words and rhythms what were basically his ideas and drift. Unlike Tarkington, GBMc was inflexible to suggestions for revising his writing, although he made many revisions on his own, as is evident in his manuscripts. But for GBMc to forgo certain iconoclasms in his plays would have amounted to a supreme irony for an author whose novels a *New York Times* editorial would pronounce innocuous—"contributions of innocent happiness."

15

"ANTHONY THE JOKER"

If McCutcheon did not have enough money to retire on by now, and he was close to being a millionaire ("close to being rendered supine by opulence," he said in his essay *Books Once Were Men*) he and Marie could have retired comfortably on the proceeds of just two of the movie sales made for him by his publishers through the agency of the American Play Company of New York. To the Famous Players–Lasky Corporation, he sold the film rights to *The Husbands of Edith* (1908), which had already earned him thousands of dollars in royalties. The rights to *City of Masks* he sold to Walter Alexander, who wished to adapt that 1918 novel as a musical. GBMc had been receiving between $5,000 and $8,000 for just one story or serial in magazines like the *Saturday Evening Post, McClure's,* and the *Delineator.* He had by now collected some magnificent paintings and first editions, all of which appreciated significantly in market values, although those were not the values he cherished. What made him run? Surely, his inherited Protestant work ethic could not entirely explain his prodigious productivity. During the 1920s until his death in 1928 he seems to have been obsessed more demonically than ever in his perennial drive to extend the genres of his writing beyond fiction, while still turning out at least one novel a year. Fortunately, not all his novels were published, although two were published posthumously.

In 1920 he revised and published, among other works, two novels he had written previously, *Anderson Crow, Detective* (illustrated by John T. McCutcheon) and *Westwind Drift.* Inspired by anecdotes about the *Lusitania, Westwind Drift* depicts some courageous passengers aboard the disabled *S.S. Doraine* adrift among German U-boats and other perils of World War I. A reviewer observed, "George Barr McCutcheon, the facile creator of mythical kingdoms, has invented a modern story stupendous enough for production by Mr. Griffith [the United Artists movie producer]."

The following year there appeared his novel *Quill's Window,* with a rural Indiana setting. The window was a name given to a cave high on a rocky cliff (there *are* rocky cliffs in southern Indiana) associated with fearful legends, including one about an invalid ex-soldier who seduces local girls.

A more substantial novel with an Indiana setting appeared in 1922. *Viola Gwynn,* set in the primitive northern Indiana of the 1830s, borrows its romantic bravura from Graustarkians but with a raciness closer to the soil. Viola is at first believed to be the half-sister of the dashing Kenneth Gwynn. Gwynn, who rides into the county with his law books in his saddle bags, turns out to be a different person—a person more suitable as a husband for Viola, of course. A *New York World* reviewer (probably Heywood Broun) observed, "Very ingeniously the author makes his villains play into the hands of the true lovers. . . . Mr. McCutcheon has risen successfully again to the expectations of those who have come to regard him as the masculine good fairy of romanticism."

McCutcheon's novel *Yollop* (1922), one of the most humorous novels of the 1920s, was re-created from another of GBMc's unproduced plays, *Mr. Smilk,* the manuscript of which has yet to be found. Smilk, a bigamist and a burglar (one appetite encouraging the other), is apprehended while ransacking the apartment of Mr. Yollop. The apprehender is the half-blind Mr. Yollop himself. At Smilk's trial, just about everybody is lampooned—not only Smilk's trollop wives but also his lawyer, the judge, and the jurors. *Yollop* (rhymes with wollop, and with good reason) hits irreverently on the irrationalities and laxities of our court system. A reviewer in the *Boston Evening Transcript* said, "The conversations between Mr. Yollop and Mr. Smilk are delicious, the behavior of the burglar's wives in court is ludicrous, the whole burlesque one of the most amusing in some time." A reviewer in the *New York Times* said, "It has frequent flashes of wit, and its hits at the faults and foibles of our system of penology are well aimed and cleverly made." On February 25, 1922, GBMc autographed a copy of *Yollop* for Booth Tarkington.

When George and Marie lived in hotel suites, as they did from time to time between apartments, George stored all but his reference books in a bonded warehouse. More characteristically, the McCutcheons lived in large, ten-room apartments near Central Park. They were now living at 125 East Seventy-second Street, for example, in a tall apartment building a couple of blocks from, and high above, the Park. The walls of at least two of the rooms, the library and the study, were lined with books, including first editions of Dickens and Thackeray. Walls not covered with book-cases were dramatized with original paintings. A Corot landscape commanded one wall of the drawing room. The dining room was dominated by a long refectory table, at which the McCutcheons entertained theater-party guests—among them, Charles Towne, Monty and Nell Flagg, Kit and Helen Morley, and other friends GBMc had made at the Dutch Treat, the Coffee House, and the Authors Club. Something of the ambience of a McCutcheon apartment emanates from a *New York Times* interview by Montrose Moses:

Behind him stretched a vista of rooms with bookcases lost in the shadows, the light now and then reflecting from the gold of sumptuous bindings. His voice modulated so as to blend with the gathering dusk of his library. [In the drawing room] high-backed chairs, carved tables and settees, and a grand piano with bulldog legs. . . . We were high above the city's noise. On a rare breeze the odor of green [cut grass] came from the Park.

When George and Marie lived near the Park, the breezes no doubt served to neutralize some of the exotic aromas in their apartments: George's Lebanon cedar oil on his leather-bound books, Marie's non-stop brew of Colombian coffee, her Egyptian cigarette smoke, and her Parisian essence-of-roses perfume. Marie was also fond of fresh-cut roses, which she distributed in slender cut-glass vases. Even when there was no special occasion to celebrate, George would come home from marketing (although they frequently ate out) with dozens of roses wrapped in green wax-paper cones.

When the McCutcheons were living in town—were not summering in Maine or wintering in Arizona—they had this apartment mostly to themselves. Bill Fay's token room—unlike the other guest room—remained almost always unoccupied. (Bill Fay, for some time on his own, was now working for the General Foods Corporation in White Plains and would later move to Boston to become that corporation's New England Sales Manager.)

GBMc and Marie kept moving from apartment to apartment not primarily because landlords kept raising the rent (as they did whenever a new McCutcheon novel was published) but because Marie's hobby of interior decorating required ever new settings. During the McCutcheons' sojourn in New York, according to GBMc's letterheads, most of the return addresses printed in boldface block capitals, they moved from the Brevoort (1911) to ONE WEST 64th STREET (1911-1914), to the Gramatan (1914-1916) to The Wolcott (1916), to 112 EAST 74th STREET (1917-1919), to 125 EAST 72nd STREET (1919-1925), to 14 EAST 60th STREET (1926-1928), to the Barclay (1928). Whenever they moved, GBMc made no demurrer, at least not aloud. He supervised the packing of his three thousand books or packed them himself. Far from complaining, he encouraged Marie in her excitements about new settings and decors, and he almost always accepted her invitations to accompany her on buying-jaunts to furniture and drapery shops.

A slave to fashion, Marie continued to attend the First Presbyterian Church, near Washington Square, and George tagged along. He loved Jehovah, loved and obeyed the Hebraic commandments, loved Jesus as the Great Exemplar though not as a Divine Presence. George was far from being a born-again Christian—did not regard himself washed in the blood of the Lamb. In GBMc's play *One Score & Ten,* the Reverend Herbert Sage is lampooned for not enforcing the Decalogue against his wayward wife –for being wishy-washy enough to look the other way.

From 1918 to 1922 the pastor at the McCutcheons' church was Harry Emerson Fosdick, a liberal professor from the Union Theological Seminary. He had been appointed by three Presbyterian congregations that merged at the First and did not require him to relinquish his credentials from the Baptist ministry. Dr. Fosdick was not so liberal politically as to condone the anarchists but he did defend certain radically Christian tenets of Eugene Debs, the socialist from Terre Haute. By October, 1920, Debs was conducting his campaign for the Presidency of the United States from his jail cell in Atlanta. He had been convicted of fomenting anarchy, but he himself was non-violent and even Christ-like in his speeches: "I have discovered that love is omnipotent," he said. "All the forces of earth cannot prevail against it. Hatred, war, cruelty, greed, and lust must all give way before it."

Dr. Fosdick's idealism pleased the disillusioned young war veterans who had prevailed in appointing him in the first place, but it naturally antagonized the politically conservative among the elders, including Andrew Carnegie (when he was not sojourning in Scotland). The McCutcheons stayed aloof, as far as is known, but one suspects they felt Dr. Fosdick had gravitated too far to the left. In May, 1922, when that liberal preacher's battles with the conservatives and fundamentalists culminated in his sermon "Shall the Fundamentalists Win?" the fundamentalists fired him. (He was eventually accepted back by the Baptists and appointed by the Rockefellers as First Pastor of the impressive new Riverside Church.)

By now McCutcheon had become, like most other Hoosiers (except for Debs and his followers) decidedly conservative in politics—had turned away from the Democratic Party of his beloved father, Captain Barr. Of course, GBMc continued to espouse, in his fiction and especially in his plays, humanitarian causes no matter how unpopular. But by temperament and conviction he was unsympathetic toward, and had virtually nothing in common with, those naturalistic writers and critics—among them, Theodore Dreiser, John Dos Passos, Djuna Barnes, Edmund Wilson, the young Clifford Odets, and the young F. W. Dupee—who would be galvanizing the chic radical left in the late twenties. GBMc alienated himself from, and was naturally ignored by, that fashionable coterie, whose literary and political criticism in such magazines as the *Nation*, the *New Republic,* and *New Masses* became the dernier cri of the New York intellectuals.

Ironically, in satirizing certain social ills and injustices, McCutcheon was as heretical as the *New Masses* left-wingers. But he parted company with "those Bolsheviks," as he and Tarkington called them, when they emerged as more politically radical in the remedy they advocated: socialism. GBMc abhorred mobocracy. Implicit in his plays (and those of his novels containing social criticism) is his consistent plea for redress of injustices through private, indeed individual, enterprise—for responsible behavior on the part of each individual.

GBMc may well have considered 1923 as one of his slack years, for he published only one novel, *Oliver October*—and that a recasting of his play *One Score & Ten.* To David Selznick he sold the film rights to *A Fool and His Money* (1913) and to the American Play Company and Charles Towne the rights to "Shard's Enemy." That story may also have been created first as a play. GBMc listed it as one of the plays in "Box 4, Hall Closet of Apartment." But, like *The Poinley Affair,* the manuscript has yet to be found.

Contrary to his usual policy, GBMc allowed *Oliver October* (1923) to appear as a serial in a magazine before the novel's publication as a book. The eight thousand dollars that *Delineator* paid him was probably not as persuasive as the editor, Charles Hanson Towne himself. Once the novel appeared it elicited mostly favorable reviews. It was quite faithful to *One

Score & Ten, the chief change being in the name of the protagonist—from Alfred Baxter Jr. to Oliver October.

One wonders whether any of the reviewers guessed that the novel had had its inception as a play. The *Boston Evening Transcript* reviewer had no reservations: "The thing we love about it," he said, "is that it is such a human book . . . so delightfully funny." The *New York Times* reviewer conceded, "It is full of humor, and its element of suspense is planted at the very beginning." But reflecting one of the reasons McCutcheon's novels failed to be noticed by reputable critics, the *Times* reviewer concluded, "Mr. McCutcheon writes to entertain, and this being so, it is only fair to judge the book from his own attitude. Observed from that angle, there is not much fault to be found with *Oliver October*." Apparently that reviewer, like many a critic among his contemporaries, did not believe in entertainment as a worthy quality of literature, despite T. S. Eliot, who (in *The Sacred Wood*) regards entertainment as an indispensable quality.

Aside from McCutcheon's neglect by the pantheon of critics who had been presided over by the late William Dean Howells, GBMc's fiction remained beneath the notice of the rising young critic Edmund Wilson. Indeed, the brilliant but dour Wilson did not believe that any member of the Dutch Treat Club or the Coffee House Club (GBMc belonged to both) possessed the quality of mind that could produce anything first-rate, as he implied in *The Twenties.* Charles Hanson Towne's sense of humor for instance, which McCutcheon regarded as agreeable, was regarded by Edmund Wilson as insipid:

This little lunch club of artists and writers [The Coffee House] had been founded by Frank Crowninshield as a sort of feeder for *Vanity Fair.* One sat at a long table with everyone else and ate an inexpensive lunch. As almost the only younger men, John Bishop and I were somewhat out of our element. I used to say that the other members were men of the eighties who had never caught up with the nineties. Charlie Towne, with his incessant insipid jokes, was the quintessence of that second-rate generation.

Obviously GBMc had no trouble in filling up his days; he was a workaholic. By 1924, if not before then, Marie must have realized that George had turned into a writing engine. More devoted than ever, she insisted he relax with the lightest kinds of diversion, for instance Broadway musicals. Early in September she had bought at the Shubert box office three tickets for the September 16 performance of Ziegfeld's *Greenwich Follies*. John Raleigh, their favorite nephew, would be visiting on his last summer fling before returning to his prep school in North Carolina. He was then only thirteen. They wanted to make him feel grown up, so they took him along to enjoy the precision kicking of the chorus flappers stepping to hit tunes by Cole Porter. Everyone in the party liked best "My Long Ago Girl" (especially GBMc, thinking of Minnie Maddern, no doubt)—also "Two Little Babes in the Woods." For several evenings the following week GBMc sang these songs to Marie's accompaniment at their grand piano with the bulldog legs.

During 1924 GBMc published another Graustarkian novel with the ominous title *East of the Setting Sun*. The novel begins in a New York City men's club. Nine members sitting near the fireplace arouse one another's curiosity about how the little Balkan principality may have fared since the War. One of the nine, a publisher, sends his best feature writer, Pendennis Yorke, to find out. By now it has become all too predictable what one would come up with, once dipping into the wells of Graustark. Pendennis returns not only with an engaging report but also with a dazzling princess, whom he has married. The influence of Thackeray is reflected not only in the reporter's name but also in his profession and character.

It was in 1924, also, that GBMc sold the movie rights to *Beverly of Graustark* through the American Play Company, which Charles Towne had recently joined. Grace Hayward of that organization was now dramatizing *Graustark*. (Miss Hayward's play would enjoy a six months' run, the following year, at the Cort Theater.) In 1924, too, GBMc was elected President of the Authors Club for the 1924–1926 term. Yet despite these apparent successes, one senses in his letters and in his increasingly long stays in Arizona a certain anomie. That he had been experiencing an identity crisis, perhaps unconsciously, is reflected in such titles as *What's-His-Name* and *City of Masks*—to say nothing of his previous pseudonyms Greaves and Clifford. (A cliff is one of the classic fantasy symbols of rejection.) Like the Arizona Indian in *Crazy Weather*, GBMc seemed to be name-traveling. Was he also entertaining, now in his late fifties, an unconscious death wish?

Early in 1924 (also the previous December) John informed George that the *Chicago Tribune* had decided to publish fiction in a series to be called Blue Ribbon Books. The publishers planned to inaugurate the series with a slim volume to be entitled *Three Yarns*. One suspects that John had some say in making the decision, for George Barr McCutcheon was invited to join the company of Booth Tarkington and G. K. Chesterton, authors of the other two yarns respectively. Here was GBMc's chance to get back at the critics—to show with a vengeance what he could do with realism. "Anthony the Joker," the story he wrote for *Three Yarns,* turned out realistic enough but also, in its psychological undertones, grimly masochistic.

"Every secret of a writer's soul, every experience of his life," observes Virginia Woolf, "is written large in his works." Does "Anthony the Joker" reveal something of GBMc's secret heart, something of his subconscious? What were his real feelings toward Marie? He would no doubt have dismissed the notion as preposterous, but subconsciously was he suffering from a niggling Calvinistic wound, from a chauvinistic recognizance that he had after all married a non-virgin? Was that why Clara had been so cool toward her?

Yet he must have been very much in love with Marie. She was still attractive, sylphlike, and virtually impeccable in her tastes. In her new mauve cloche, she looked like a *Vogue* fashion model. Daisy McCutcheon must surely have been one of the beautiful wives that Monty Flagg, artist and Biddeford Pool neighbor, had in mind when, in his chapter on friends' wives in *Roses and Buckshot,* he observed, "There are so many beautiful women in America these days!" As George sat beside Marie in church, he must have been very proud of her, but was he also jealous? No wife was ever more faithful than Marie Van Antwerp Fay McCutcheon, no matter how many men's flattering glances followed her. Thus GBMc may only have been fantasizing, in "Anthony the Joker," about what a non-convivial husband's life *might have been like* in a fashionable Central Park apartment, with a glamorous francophile wife who in several traits—except for conjugal infidelity—resembled Marie. In "Anthony the Joker" the glamorous, sylphlike, cigarette-smoking Cora Vandoon from the French Quarter of New Orleans arrives in New York City in search of a husband.

New Orleans had gallantly offered her a score or more [of prospective husbands] but there was one thing lacking in all of them: money. Men who have no money at all inevitably become the fathers of large and *exciting broods of children.* [Emphasis added.] Anthony was denied this most primitive of all achievements. . . . He was forty-six; he had asked some fifteen or twenty women at odd times to marry him, and he was still a bachelor when Cora Vandoon came to town looking for a husband.
[After their marriage] the Anthony Blacks lived on the top floor of

a fashionable apartment building, a stone's throw away from Central Park. For the first two or three years of their married life, Anthony and Cora kept step. She was forced to lag a little, it is true, because Anthony was a slow mortal. He was an honest, upright fellow, and he prided himself on his gifts as a story teller, but he was never so dull as when he tried not to be dull. . . . If he had possessed that rare gift [a sense or humor] he would never have married Cora. He would have got the point of the joke before it was too late.

All too diffidently GBMc had always perceived himself as a provincial, sometimes boring, interloper in the urban society he often found himself in. In at least two of the Dutch Treat Club skits, he had been cast in risible, clownish roles. As bumptious and banal as the provincial William Gunn, Esquire, of "The Waddleton Mail," Anthony Black turns out to be also a practical joker and a cuckolded clown, a *pagliaccio:*

Cora was not in love with Anthony and never had been. She endured him for two years and then fell in love with a man who claimed to understand her. That is one of the oldest claims in the world and seldom fails to cause mischief. For two or three years she went on being understood and mis-understood by successive admirers. . . . Anthony was so upset by the fear that her love for him was waning that he purchased the string of pearls she had been coveting . . . but was forced to go to Tiffany's with her the next day to prove to her that they were genuine [not a practical joke].

And then there was the time when he suffered a simulated attack of heart disease and fell (somewhat carefully to be sure) to the floor and pretended to be dying in great agony—and suspense, as it turned out, because of the extraordinary and tearless interest she took in the prolonga-tion of his death struggles. . . .

"See here, Cora. I can't stand this sort of thing [your infidelities] any longer," he burst out. "If you don't love me any longer, say so. It's getting on my nerves. Dr. Gage says I'm in pretty bad shape. My heart's bad. He says I need a change, a long rest . . . away from New York awhile. . . . Of course, you haven't noticed for the good reason that you seldom have a meal with me. Breakfast in bed, luncheon downtown with people I don't like. . . . You are always too tired to go to the theater with me. . . . You're going to have tea with Blatchford now. Just you two alone. Same as you used to with Hillis and Granby and God knows with how many others. . . . They never ask me to their dinner parties. . . . Haven't you any consideration for Blatchford's wife?"

Cora laughed. "She has fish of her own to fry . . . her and young Thompson. My dear Anthony, she doesn't in the least mind how much I play around with her husband."

One morning, the Blacks' butler finds that Anthony really has suffered an attack, this time a stroke. The butler phones Dr. Gage, then goes downstairs to the Blatchfords' apartment to inform Cora. Cora upbraids him for not realizing that it's all one of Anthony's practical jokes. But she later goes to Anthony's room in the hope that the attack is real. She finds that he has indeed suffered a paralytic stroke and that his mouth is twisted in a ghastly sardonic sneer. She hires a couple of nurses and rests assured that "Anthony was safely out of her way for the time being. . . . She became gayer than ever." Within three months, Anthony recovers enough to move about the apartment. He keeps looking out the window to the courtyard fourteen stories below.

One night Cora attends without Anthony a theater party with the Blatchfords and others, followed by a midnight champagne supper at the Blatchford apartment.

"How is good old Saint Anthony tonight, Cora?" someone loudly and jovially inquired.

"He's getting better and better every day," replied Anthony's wife without removing the cigarette from her scarlet lips.

Blatchford sat at the head of the long refectory table, his back to the single window in the west end of the room. . . . Cora sat on her host's right. . . . Cora half rose from her chair, her gaze fixed on Bliss, the butler, who was standing as if petrified . . . staring beyond her in the direction of the window.

"What is the matter, Bliss?" she called out. "What are you looking at?"

"I could swear I saw a man standing outside there on the window ledge . . . leastwise his legs. . . ."

Blatchford struggled to his feet, overturning his chair in haste.

There was a rope around Anthony's neck. . . . Afterward they found a little placard pinned to his waist. On it was printed in bold, clumsy letters: "Eleven o'clock. I thought it would be a good joke to come to the party uninvited. Throw me out if you don't care to have me around."

I fear I have neglected to mention the fact that the Blatchford apartment on the thirteenth floor of the building was immediately below that of the Anthony Blacks.

"Anthony the Joker" sounds ominously like McCutcheon's death wish. Was it only a coincidence that he took pains, this same year, to write his will? He requested, incidentally, that his body be cremated and the ashes buried in the family plot in Lafayette. Most of his property he left "to my beloved wife, Marie." His beneficiaries included "my stepson, William Pickman Fay, whom I have reared, educated, and loved as my own son." He left only $100 to John T. "as a token of my love for one not in financial need." He kept making lists and inventories—"Royalties, 1925," *My Pictures*, "Books in the Hall Closet of the Apartment," "Manuscripts in Box #4."

16

CURTAIN

If GBMc was beginning to feel the chest pains symptomatic of his weakening heart, he said nothing to Marie. If he felt disheartened by his failure to get any of his plays produced on Broadway, he gave no sign of it. He appeared more cheerful than ever among his friends at the Dutch Treat Club. He dined with some of them on November 16, 1925, at the Coffee House: Charles Towne, Christopher Morley, Julian Street, Otis Skinner, Irvin Cobb, and George Putnam.

Almost simultaneously with the publication of Dreiser's novel *An American Tragedy,* there appeared McCutcheon's *Romeo in Moon Village,* one of his last flings at the writing of romance. The errant Romeo Egerton, in mending his picaresque ways, wins back his Eulora, his true love. Reviewers dismissed this romance with complimentary but very brief notices—no doubt justifiably. Typically they said, "The fact that *Romeo in Moon Village* has no serious significance does not in the least detract from its entertaining qualities." Other brush-off notices mentioned the book's "delightful streak of whimsicality," "jovial humor," and "McCutchoen's facility in bringing humor, often farce, to bear." That last observation appeared in the new, American *Saturday Review of Literature,* launched under the editorship of Henry Seidel Canby of Yale and the Dutch Treat Club.

Among the Dutch Treat Club members GBMc most frequently fraternized with, besides Charley Towne and Monty Flagg, was Christopher ("Kit") Morley. The affinity, which was mutual, was probably not attributable to Morley's interest in melodrama. Morley did not know that GBMc had written melodramas, and GBMc was probably not aware that Morley would be trying to revive melodrama in 1928 and 1929 at a theater in Hoboken. Rather, GBMc exchanged notes with Morley on their mutual affliction with bibliomania. Long before both authors had emigrated to New York City (Morley from Pennyslvania), each had developed a love for books not only as literature but also as artifacts to be collected. Morley, the author of *Parnassus on Wheels* (1917) and *The Haunted Bookshop* (1919), shared with GBMc some of the excitements of acquiring first editions or fine editions or both.

The motto on McCutcheon's bookplate was "Books Once Were Men." Marie had had the plates designed and engraved in Chicago the year after they were married and had surprised George with a set of them. She may have heard George utter the truism, although he himself disclaimed having composed it. He had been keeping notes about his experiences and acquisitions as a bibliophile, no doubt intending to gather them, one day, into an essay. In 1925 he wrote such an essay and named it "Books Once Were Men."

My book-plate reads, Books Once Were Men [the essay begins]. I am sorry to say, the apothegm is not original with me. A great many years ago someone with a profound mind wrote that simple line of one-syllable words; he lived in an age when men put themselves into books as they wrote them, and their readers, to a certain degree, did the same as they read them.

Then, attempting to take the curse off the apparent male chauvinism of that opening and title, GBMc adds,

She [my wife] finds herself almost completely surrounded by the 3,000 men who stand in gallant array around my library, outwardly mute but inwardly vociferous . . . neat-looking gentlemen all, in snug levant garments and trimmings of gold. To be sure, she has to think of Charlotte Brontë, Jane Austen, Fanny Burney, and others as men . . . they are attired in the same fashion, feel the same to the touch, and speak with a strong masculine persuasiveness—well it was [a] she [Marie] who dug up that old saying about books being men.

To make sure the reader understands that McCutcheon has not just collected but has actually read these books, GBMc now shares some autobiographical reminiscences:

Like most boys of that day, I read Dickens, Thackeray, Scott. . . .
Whether we liked it or not, we were brought up on good literature out
there in the Middle West. We took it, I suppose, in much the same way
we took grammar and mathematics, Virgil, and other hardships. . . .
Strange to relate we were surprised to find after we had grown up that
we remembered Dickens and Thackeray and Scott. . . .

Marie's attitude toward some of GBMc's book purchases is reflected
in this revelation:

Some men collect rare books as an investment. On the other hand, their
wives as a rule look upon it as a crime. . . . Many an otherwise domineering
husband, open-faced as a clock, becomes a stealthy conniving coward
when it comes to introducing a new book or two into his collection.

McCutcheon interlards his exposition with anecdotes about how
collectors come by their treasures, some by serendipities in used-book
shops. One of the humorous anecdotes concerns the man who has surreptitiously collected erotica. Guilt-ridden, he keeps them locked in a
closet and thinks of their authors as "coarse individuals with all the ten-
dencies of perverts and without the decency of ordinary prostitutes."
When the collector reaches the age of seventy, he fears for what his wife
and children would think when, after his death, they opened the private
closet. Desperately trying, but failing, to sell the erotica to a book dealer
(apparently these were the days before so-called adult book shops), he
ends up paying the dealer to take the contraband off his hands.

The essay is laced with sententious quotables: "One of the real joys
of book collecting is in the search." "Books are the visible ghosts of men's
minds." "You may buy them and sell them, but you cannot make slaves
of them."

Finally, the prose rhythms in this essay remind one of those in
McCutcheon's short story "Courage":

I like the feel of those old books. I like to pick one of them up and say
to myself, "This is Goldsmith" or any of a hundred others . . . for it is
Dr. Goldsmith, not in the flesh, to be sure, but in a far more enduring
form. . . . The man puts himself upon those sheets as surely as he draws
the breath of life.

Of course, that kind of prose also evokes pre-television eras, when sentiments floated into one's mind with the tranquillity of summer clouds or burned brightly as the firelight before one's easy chair on a winter's evening.

Ironically, McCutcheon did not submit "Books Once Were Men" to the *Atlantic* or to *Harper's,* where he might at last have been published. Instead, he sent it to the *Saturday Evening Post,* where it was published in the September, 1925, issue. That was probably the wrong outlet if he was hoping to impress intellectuals. Still, Kate Douglas Wiggin read it and wrote him a congratulatory note. She added, "Why didn't I keep first editions of everything, myself!" A few years after McCutcheon's death Frank Dodd published a clothbound memorial edition of *Books Once Were Men.* In this unabridged version, one can learn of McCutcheon's provenance—of specific authors and books he read and cherished.

In December GBMc and Marie wintered in Arizona again. "I shall be here for a couple of months," he wrote on stationery of the San Marcos Hotel, Chandler, Arizona, to a rare books dealer in Chicago. "By the way, your copy of Wordsworth's 'An Evening Tale' does not quite come up to the mark." Just before leaving for Chandler, GBMc wrote a thank-you letter to George Ade, who had sent the McCutcheons his latest photograph: "I wouldn't take anything for it," GBMc jested, "except chloroform...." Then seriously: "Arizona is delightful. Marie and I wish you could join us.... Marie sends her best and adds that if this photograph is the best you can do, God save you!" Apparently, Marie had a sense of humor, too. It was not characteristic of GBMc to put words in her mouth.

Quite affluent by now, McCutcheon owned a Packard limousine and employed a chauffeur who doubled as a butler at dinner parties. The man's name, Clotworthy, must have sounded foreboding to GBMc, who was now sensitive to the ominousness of "clot." One Thursday in March, 1926, Clotworthy found a brief typewritten manuscript kicking around (GBMc's phrase) on the sidewalk of Thirty-seventh Street between Madison and Fifth Avenues. By an almost incredible coincidence, the manuscript happened to be one by McCutcheon that he had sold through an agent and that had been lost on its way to the studio of an illustrator. McCutcheon had it delivered to the buyer immediately, of course, but offered to buy it back for ten times what it had sold for "so that I could destroy it."

Why this compulsion to destroy? Did he now regard his acceptances by the *Saturday Evening Post* as mockeries, as reminders that he would never make it into the *Atlantic* or *Harper's?* Even James Whitcomb Riley (whose "Little Orphan Annie" with its refrain "The Gobble-uns'll git you ef you don't watch out" GBMc as a child was required to memorize and recite) had breached the pages of the *Atlantic*. Most of GBMc's Indiana contemporaries had by now made it on Broadway—Ade, Tarkington, David Graham Phillips, William Vaughn Moody, to say nothing of Cole Porter and the critic George Jean Nathan, one of the first to recognize the achievement of Theodore Dreiser. In April, 1926, with all GBMc's financial security—indeed, with an affluence rare among his contemporary writers—why would he sell at auction, as he did, his collection of cherished first editions? And for the one novel he published that year, why would he settle on a title like *Kindling and Ashes?*

Consciously or unconsciously McCutcheon invested that novel with some revealing symbolism, although the story is realistic on its surface. It is the story of the bitterness between the no-account Bennie Jaggard and the snobbish Waynes. When it becomes known that Jaggard has trifled with but has not married Barbara Wayne, he is murdered by one of her brothers. Did GBMc identify with the no-account Bennie, did Barbara represent the critical recognition that had eluded him, and did the murderous Wayne brothers represent the critics? Whatever the answers, and for whatever reasons, the novel was virtually ignored by critics and reviewers. Only the *Boston Evening Transcript* accorded it a brief notice: "A really remarkable story exceptionally well done." Perhaps the quasi-invisibility of *Kindling and Ashes* lay in its format as a tabloid marketed on newsstands.

The McCutcheons spent the Christmas of 1926 in Arizona, again, but early the following week, much earlier than was their custom, they returned to New York. Aside from Marie's restlessness when she was not in the City, both of them wanted to see Minnie Fiske's interpretation of Mrs. Alving in Ibsen's *Ghosts* on January 10, 1927. They were glad they braved the New York winter, for Mrs. Fiske's performance proved quite rewarding—indeed, with its consummate understatement, it proved to be another of her triumphs even if the play did not succeed commercially. Marie did not realize that this would be George's last glimpse of Minnie. George almost surely had premonitions. The last night out together for the McCutcheons themselves would occur on October 8, 1928, when, at the Music Box Theatre, they would enjoy Cole Porter's musical revue *Paris,* with its hit tune "Let's Fall in Love."

The last novels to be published during GBMc's life were *The Inn of the*

Hawk and the Raven (1927) and *Blades* (1928). One wonders what those predacious titles adumbrated in the stricken McCutcheon. The *Inn* was the last, and perhaps the most entertaining, of the Graustarkians, as most of the reviewers conceded. *Blades* is the story of Barnaby Blades, an intelligent athlete who becomes disenchanted with a New York enchantress, turns noble savage, and heads for the hinterland, where he finds a purer romance and religion. A reviewer in the London *Times Literary Supplement* praised the book: "Here is that *rara avis,* a novel with freshness . . . written with a light touch and an alert sense of humor."

To the end of GBMc's life, there seemed to be no deterioration of his mind—only of his heart. Even his posthumously published novel, *The Merrivales* (1929), reflects his sustained mental alertness. Ursula, the eighty-two-year-old protagonist of that novel, shrewdly manipulates her children's and grandchildren's love affairs. "The age of that heroine must not serve to keep McCutcheon enthusiasts away," observed a reviewer in the *New York Times.* "For her spirit and energy, her will and understanding, are ever youthful." For GBMc, Ursula was probably an idealized Clara.

It was about this time that GBMc received a letter from Bernhardt Wall, the Lime Rock, Connecticut, etcher, who had been publishing limited editions of ornately decorated Words of Wisdom by and about celebrated Americans. Wall requested GBMc to contribute, to a proposed new brochure, about one hundred words that would represent a distillation of "George Barr McCutcheon's experience as a writer." Ordinarily GBMc threw such requests away, but in this instance he obliged with "Blind Man's Buff":

Blind Man's Buff! The game we are all playing with our eyes wide open—the everlasting game of groping in darkness for the things that are about us, that mock and elude us, that impishly lead us to great heights and far corners and leave us there to die of hunger, with limitless invisible stores just beyond our reach. With outstretched arms we go in circles, ready to clasp knowledge, power, opportunity, fame—elusive dodgers in this endless game of Blind Man's Buff, ever tricking us, ever vanishing before our straining eyes, ever stepping out of our grasp as we think we have our hands upon them. Always for us this game is just beginning—this game of catching phantoms. And yet we go on, and will go on forever playing this game, each in his own way, for no matter what the rest of the world may say of us, we come to the end knowing that we have not found all that we set out to find.

In May, 1927, GBMc's physician, in consultation with a specialist, confirmed what GBMc had suspected for a long time and had kept from Marie—his heart condition was critical. He was put on medication, but no medicine can heal a heart ravaged by failure to elicit, for a life's work, any truly critical appreciation, to say nothing of esteem. One of the inextinguishable traits of human nature, as William James among others observes, is the craving to be recognized, and there is a persistent relation between disappointed expectations and heart attacks. Physicians know that the most incurable persons are the frustrated. The frustrated artist, for example, will not be satisfied with fame or riches or even achievement in another field. The only true success kept eluding McCutcheon: the failed playwright—or, what was tantamount, the unproduced playwright—confronted the inevitable prognosis of heart failure.

It happened on October 23, 1928. He had been attending a Dutch Treat Club luncheon at the Hotel Martinique. The meal was not quite over. He staggered to a restroom and collapsed. Charley Towne and Monty Flagg hurried after him, but Bud Kelland and Walter Trumbull happened to be the first to reach him. They found him dead.

After a brief funeral in New York City, the next day, his body was cremated and the ashes were sent home for burial in the family plot in Spring Vale, Lafayette. Theodore Roosevelt Jr. wired his condolences ("my deepest sympathy") to John at the *Chicago Tribune*. News of McCutcheon's death appeared on the front pages of most American and British newspapers.

George Ade wrote from Hazeldon, his Indiana estate, to John:

I was terrible *[sic]* shocked and grieved to learn of the sudden death of George. I wired Mrs. McCutcheon and tried to keep track of the funeral arrangements but I am greatly worried now for fear that I should have shown up at Lafayette. . . . I want you to know that I would have been at Lafayette if I believed that I was expected. George and I were such good friends in the old days that I was in readiness to start down but I was really in doubt as to whether I should go or not.

EPILOGUE

As a person George Barr McCutcheon was decent, affectionate, and responsible—"a kind and lovable gentleman," as Meredith Nicholson said in his eulogy in the *Indianapolis Star* on October 24, 1928. McCutcheon was prodigiously industrious. He probably should not have published novels that he himself knew were slight, but he never gave up trying for distinction in his plays. Yet it hardly needs to be said that as a playwright he does not rank at the top with Shaw and Wilde. He remains nonetheless a creditable minor playwright, who deserves to be reckoned with.

What can never be taken away from him is his contribution to popular culture—contributions through humorous melodrama, through short fiction, and even through some of his novels. In *The Melodramatic Imagination* (1976) Peter Brooks may be extravagant in beguiling us with his notion that melodrama "is a popular influence that higher literature must regard with envy." Perhaps Eric Bentley and Frank Rahill reflect a more balanced view in stating that "the theater can benefit from productions of popular plays as well as of literary masterpieces." Surely, McCutcheon's plays can delight and instruct both sophisticated and unsophisticated audiences.

McCutcheon contributed not only to popular culture but also—in his satire of irrational mores—to social criticism, to the ongoing moral dialectic. Everywhere in his writing one finds castigations of monopolies whether individual or institutional. He satirized senseless slaughter of wildlife *(Brood House* and *Black Is White).* He lampooned the irrationalities

168

of mobs and the hypocrisies of certain organized religions *(One Score & Ten, Oliver October, The Double Doctor)*. He called attention to laxities in our penal system *(Yollop)*. He burlesqued the undertaking industry and people's prurience toward death *(One Score & Ten* and *The Flyers)*. He dealt compassionately with the social problems of alcoholism *(Sherry)*, euthanasia *(From the Housetops)*, and abandoned children *(The Man Who Loved Children* and *Mr. Bingle)*. In *Kindling and Ashes* and in "Mr. Hamshaw," among other short stories, he deflated snobbery. Indeed, all McCutcheon's writings reflect his social conscience and his gentle reminder that we must love one another or perish, a theme of universal importance.

Never didactic, McCutcheon's oblique instruction consists in making us laugh at ourselves. He demonstrated his knowledge of the distinction between humor and wit, the first emanating from idiosyncrasy of character, the second from pleasant disappointment of expectation (Henri Bergson's and Max Eastman's well known definition). GBMc filled his essays with delightful wit, especially irony and paradox, and he can often compete with G. K. Chesterton, if not quite with Mark Twain. McCutcheon's wit will probably stand up longer than George Ade's. Wit and humor permeate virtually all of GBMc's writings regardless of genre.

Some persons, not a few critics and reviewers among them, are by nature too dour to appreciate wit or humor or both—simply do not vibrate to those wavelengths, as Jung observed. Indeed, they are often offended when the wit extends to satire—to irreverent ridicule of their most sacred irrationalities. This phenomenon may well explain how GBMc's best novels elicited conflicting, sometimes diametrically opposite, verdicts. His novel *Black Is White*, for example, elicited verdicts that ranged from "his strongest and best" down to "not worth discussing." Again, commenting on *The Inn of the Hawk and the Raven*, primarily a Graustarkian piece but laced with wit and humor, a *New York Times* reviewer pronounced it "a rather foolish story." But a reviewer in the *Times Literary Supplement* of London said, "The occasional characters are excellently done. If Mr. McCutcheon were always as humorous as that, it would be a literary creation." And Will Cuppy, author of *The Decline and Fall of Practically Everybody*, reviewing McCutcheon's book in the *New York Herald Tribune*, praised it without reservation and applauded McCutcheon's "power and charm." Of course, it takes a humorist to recognize a humorist. To work a twist on E. B. White's dictum about "one man's meat," one Edmund Wilson's "insipidity" may be a Will Cuppy's "power and charm."

The writer of the *New York Times* editorial of October 24, 1928 (the day after GBMc died) damned him with faint praise. But the *Times* 1928 assessment needs re-examining from the perspective of the 1980s. For "fashions are subject to change," as Dr. Johnson observed in his *Lives of the Poets.* McCutcheon's "contributions of innocent happiness," as the *Times* put it, need not be limited to audiences of "college boys, kitchen maids, and daughters of millionaires." GBMc's fiction gave pleasure to many readers. His plays, once produced, can give even more pleasure and enrichment.

Finally, McCutcheon must be applauded for his humor of self-deprecation and his civilized sense of balance, indispensable sensitivities in any writer, as Mark Van Doren observes:

Humor is the indispensable ingredient in art as it is in life. Just as we cannot take anyone seriously who lacks the sense of humor, so we cannot take a poet [or playwright] who lacks this sense. Humor is the final sign and seal of seriousness, for it is proof that reality is held in honor and in love.

NOTES

ABBREVIATIONS

DFM–*Drawn from Memory*, autobiography of John T. McCutcheon; IN/PUR–Indiana Collection, Purdue University; UT/HRC–University of Texas Humanities Research Center; BEI/Y–Beinecke Library, Yale University; BERG/NY–Berg Collection, New York Public Library; NEW/CHI–Newberry Library, Chicago; LL/IU–Lilly Library, Indiana University; TCHA–Tippecanoe County Historical Association; *NYT–New York Times;* CT–*Chicago Tribune; LAF/J–Lafayette* (Indiana) *Journal; LAF/C–Lafayette* (Indiana) *Courier; J & C–Lafayette Journal & Courier.*

PROLOGUE

GBMc interviewed by Joyce Kilmer, *NYT*, August 1, 1915, p. 16; James Woodress, *Booth Tarkington: Gentleman from Indiana,* pp. 14ff and 215; Isaac Marcosson and Daniel Frohman, *Charles Frohman: Manager and Man,* p. 81; Peter Brooks, *The Melodramatic Imagination,* p. ix. Howells was not above trying his own hand at romantic plays–e.g., *Samson* (1874) and *Yorick's Love* (1878). For Howells's quarrel with romantic fiction see Kenneth Lynn, *William Dean Howells* (Harcourt Brace Jovanovich, 1970), p. 315. As for Henry James, Leon Edel writes "After James had passed four of his plays around the London theaters in vain, he published them in two volumes, acknowledging a humiliating confession of defeat." *Henry James: The Treacherous Years* (Lippincott, 1969), p. 25.

CHAPTER ONE

DFM, pp. 18, 21, 28, 47; William Reser, "A Short Excursion into the Past," TCHA, p. 9; Sarah Bowerman, "George Barr McCutcheon," *Dictionary of American Biography,* 2: 12ff; Barbara Hawkins, *Dr. Elias B. Glick,* TCHA, p. 1; H. B. Knoll, *The Story of Purdue Engineering,* p. 21; Purdue's Ninth Annual Register, p. 73; *Books Once Were Men,* p. 7; *Several Short Ones,* unpaginated, TCHA; GBMc's holographic mss. "My First Party" and "My Maiden Effort," also his report card of May, 1876, in UT/HRC. "Deadeye Dick" is alluded to in *Mr. Bingle,* p. 131;

171

"Oliver Optic" in *Brewster's Millions*, pp. 19, 52, 173. GBMc's parents' disapproval of dime novels is mentioned in Jean Maury's *Boston Evening Transcript* interview "What GBMc Thinks About," p. 24. Early on, GBMc mastered such spelling demons as "accommodate," "embarrassed," "occasion," "occurrence," and "perseverance."

CHAPTER TWO

J. H. McKee, "Famous Family Once Jailers," p. 4; DFM, pp. 26, 40, 179 (the escapee, Douglass Kramer, was a horse thief). On Annie Pixley, see Gelett Burgess, ed. *My Maiden Effort*, p. 172. Other sources for this chapter: Fred Kelley, *George Ade: Warm-Hearted Satirist*, pp. 68ff; Paul Fatout, "Mark Twain Comes to Lafayette," TCHA *Weatenotes*, p. 1; Isaac Marcosson and Daniel Frohman, p. 81; GBMc's holographic mss. "How I Retired from the Stage," "Lucky It Was a Dream," and "The Marriage Models" UT/HRC. In the *Biographical Record & Portrait Album*, TCHA, p. 624, the McCutcheons are described as "strict old school Presbyterians"; and the Glicks, p. 595, as "registered Republicans." Information on melodrama: Peter Brooks, *The Melodramatic Imagination*, pp. 24ff; Eric Bentley, *Life of the Drama*, pp. 195ff; Frank Rahill, *The World of Melodrama*, p. 262. "Melodrama," writes Brooks, "is of the utmost importance to an understanding of Balzac, Dickens, Conrad, and Henry James; indeed, to an important and abiding mode in the modern imagination."

CHAPTER THREE

DFM, pp. 28, 29, 179, 181; E. F. Harkins, *Little Pilgrimages among the Men Who Have Written Famous Books*, pp. 290ff. Purdue's First Annual Register, pp. 22-23; Lafayette, Indiana, School Corporation's *Annual Report to the Trustees, 1882*, TCHA, pp. 18-19; Cecil Webb, *Historical Growth of the Schools of Lafayette* (Lafayette, Indiana, School Corporation, 1972), p. 11; H. B. Knoll, pp. 6, 13, 26; William Hepburn and Louis Sears, *Purdue University: Fifty Years of Progress*, pp. 177ff. On Minnie Maddern: Frank Carlos Griffith, *Mrs. Fiske*, p. 24; Archie Binns and Olive Kooken, *Mrs. Fiske and the American Theater*, pp. 24, 26, 397; *New Columbia Encyclopedia, 4th ed.*, p. 956. GBMc's holographic mss. *Vashti*, IN/PUR; "The Countess Thalma" and "Miss Divinity," UT/HRC.

CHAPTER FOUR

GBMc's holographic mss. *Buck & Gagg*, BEI/Y; *Midthorne, The Reef Bell, A Mythological Malady*, and *Judith Verne*, IN/PUR.

CHAPTER FIVE

"Perunius Skinner" in *Several Short Ones*. GBMc's ms. "How I Retired from the Stage" (UT/HRC) was published (and garbled) in *Second Book of the Authors Club* (The Authors Club, New York, 1920), pp. 343ff. When Jessie died, in 1964, she was at least eighty-one, according to the birthday party described in DFM, p. 180, and to a picture inscribed "Jessie McCutcheon, age 1" in the 1864 photo album of Lafayette attorney Coffroth, UT/HRC. OTHER SOURCES for this chapter include DFM, p. 54, and Jean Maury's interview "What GBMc Thinks About," p. 24.

CHAPTER SIX

The three McCutcheon brothers always inscribed "To Mother" their first-off-the-press books, several of which are in UT/HRC. For GBMc's participation in local plays, see Bernard Sobel, *Broadway Heartbeat*, p. 50; Harkins, p. 288; *LAF/C*, May 15, 1900, p. 5; December 5, 1900, p. 5; February 6, 1901, p. 4. In *Before I Forget* (Dodd, Mead, 1950), p. 560. Isaac Marcosson writes that despite rumors to the contrary Charles Frohman and Maude Adams were not married. GBMc's ms. *George Washington's Last Duel*, IN/PUR. Lafayette, Indiana, provided one of the underground stations for fugitive slaves. A letter of instructions by GBMc to his New York secretary (July 8, 1911) is in the Fales Library, New York University. According to John Raleigh, "Uncle George was left-handed." OTHER SOURCES: James Kopka, "George Barr McCutcheon and the Graustark Legacy," p. 8; Richard de Hart, *Past & Present of Tippecanoe County* (Indianapolis: Bowen and Company, 1909), pp. 403ff; Richard Roberts, "The Literary Life of GBMc," pp. 43ff; Howard Baetzhold, "Charles Major: Hoosier Romancer," p. 34; also the Julia Marlowe ed. of Charles Major, *When Knighthood Was in Flower* (Indianapolis: The Bowen-Merrill Company, 1898), p. iv.

CHAPTER SEVEN

GBMc's pasted-up clippings of "The Waddleton Mail" and the ms. of "The Scaffold" are in UT/HRC. GBMc's reviews of Opera House productions are in the following order: *LAF/J*, Oct. 6, 1890, p. 1; Oct. 10, 1890, p. 1; Feb. 23, 1892, p. 2; *LAF/C*, Feb. 7, 1893, p. 1; Jan. 10, 1894, p. 8; Oct. 17, 1899, p. 2. On George Ade: Fred Kelley, p. 68; Lee Coyle, *George Ade*, p. 24. The society page (4) of the *LAF/C* for Nov. 9, 1889, reports: "The regular first-nighters at the Opera House have become familiar. George Ade, one of the confirmed, is usually accompanied by the McCutcheon boys." Ade and GBMc were accompanied on March 14, 1889, by the Ruger sisters, according to a social note in the *LAF/C*, March 15, 1889, p. 4. In a brief "Autobiography" in Terence Tobin, ed. *Letters of George Ade*, p. 14, Ade tells of his move to Chicago. James DeMuth writes, "Ade was an enthusiastic patron of vaudeville and the popular stage. He knew many of the entertainers, and he counted among his closest friends the renowned blackface comics George Thatcher and Willis Sweatman." *Smalltown Chicago: The Comic Perspective of Finley Peter Dunne, George Ade, and Ring Lardner*, p. 57. OTHER SOURCES: Kopka, p. 8; Roberts, p. 43; *Biographical Record & Portrait Album*, p. 627.

CHAPTER EIGHT

On the Chicago Exposition: Stanley Appelbaum, *The Chicago World's Fair of 1893*, passim; DFM, pp. 70, 75; Charles Fanning, *Finley Peter Dunne and Mr. Dooley: The Chicago Years*, pp. 28ff. "In 1893 Chicago's police force was demonstrably corrupt," writes Fanning, p. 57. GBMc's ms. *The Bachelor Lamb*, IN/PUR. His verses dated "23 March 1896," *Several Short Ones*. His mss. "The Ante-Mortem Condition of George Ramor" and "The Winning Shot" are in UT/HRC, as are Jessie's memorabilia, the *LAF/C* letterhead, and the pasted-up pages of "The Wired End" from the *LAF/C*, July 21, 1897. GBMc occasionally vacationed on the Kankakee River at Aroma Park, Illinois, so that the setting of "The Wired End" may have been inspired by a composite of the Wabash and the Kankakee shores. GBMc's *The Double Doctor*, from holographic ms. in IN/PUR, also in Lazarus, ed., *The*

Indiana Experience, pp. 300ff. Notices on the society page (4) of the *LAF/C:* about GBMc and Ben at a Sigma Chi dance, Apr. 21, 1898; about a party of Jessie's, Dec. 23, 1898; about Jessie's summer with Clara, May 20, 1898; about Ben's homecoming, June 21, 1898. Other supportives: Dec. 29, 1897 and Sept. 13, 1898. OTHER SOURCES: DFM, pp. 181, 183; John McCutcheon Raleigh's letter to A. L. Lazarus, Sept. 6, 1979. On the challenges of writing successful farce, see Dion Boucicault as quoted by William Winter, *Other Days* (New York: Moffat, Yard, & Company, 1908), chapter 4, passim.

CHAPTER NINE

John's recognition of GBMc; "Brothers under the Skin," *Collier's,* Apr. 11, 1925, p. 14. Victor Jones, "Why Richard Greaves?" *Midwestern Miscellany,* Nov., 1977, p. 7. Ade's and GBMc's readings at English's Opera House reported in the *Indianapolis Sentinel,* May 31, 1902, pp. 1, 3; *Indianapolis News,* May 30, 1902, p. 12; *Indianapolis Journal,* May 31, 1902, p. 7. Farewell editorial in *LAF/C,* Apr. 21, 1902, p. 4. Farewell party fictively reconstructed from social notes in *LAF/C,* Feb. 15, 1902, et al. GBMc's review of *The Sultan of Sulu* in *LAF/C,* Apr. 25, 1902, pp. 1, 2. Chicago residences of the McCutcheons in *Who's Who in America,* 1901 through 1907. Quotations from *Brewster's Millions* (1903), pp. 1, 2. James Hart on Winchell Smith in *Oxford Companion to American Literature, 4th ed.,* p. 781. On the failure of the play adaptation in London: Marcosson and Frohman, p. 308. Quotations from *The Sherrods* (1903), pp. 189, 198, 343. REVIEWS: of *The Sherrods* in the *Philadelphia Item* and the *Cleveland Leader* quoted in *The Bookman,* Jan. 1904, p. 18; reviews of *Daughter of Anderson Crow* in *NYT,* Oct., 1907, and in the London *Saturday Review,* Nov. 17, 1907, quoted in the *Book Review Digest* (1908). GBMc's correspondence with the Dodds, UT/HRC. *Note:* GBMc's letters in BERG/NY are not now released; for whatever reason, the American Play Company prefers to keep them confidential.

CHAPTER TEN

On Chicago and Lawrence Proudfoot: Joseph Kirkland, *Story of Chicago* (Chicago: Dibble Co., 1892), p. 276. On Marie: John McCutcheon Raleigh's letters to A. L. Lazarus, June 28, July 11, Aug. 2, 1978; Lazarus's phone interviews with Theodora McCutcheon, July 27, 1978, and Nov. 28, 1979. On GBMc's burning copies of *Several Short Ones:* Jacob Blanck, *Bibliography of American Literature,* p. 112. On the Little Room: Harriet Monroe, *A Poet's Life,* p. 197; Wallace Rice's invitation to GBMc, also the "Revelry in Graustark" playbill, UT/HRC. On the Whitechapel Club: Blair and Hill, *America's Humor,* p. 384. GBMc's mss. "The Gloaming Ghosts" and "The Wedding Journey," BEI/Y. A copy of the American Art Association's catalogue *The Renowned Collection of First Editions of Dickens and Thackeray* [circa 1926] with some of GBMc's holographic annotations in the Rare Books Collection, Stanford University Library. Highlights of GBMc's will: *NYT,* Nov. 15, 1928, p. 19. GBMc's correspondence: with Riley and with J. A. Woodburn, LL/IU; with Hamlin Garland, University of Southern California Library; with brother John T., NEW/CHI. OTHER SOURCES: "The Flodden Field of Fiction" quoted by Howard Baetzhold in "Charles Major: Hoosier Romancer," p. 7; Carl Van Doren, *Many Minds,* p. 18; Terence Tobin, p. 7 (Tobin adds that Ade took more pains with his short stories in *In Babel*); Julian Street, "When We Were Rather Young," pp. 10ff; John T. McCutcheon, *In Africa: Hunting Adventures in the Big Game Country,* p. 99; Jean Holloway, *Hamlin Garland,* p. 107. REVIEWS:

of *Nedra*, the *New York Independent*, Nov. 16, 1905, p. 1154; of *Cowardice Court*, the [New York] *Critic*, June, 1905, p. 573; of *Jane Cable*, *The Bookman*, Nov., 1905, p. 248; of *The Husbands of Edith*, *NYT*, Jan. 13, 1908, p. 341; of *The Alternative*, *NYT*, June 12, 1909, p. 376; of *Truxton King*, *The Bookman*, Oct., 1910, p. 195.

CHAPTER ELEVEN

On New York in 1910: George Constable et al., *This Fabulous Century*, vol. 1; Moses King, *King's Views of New York 1896-1915;* Dutch Treat Club Yearbooks, LL/IU; Rupert Hughes, *The Real New York;* Arthur Maurice, *The New York of the Novelists;* Brander Matthews, *These Many Years.* On Mrs. Fiske: Griffith, p. 113; Binns and Kooken, p. 55; Charles Hanson Towne, *This New York of Mine*, p. 218; Library of Congress Register of Mrs. Fiske's Papers, p. 3; review of *Salvation Nell* quoted by Constable, p. 256. On Theodore Roosevelt: John T. McCutcheon, *In Africa...*, passim; Julian Street, *The Most Interesting American*, pp. 19, 27, 29. GBMc's "The Wrath of the Dead," in *Her Weight in Gold & Other Stories* (1911 ed.), pp. 77ff. Quotations from *Brood House* (privately printed) in this order: pp. 44, 92-93, 26, 30, 46, 12, 170ff. Marie's letter to Jessie in Jessie's memorabilia, UT/HRC. George Bernard Shaw is quoted by Craig Timberlake in *The Bishop of Broadway*, p. 108. Charles Dudley Warner, "A-Hunting of the Deer," *In the Wilderness*, p. 63. James Kopka, "A Visit with Evelyn McCutcheon," *LAF/C*, March 19, 1978, p. 10. REVIEWS: of *The Rose in the Ring*, *Life*, Dec. 8, 1910, p. 146; of *Black Is White*, *NYT*, March 15, 1914, p. 124, and June 14, 1914, p. 276; *Springfield* (Massachusetts) *Republican*, July 25, 1914, p. 4; and the *Boston Evening Transcript*, March 18, 1914, p. 9.

CHAPTER TWELVE

Ms. of *The Flyers*, IN/PUR. Copy of the court order in favor of the Fiskes, UT/HRC. Charles Frohman is quoted by Isaac Marcosson, *Before I Forget* (Dodd, Mead, 1959), p. 560. OTHER SOURCES: Marcosson and Frohman, p. 87; Timberlake, p. 143; Daniel Watermeier, *Between Actor and Critic: Selected Letters of Edwin Booth and William Winter* (Princeton University Press, 1971), p. 259; Isaac Marcosson, *Adventures in Interviewing* (New York: John Lane, 1920), p. 290; Woodress, p. 82; Dixon Wecter, *Saga of American Society*, p. 36 and passim; George Jean Nathan and H. L. Mencken, *The American Credo*, p. 67. REVIEWS: of *The Flyers*, *NYT*, Jan. 16, 1912, p. 8, and the *Rochester* (New York) *Union & Advertiser*, Jan. 16, 1912, p. 11; of *The Hollow of Her Hand*, *Boston Evening Transcript*, Oct. 23, 1912, p. 24. A copy of this novel inscribed to James Montgomery Flagg, UT/HRC. The *Brooklyn Eagle* review of Tarkington's *The Man From Home* is quoted by Constable, p. 256, emphasis added.

CHAPTER THIRTEEN

Ms. of *The Man Who Loved Children*, BERG/NY, by permission quoted in this order: pp. 85, 58, 23. Excerpts from *Mr. Bingle* in this order: pp. 305, 188-89, 193ff. GBMc's letters and telegram to Riley and Eitel, LL/IU; Eitel's response is tipped into GBMc's copy of *Her Weight in Gold*, UT/HRC. On Riley's problems with alcohol: Richard Crowder, *Those Innocent Years*, pp. 138-39 and passim; problems with gout or syphilis: Jared Carter, "Defrosting the Punkin: Another Look at Riley," pp. 29-30. Tarkington's letters to Hamlin Garland and Julian Street in Woodress, pp. 254ff. Marie's sterility is revealed in GBMc's letter to his brother John, May 3, 1913, NEW/CHI. John T.'s letter to Charles Dawes, May 11, 1914, Northwestern University Library. Some of the novels GBMc inscribed for Marie are in the UT/HRC, as are GBMc's typescript *My Pictures* and "Article for the *New York Sun.*" GBMc's correspondence with Brander Matthews is in the Butler Library, Columbia University. GBMc's letter nominating Hamlin Garland to the Century Club is in the University of Southern California Library. GBMc's "Tribute to Howells" in in the Houghton Library, Harvard University. The report "Art Auction" is in the *NYT*, Jan. 19, 1927. OTHER SOURCES: William Dean Howells, *Imaginary Interviews*, p. 296; George Arms, "Howells" in Max Herzberg, ed., *The Reader's Encyclopedia of American Literature* (New York: Thomas Y. Crowell Company, 1962), p. 492; S. N. Behrman, *Duveen*, pp. 10, 21, 30; Arthur Maurice, *Fifth Avenue* (Dodd, Mead, 1918), pp. 27, 128, 160; James Montgomery Flagg, *Roses and Buckshot*, p. 114; Joyce Kilmer, ed., *Literature in the Making*, pp. 157ff; Montrose Moses, "George Barr McCutcheon," *NYT*, July 21, 1912, pp. 417ff; Margaret Case Harriman, *Blessed are the Debonair* (New York: Rinehart, 1956), p. 144, Walter Jackson Bate, *The Achievement of Samuel Johnson* (New York: Oxford University Press, 1961), p. 182. Mencken and Nathan are quoted by John McAleer in *Rex Stout* (New York: Little, Brown & Company, 1977), p. 131. REVIEWS: of *Mary Midthorne, NYT,* Sept. 24, 1911, p. 570; of *A Fool and His Money, NYT,* Oct. 26, 1913, p. 670; of *Mr. Bingle, NYT,* Dec. 30, 1915, p. 570.

CHAPTER FOURTEEN

Ms. of "Courage" in the University of Arizona Library. Following at UT/HRC: typescript of "Pour la Patrie" and holographs of "Lines to Julian Street" and "How I Retired from the Stage." Excerpts from *One Score & Ten* (privately printed) in this order: pp. 216, 45-46, 151, 220. GBMc's letters to Ade, IN/PUR, Oct. 13, 1915; Apr. 25, 1918; Nov. 20, 1923. OTHER SOURCES: Betty Shannon, "Maker of the Good Fairy," *American Magazine*, June, 1918, pp. 54-55; Flagg, p. 58; Charles Hanson Towne, *This New York of Mine*, p. 186 and his *So Far So Good* (New York: Julian Messner, 1945), pp. 223, 225; Alan Downer, ed., *On Plays, Playwrights, and Playgoers: Selections from Letters of Booth Tarkington to George C. Tyler and John Peter Toohey, 1918-1925*, pp. 7, 9, 11, 14, 18, 70; W. J. Stuckey, *The Pulitzer Prize Novels: A Backward Look*, pp. 209, 213-14; William Pickman Fay's report in Harvard Class of 1915 Twenty-Fifth Anniversary Report, p. 219. REVIEWS: of *Green Fancy, NYT*, Sept. 16, 1917, p. 22; of *Sherry, NYT,* Sept. 21, 1919, p. 474, and [New York] *Outlook*, Nov. 12, 1919, p. 307.

CHAPTER FIFTEEN

Excerpts from "Anthony the Joker" in this order: pp. 7ff, 14-15, 25-27. GBMc's correspondence with Towne and his secretary, Apr. 26, 1922, in the Butler Library, Columbia University. GBMc's royalty ledgers were for sale, in 1979, by the Serendipity Bookstore, Berkeley, California. Various inventories both holographic and in typescript are in the McCutcheon Collection, UT/HRC, as is John T. McCutcheon's letter of Dec. 24, 1923. OTHER SOURCES: Flagg, p. 213; Towne, *So Far So Good,* p. 197; Loetscher, *The Broadening Church*, pp. 108-9; Edmund Wilson, *The Twenties,* p. 49; although Wilson remains valid as a critic most of the time, at Harvard he was found wanting as a teacher and a person. Howard Mumford Jones writes, "Tell it not in Gath, publish it not in the streets of Askelon—the students and the faculty found him disappointing." *An Autobiography* (University of Wisconsin Press, 1979), p. 262; Virginia Woolf, quoted by Leon Edel in his *Literary Biography,* p. 55; Montrose Moses' interview with GBMc, *NYT,* July 21, 1912,

p. 418; Eugene Debs's interview with C. W. Wood, Oct. 3, 1920, quoted in James Boylan, *The World and the Twenties* (New York: Dial Press, 1973), p. 43; "Dutch Treat Club," *NYT*, Feb. 8, 1919, p. 5; "Well Known Actors Act Their Own Plays in Movies," *Saturday Evening Post*, Apr. 6, 1935. REVIEWS: of *Westwind Drift, New York Post*, Dec. 11, 1920, p. 8; of *Viola Gwynn, New York World*, Oct. 22, 1922, p. 22, and the London *Times Literary Supplement*, Nov. 23, 1922, p. 726; of *Yollop, Boston Evening Transcript*, March 18, 1922, p. 6, and *NYT*, March 5, 1922, p. 19; of *Oliver October, Boston Evening Transcript*, Aug. 18, 1923, p. 5, and *NYT*, Aug. 26, 1923, p. 26.

CHAPTER SIXTEEN

Excerpts from *Books Once Were Men* (1931 ed.) in this order: pp. 3, 11, 7, 36, 41–42, 4. Holograph of "Blind Man's Buff," Fales Library, New York University. Kate Douglas Wiggin's letter to GBMc, UT/HRC; as are GBMc's letters from Arizona, his unpaginated journals (including the entry "so that I could destroy it"–the ms. Clotworthy discovered), and the Coffee House memento of Nov. 16, 1925 tipped into GBMc's copy of Merrick's *While Paris Laughed.* GBMc's letter to Ade, Oct. 19, 1926, and Ade's letter to John T., Oct. 29, 1928, are in IN/PUR. REVIEWS: of *Romeo in Moon Village, NYT*, Nov. 29, 1925, p. 26, *Literary Review*, Nov. 7, 1925, p. 9, and *International Book Review*, Nov., 1925, p. 26; of *Kindling and Ashes, Boston Evening Transcript*, Sept. 22, 1926, p. 4; of *The Inn of the Hawk and the Raven, Saturday Review of Literature*, Aug. 6, 1927, p. 17; of *Blades*, London *Times Literary Supplement*, Dec. 13, 1928, p. 992; of *The Merrivales, NYT*, Sept. 29, 1929, p. 18.

EPILOGUE

Peter Brooks, *The Melodramatic Imagination*, pp. ixff; Frank Rahill, *The World of Melodrama*, p. 262, quoting Bentley. Mark Van Doren on humor: introduction to Carl Sandburg, *Harvest Poems* (New York: Harcourt, Brace, 1960), p. 3. The playwright and critic Lessing said in his *Hamburgische Dramaturgie*, "Those who only feel, weep; laughter comes from those who think." OTHER REVIEWS: of *The Inn of the Hawk and the Raven: NYT*, Aug. 7, 1927, p. 12, London *Times Literary Supplement*, Dec. 1, 1927, p. 912, and the *New York Herald-Tribune*, Aug. 21, 1927, p. 12–the last by humorist Will Cuppy.

SELECTED BIBLIOGRAPHY

Appelbaum, Stanley. *The Chicago World's Fair of 1893.* New York: Dover Publications, 1980.

Baetzhold, Howard. "Charles Major: Hoosier Romancer," *Indiana Magazine of History* 51 (March, 1955): 1.

Banta, Richard E. "George Barr McCutcheon" in *Indiana Authors and Their Books.* Crawfordsville, Indiana: Wabash College, 1949.

Barzun, Jacques. "Henry James, Melodramatist," *The Question of Henry James,* ed. F. W. Dupee. New York: Henry Holt, 1945.

Behrman, S. N. *Duveen.* New York: Random House, 1951.

Belasco, David. *The Theater through Its Stage Door.* New York: Harper & Brothers, 1919.

Bentley, Eric. "Melodrama," *The Life of the Drama.* New York: Atheneum Publishers, 1964.

Binns, Archie, and Olive Kooken. *Mrs. Fiske and the American Theater.* New York: Crown Publishers, 1955.

Blair, Walter, and Hamlin Hill. *America's Humor.* New York: Oxford University Press, 1978.

Blanck, Jacob. "George Barr McCutcheon," *Bibliography of American Literature.* New Haven: Yale University Press, 1973.

Blum, Daniel. *Pictorial History of the American Theater, 1900-1950.* New York: Greenberg Publishers, 1951.

Bond, Carrie Jacobs. *The Roads of Melody.* New York: D. Appleton & Company, 1927.

Brooks, Peter. *The Melodramatic Imagination.* New Haven: Yale University Press, 1976.

Brooks, Van Wyck. *America's Coming of Age.* New York: E. P. Dutton, 1915.

Burcal, D. E. "Opera House, First Lafayette Theater," *Lafayette Journal and Courier,* June 27, 1975.

Burgess, Gelett, ed. *My Maiden Effort.* Garden City, New York: Doubleday, Page & Company, 1921.

Carmody, John, et al. *Indiana: A Guide to the Hoosier State.* New York: Oxford University Press, 1973 (first published 1937).

Carter, Jared. "Defrosting the Punkin: Another Look at Riley," *Indiana Writes* 2 (fall, 1977): 2.

Constable, George, et al. *This Fabulous Century, vol. 1. 1900-1910.* New York: Time-Life Books, Inc., 1969.

Coyle, Lee. *George Ade.* New York: Twayne Publishers, 1964.

Crowder, Richard. *Those Innocent Years.* Indianapolis: The Bobbs-Merrill Company, 1957.

DeMuth, James. *Small Town Chicago: the Comic Perspective of Finley Peter Dunne, George Ade, and Ring Lardner.* Port Washington, New York: Kennikat Press, 1980.

Downer, Alan. *On Plays, Playwrights, and Playgoers: Selections from Letters of Booth Tarkington to George C. Tyler and John Peter Toohey, 1918-1925.* Princeton: Princeton University Library, 1959.

Edel, Leon. *Literary Biography.* Toronto: University of Toronto Press, 1957.

Fanning, Charles. *Finley Peter Dunne and Mr. Dooley: The Chicago Years.* Lexington: The University Press of Kentucky, 1978.

Fatout, Paul. "Mark Twain Comes to Lafayette," *Weatenotes* 12 (February, 1978): 2.

Flagg, James Montgomery. *Roses and Buckshot.* New York: G. P. Putnam's Sons, 1946.

Frohman, Daniel. *Daniel Frohman Presents: An Autobiography.* New York: Kendall and Sharp, 1935.

Gassner, John, ed. *Ideas in the Drama.* New York: Columbia University Press, 1964.

Gill, Brendan. "A Biographical Essay on Cole Porter" in Robert Kendall, ed. *Cole.* New York: Holt, Rinehart & Winston, 1971.

Griffith, Frank Carlos. *Mrs. Fiske.* New York: Neale Publishing Company, 1912.

Grimstead, David. *Melodrama Unveiled: American Theater and Culture, 1800-1850.* Chicago: University of Chicago Press, 1968.

Harkins, E. F. *Little Pilgrimages among the Men Who Have Written Famous Books.* Boston: L. C. Page Company, 1903.

Hawkins, Barbara. *Dr. Elias B. Glick.* Lafayette, Indiana: Tippecanoe County Historical Association, 1976.

Hepburn, William Henry, and Louis Sears. *Purdue University: Fifty Years of Progress.* Indianapolis: Hollenbeck Press, 1925.

Holloway, Jean. *Hamlin Garland.* Austin: University of Texas Press, 1960.

Howells, William Dean. *Imaginary Interviews.* New York: Harper & Brothers, 1910.

Hughes, Rupert. *The Real New York.* New York: Smart Set Company, 1904.

Jones, H. M. *An Autobiography.* Madison: University of Wisconsin, 1979.

Jones, Victor H. "Why Richard Greaves?" *Midwestern Miscellany* 5 (November, 1977): 1.

Kelley, Fred C. *George Ade: Warm-Hearted Satirist.* Indianapolis: The Bobbs-Merrill Company, 1947.

Kilmer, Joyce, ed. *Literature in the Making.* New York: Harper & Brothers, 1917.

King, Moses. *King's Views of New York 1896-1915.* New York: Arno Press, 1980.

Knoll, H. B. *The Story of Purdue Engineering.* Lafayette, Indiana: Purdue University Studies, 1963.

Kopka, James. "George Barr McCutcheon and the *Graustark* Legacy," *Indiana English Journal* 6 (winter, 1972): 2.

Kriebel, Robert. "Old Lafayette," *Lafayette Journal and Courier,* August 12, 1979.

Lazarus, A. L., ed. *The Indiana Experience.* Bloomington: Indiana University Press, 1977.

Loetscher, Lefferts. *The Broadening Church.* Philadelphia: University of Pennsylvania Press, 1954.

Marcosson, Isaac, and Daniel Frohman. *Charles Frohman: Manager and Man.* New York: Harper & Brothers, 1916.

Marker, Lise. *David Belasco.* Princeton: Princeton University Press, 1975.

Matthews, Brander. *These Many Years.* New York: Charles Scribner's Sons, 1919.

Maurice, Arthur B. *The New York of the Novelists.* New York: Dodd, Mead, 1916.

Maury, Jean West. "What George Barr McCutcheon Thinks About," *Boston Evening Transcript,* December 10, 1927.

McCutcheon, John T. *Drawn from Memory.* Indianapolis: The Bobbs-Merrill Company, 1950.

———. *In Africa: Hunting Adventures in the Big Game Country.* Indianapolis: The Bobbs-Merrill Company, 1910.

McKee, J. H. "Famous Family Once Jailers," *Lafayette Journal and Courier,* August 18, 1962.

McQuillen, David K. "The Lafayette Opera House," vertical file no. 7216, Lafayette, Indiana: Tippecanoe County Historical Association archives.

Minnie Maddern Fiske: A Register of Her Papers in the Library of Congress. Washington, D.C.: Library of Congress, 1962.

Monroe, Harriet. *A Poet's Life.* New York: The Macmillan Company, 1938.

Morley, Christopher. *John Mistletoe.* New York: Doubleday, Doran & Company, 1931.

Moses, Montrose. "George Barr McCutcheon," *New York Times Book Review,* July 21, 1912, sec. 6.

Nathan, George Jean, and H. L. Mencken. *The American Credo.* New York: Alfred A. Knopf, 1920.

Nicholson, Meredith. *The Hoosiers.* New York: The Macmillan Company, 1900; 1916.

Page, Thomas Nelson. *Elsket & Other Stories.* New York: Charles Scribner's Sons, 1891.

Rahill, Frank. *The World of Melodrama.* Philadelphia: University of Pennsylvania Press, 1967.

Roberts, Richard R. "The Literary Life of George Barr McCutcheon," *Indianapolis Star Magazine,* April 26, 1964.

Shannon, Betty. "The Maker of the Good Fairy," *American Magazine,* June, 1918.

Shepherd, Jean, ed. *The America of George Ade.* New York: G. P. Putnam's Sons, 1961.

Sobel, Bernard, *Broadway Heartbeat.* New York: Hermitage Press, 1953.

Street, Julian. *The Most Interesting American.* New York: The Century Company, 1916.

———. "When We Were Rather Young," *Saturday Evening Post,* August 20, 1932; November 19, 1932.

Stuckey, W. J. *The Pulitzer Prize Novels: A Backward Look.* Norman: University of Oklahoma Press, 1966.

Sullivan, William G. *English's Opera House.* Indianapolis: Indiana Historical Society, 1960.

Tarkington, Booth. "Great Men's Sons" in A. L. Lazarus, ed. *The Indiana Experience.* Bloomington: Indiana University Press, 1977.

———. *The World Does Move.* Garden City, New York: Doubleday, Doran & Company, 1929.

Timberlake, Craig. *The Bishop of Broadway: The Life and Work of David Belasco 1853-1931.* New York: Library Publishers, 1954.

Tobin, Terence, ed. *Letters of George Ade.* Lafayette: Purdue University Press, 1973.

Towne, Charles Hanson. *This New York of Mine.* New York: Cosmopolitan Book Corporation, 1931.

Van Doren, Carl. *Many Minds.* New York: Alfred A. Knopf, 1924.

Warner, Charles Dudley. "A-Hunting of the Deer," *In the Wilderness.* Boston: Houghton, Osgood and Company, 1878.

Wecter, Dixon. *Saga of American Society.* New York: Charles Scribner's Sons, 1937.

Wilson, Edmund. *The Twenties.* New York: Farrar, Straus & Giroux, 1975.

Winter, William. *Vagrant Memories.* New York: Doran and Company, 1915.

Woodress, James. *Booth Tarkington: Gentleman from Indiana.* Philadelphia: Lippincott and Company, 1954.

INDEX